W9-ASI-859

To Roy:
with warm personal and
professional
regards.

Ibrahim J. Rubama

Trauma
at Home

After 9/11

Edited by
Judith Greenberg

University of Nebraska
Press: Lincoln and London

Jill Bennett, "The Limits of Empathy and the Global Politics of Belonging," originally appeared in longer form in "*Tenebrae* after September 11: Art, Empathy, and the Global Politics of Belonging," in *World Memory: Personal Trajectories in Global Time,* ed. Jill Bennett and Rosanne Kennedy (Hampshire: Palgrave MacMillan, 2002). Reprinted with permission.

Geoffrey Hartman, "On That Day," originally appeared in Geoffrey Hartman, *Scars of the Spirit: The Struggle against Inauthenticity* (New York: Palgrave, 2002). Copyright by Geoffrey Hartman. Reprinted with permission of Palgrave.

Toni Morrison, "The Dead of September 11," reprinted by permission of International Creative Management, Inc. Copyright © 2001 by Toni Morrison.

Susannah Radstone, "The War of the Fathers: Trauma, Fantasy, and September 11," originally appeared in *Signs* 28, no. 1 (2002). Reprinted with permission.

Photographs by Lorie Novak © Lorie Novak 2001. Reprinted with permission. Photographs by Diana Taylor, Tony Savino, Mark Seliger, and Larry Towell reprinted with permission.

Library of Congress Cataloging-in-Publication Data
Trauma at home : after 9/11 / [edited by] Judith Greenberg.
p. cm.
Includes bibliographical references.
ISBN 0-8032-7108-5 (pbk. : alk. paper)
1. September 11 Terrorist Attacks, 2001.   2. Psychic trauma—United States.
3. Psychic trauma—New York (State)—NewYork.   I. Greenberg, Judith, 1966–
HV6432.7.T83 2003
155.9'35—dc21
2002032092

"N"

To Claire—and all the children of the world.
In the hope for a peaceful future.

Contents

Remember Life with Life:

Illustrations

Acknowledgments

This book emerges from a tragedy. It was conceived as a response to the deaths of over three thousand people killed in the attacks on the World Trade Center, the Pentagon, and the plane that crashed in Pennsylvania on September 11, 2001. In her poem included in this volume, Toni Morrison writes, "I must not claim false intimacy or summon an overheated heart glazed just in time for the camera. I must be steady and I must be clear, knowing all the time that I have nothing to say—no words stronger than the steel that has pressed you into itself; no scripture older or more elegant than the ancient atoms you have become." Morrison articulates a struggle of finding words to address the dead. I think that many have felt ill-equipped to speak or write in response to September 11. Yet words—reading, writing, and discussing—are our ways of making sense. Inasmuch as silence overwhelms us, we yearn to return to dialogue. It is in this yearning for dialogue that this book has come into being.

Dialogue, of course, can create dissent. The process of inviting contributors introduced me to views different from my own and from those I encountered in my circles in New York. Listening to and exchanging e-mail messages with the contributors of this book created a larger community for sharing the aftermath of September 11. I hope that the book can in turn provide such a larger community for its readers, who may encounter positions they have not considered in the isolation of their own reactions.

I am extremely grateful to all of the contributors to this book. For many, especially those who exposed their own traumas in personal essays, the writing experience was emotionally draining. I thank them for their hard work. Some have told me that the writing process proved somewhat cathartic; I think all are still in the process of working through.

The idea for this book emerged during a walk I took through Riverside Park with Marianne Hirsch (and my daughter, Claire) a few weeks after

September 11. Marianne, originally my teacher when I was an undergraduate at Dartmouth, has become over the years a trusted mentor and friend. We shared our feelings of frustration with some of the initial reactions, published and unpublished, to the events. Since we had both written about trauma and were living in New York, we remarked that it ought to seem natural to write about the events. Yet we felt a pervasive numbing, the impossibility at that time of putting our shock to words. "Why don't you edit a collection?" Marianne volunteered. "And I'll contribute something." And there this book began. I want to offer a special thanks to Marianne; without her, that walk through the park, and her suggestions along the way, this book would not be.

Some of the pieces in this book have previously appeared elsewhere, and I am grateful to all who allowed me to reprint them here. A special thanks goes to Toni Morrison and Suheir Hammad for generously allowing us to reprint (free of charge) the beauty of their poetry. Toni Morrison's "The Dead of September 11" originally appeared in *Vanity Fair* magazine. Her assistant, Renée Boatman, and Betsy O'Brien at International Creative Management, Inc., were particularly helpful in granting me reprint permission. For reprint permissions, I also want to thank Jennifer Nelson at Palgrave/Macmillan (for Jill Bennett's essay); Davinder Bhamra at Palgrave/St. Martin's Press (for Geoffrey Hartman's essay); and Perry Cartwright at the University of Chicago Press (for portions of Susannah Radstone's essay). I must confess that I unconsciously borrowed the title *Trauma at Home* from my graduate school friend and colleague Margery Sokoloff, whose scholarship I admire and who graciously "lent" the title to me.

This book would not be as effective without the photographs included. Lorie Novak's photographs of the missing person fliers posted around New York add a visceral dimension to this book. Diana Taylor, who has also written on photography and September 11, shared her photograph for Marianne Hirsch's essay. I am grateful to Tony Savino for permission to include his photograph from the "Here Is New York" show and to Stephanie Schennpe at "Here Is New York" for her help. Thanks go to Michael Shulman at Magnum Photos for granting me permission to reprint Larry Towell's photograph and to Shelter Serra and Mark Seliger for permission to reprint Seliger's photo in my own essay.

Thanks also go to the staff at the University of Nebraska Press for the confidence in this project and all of the work along the way.

I cannot imagine the process of absorbing the past six months and of writing and editing this book without my dear friends and family. Many called from across the country, overseas, and down the street to check in and helped me feel less isolated, especially in those early days. A special thanks goes to my dear friends Nina Greenberg and Kathryn Potts, who helped my process of working through, shared many discussions about the events and the various shows dedicated to them around the city, and listened to me talk about the process of putting this book together. An extra thanks goes to Nina for her keen editorial eye. Adrienne Defendi provided me with many useful resources about photography and September 11 along with endless enthusiasm for the project.

To my parents, Robert and Maida Greenberg, I extend deep thanks for their unwavering support in this project, as in all of my endeavors. My mother, a psychoanalyst, provided me with numerous e-mails about psychoanalytic contacts, September 11–related talks, reading material, and, most important, the inspiration of her remarkable capacity for empathy. My philosopher father paid the same careful and loving attention to this book as he does to everything I do. A special thanks goes to my brother David for his meticulous editing of my essay and his general editorial wisdom and good sense. Both he and his fiancée, Suzanne, were enthusiastic about this book from the start. Thanks too go to my brother Jonathan and his wife, Megan, for their support. Finally, deep thanks go to Ira for his many readings and opinions, e-mail searches, support, foot rubs, and, most of all, for being my safe home.

Introduction

By the time this book appears on the shelves, more than a year will have passed since September 11, 2001. The writers and readers of the essays will be at different places, places we cannot yet anticipate, as many of the essays observe. At the time of this book's composition, roughly six months after the attacks, Dori Laub acknowledges that the "truth" of 9/11 is "still fragmented, piecemeal, and disorganized, a story in search of a voice." If the essays cannot document some fixed "truths" (and none claims to), what they can show are attempts to construct narrative, to find a voice, to create a "thread thrown between your humanity and mine," as Toni Morrison writes to the dead of 9/11.

Time became crucially important on 9/11. For people in the Twin Towers, where they were located and what time they tried to leave were facts of life and death. An awareness of temporality marks many of the essays: some are written in journal form, exposing the process of their formation; many essays contemplate the changing nature of their authors' responses and the need for time to assess this moment. The unpredictable reappearance of the past and a confusion of time, of course, are central concerns for trauma theory. At the heart of the structure of the reception of trauma lies a delay—experiences that resist knowing can return belatedly. As we construct narratives, we can look at how delays not only give us time to mourn but also complicate the very notion of 9/11 as a fixed "event." "Memory is, after all, a process and is everlasting only when it remains a process and not a finished result," James Young reminds us in his essay.

The book's title itself emerged as a work in progress. And while publication grants the title a kind of permanence, it still possesses an unfinished quality, given the instability of the terms "home" and "trauma." For me, "trauma at home" originally meant the arrival of massive violence in my backyard—in downtown New York. We see this meaning in the essays about encountering the Twin Towers, the detritus of ground zero, and the sites of mourning around the city, through viewing photography, watching television, cleaning up, escorting victims' families, looking from the viewing platform, or other forms of witnessing. "Trauma at home" also indicates how we absorb public trauma in our private homes and our psyches. This valence is evident in the essays that address how the news of the deaths of others evoked echoes of personal loss, awakened prior traumas, and translated unconscious fears and fantasies into reality.

A third meaning of the title is intertwined throughout the book: a reference to our national and transnational homes. Many of the essays examine the echoing of prior historical events—the Holocaust, Vietnam, Hiroshima and Nagasaki and the onset of the nuclear age. Also mentioned in the book and relevant to the title is the fact that America has its own traumas of slavery and racism embedded in its fabric of "home." Going back further in time, the homeland of America rests on the trauma of Native Americans. Feelings about home and trauma are not unrelated to one's identity position in this community or "home."

"Home" is traditionally ascribed a feminine space. Several essays comment upon the dominance of male figures, heroes, and power struggles in the aftermath of 9/11 and call attention to the need to expand the narratives told. Much as Judith Herman's influential book, *Trauma and Recovery*, brought attention to experiences of sexual and domestic violence and how women victims shared symptoms with combat veterans, political prisoners, and survivors of concentrations camps, we should remember that trauma occurs in the home for far too many women and children. This book recasts a sphere traditionally linked with the feminine and safety in light of the reality of violence, perpetrated by men, as was the case of 9/11. This book includes many women's voices—and photographs—to expand and shift existing discourse. They call for new narratives and unmask the gendered assumptions behind fantasies and stories at play.

Home itself is a complex concept. Suheir Hammad's poem portrays the multitude and diversity of homes traumatized by 9/11 and reveals the complexity of the term "home"—not only for a Palestinian American but for many whose sense of identity and homeland remains unsettled. Other essays critique a stable sense of home and call attention to the role of the refugee and the homeless.

The book is divided into six sections. The first three sections concentrate on historicizing, narrating, and witnessing 9/11. The next three sections focus on psychological dynamics and ideological frameworks at work in acts of reception. But such neat separations of categories fall apart upon reading the essays, for issues bleed into one another and the boundaries between them remain fluid.

The first section, "Impact," sets the impact of 9/11 in both a historical context and New York. The twentieth century, of course, witnessed the repetition of waves of violence. Geoffrey Hartman reminds us that time does not alleviate global misery or ensure progress in countering violence. Our post-Holocaust consciousness casts history as "one single catastrophe which keeps piling wreckage upon wreckage" and refuses attempts to fashion it into a meaningful configuration, as Walter Benjamin describes in Richard Stamelman's essay. Stamelman introduces Benjamin's view to suggest that history can be recast as a kind of "ground zero." This section looks at the events of 9/11 in light of conceptions of history, progress, and meaning making. Hartman brings to bear his knowledge of Western thought and literature on the cultural, philosophical, aesthetic, and spiritual forces behind 9/11. He speculates about what could have motivated the terrorists—how can violence cloak itself as spirituality? Stamelman analyzes how historical spaces are transformed into what Pierre Nora calls "*lieux de mémoire*," memory sites. "Many are the battlefields, the monuments, the cultural icons, the architectural spaces, even the killing fields whose image and icons have been transferred to T-shirts, hats, pens, metal souvenirs, coffee cups, and drinking glasses designed to be carried away as souvenirs and mementos," Stamelman observes. One such example is the series of advertisements by designer Kenneth Cole that use 9/11 to fill in the memory site with its products. My own essay explores the impact of the missing of 9/11, the still unknown wounds to New York and New Yorkers, and the role of distance in responding to trauma. I consider the transmission of such a history of fragments and wreckage to our children.

The second section, "Reporting," examines ways in which various narratives have come to fill in experience. Focusing on the "Portraits of Grief" section that appeared in the *New York Times*, Nancy K. Miller studies the kinds of narratives told about the victims, the development of the section itself, and the general features of the profiles in order to ask questions about storytelling and 9/11. Whose stories are told? Who is mourning in these stories? What's the real story of the survivors? Discussing the scrapbook-like nature of the portraits, Miller focuses on her own attachment to the "scraps" of the portraits section that she retains and wonders how she relates to these narratives when none resembles her own. Other essays in this section challenge post-9/11 narratives in different ways. According to Peter

Brooks, there has been another more insidious narrative in the wake of the attacks. As a response to the vulnerability created, the Bush administration cloaked its Republican agenda behind the mantle of a war on terrorism, a masquerade akin to the manipulation of mourning for political mischief in Shakespeare's *Julius Caesar*. For James Berger, narrative and language fail in the face of trauma, and yet acts of naming have come to fill in or form around the experience. His essay claims that the specific words used cannot be precise but instead are reflective of our processes of mourning. Drawing on queer perspectives that integrate nonnormative dimensions of emotional response, Ann Cvetkovich calls for narratives that make room for both the emotional complexity of responses and political activism. Of particular interest to her is how oral testimony will be used to expand understandings and questions raised about 9/11—how we can connect the cataclysmic moment to the texture of everyday life.

"Commentators have agreed that the September 11 attacks were 'the most photographed disaster in history,'" Marianne Hirsch tells us. The third section, "Photographing," looks at the role of pictures in the aftermath. Hirsch discusses her need to take pictures and yet her discomfort with doing so. Her examination of the relationship between photography and trauma points out features of the photograph that make it particularly suited for communicating the wound of trauma, such as its elegiac stopping of time, its ability to hold on, its deferral of understanding, and its conveyance of an absent presence. After analyzing a number of rich photographs from the aftermath, Hirsch proposes that only time will reveal which images come to symbolize 9/11 and that the debates about what is appropriate to photograph are as instructive as the images themselves. Lorie Novak, whose photos also appear in Hirsch's essay, shares some of her images of memorials to 9/11. As a photographer who works on the relations among family snapshots, memory, and identity, her images of the missing person fliers, the comments written on them, and the items placed around them provide opportunities to think about processes of mourning in and around New York City. E. Ann Kaplan also took pictures of downtown New York, where she lives, and discusses her own relationship to these sites of mourning. "Given trauma's peculiar visuality as a psychic disorder, this event seemed to feed trauma by being so highly visible in its happening," she observes. (Kaplan's pictures are not included in her essay out of fear that they would suffer in the translation—a decision that reflects the difficulty of capturing the extraordinariness of the images in the snapshot.) While Novak has said that the camera acted as a shield from experiencing the memorials in their immediacy, Kaplan found that it helped her make real what she could not otherwise comprehend. She critiques academic responses that overly theorize or distance the experience and fail to address a kind of specificity of and emotional response to the events.

"Imagining," the fourth section, looks at various psychic dynamics at work in our reactions. For Claire Kahane, on 9/11 our "primal fears uncannily became history." Kahane proposes that what lay behind the frequently heard comment "it's just like a movie" was the ability for films to encode our preexisting anxieties. Our "fascination with the abomination," as Joseph Conrad put it in *Heart of Darkness*, pulls us to Hollywood and, on that day, to the horrifying images on television. "We looked at what we couldn't see and lost our bearings," Kahane writes. Susannah Radstone too observes how films uncannily predicted the attacks and stresses the role of fantasy in our responses. The problem with referring to the attacks as traumatic, she finds, is that it tends to feminize the subject as victim and to determine the scar to be unreadable, elusive of meaning. Instead, Radstone looks at the role of unconscious fantasy life in the construction of meanings of 9/11 and the role of gender in fantasies of invulnerability and competing masculinity (a "battle of the fathers").

Picking up on the critique of creating a traumatized victim, Orly Lubin urges a shift from thinking nostalgically about innocent victims to take into account the role of the community and the trauma of "the horror of being in power." For Lubin, the Naudet brothers' film *9/11* illustrates an American reliance upon narrative conventions: the film generated a desired form of community and testimony for the spectator. Those who belong to communities of power must recognize their burden of accountability, she agues, and must work to get rid of power by refusing to define the existence of an Other and shifting frequently one's identity position. Jill Bennett's essay also takes on communities' creations of an Other for political ends. Like Lubin, she renders problematic the creation of an American "imagined community" of a victim class based on nationality. "When trauma is coextensive with nation, where do the limits of empathy lie?" she asks. Bennett turns our attention to the global dimensions of the trauma, which, in Australia, allowed political conservatives to assume power by casting Afghan asylum seekers as dangerous terrorist threats. Bennett examines the nature of empathy and identification: how the victim with a shared identity receives empathy while the alien body, such as the Afghan refugee or homeless person, is cast adrift. September 11 changed not only "home," she argues, but also our global community. She asks what it's like to inhabit the space of the refugee.

Following this attention to the place of the refugee, Suheir Hammad's

xxii   INTRODUCTION

poem "first writing since" articulates an alienation from America, the complicated feelings of an Arab New Yorker who embraces her city after the attacks: " 'my brother's in the navy,' i said. 'and we're arabs.' 'wow, you got double trouble.' word." Hammad also captures the transformation of the day—"sky where once was steel. / smoke where once was flesh"—and the anxiety created—"there is death here, and there are promises of more." Yet she concludes with an affirmation of life and survival, pointing out how the very act of reading her poem testifies to rising from the ash and looking for peace and justice.

"Echoing," the fifth section of this book, picks up on the investigation of international connections and the search for justice. In it, Michael Rothberg proposes that Cathy Caruth's insights regarding the structure of trauma as a mode of reception can be used to bridge disparate historical experiences. He finds that Hammad's poem illustrates the unique ability of art to respond to trauma and, in this case, to unsettle "trauma at home" and manifest a "double position" as insider and outsider, simultaneously at home and in exile. Elizabeth Baer also looks at the complexity of the term "trauma at home," discussing the role of war in her life and work. Baer interweaves quotations from a 1950s brochure about the potential harms of nuclear fallout with her description of forms of fallout of war during her lifetime—World War II (the Holocaust in particular), Vietnam, and 9/11—to trace how wars unsettle a sense of "home." September 11 reinforces Baer's commitment to teach about war, and the Holocaust in particular, so that we recognize our capacity to repeat acts of hatred, injustice, and genocide. The echoing on 9/11 of previous violence felt all too real to Irene Kacandes, who bravely shares how the attacks reawakened what was still her raw encounter with the brutal murder of her close friends, Dartmouth professors Susanne and Half Zantop, the previous year. She writes, "radically different traumata can be experienced as similar by those who have already been traumatized." Kacandes follows Toni Morrison's phrase of "throwing a thread between your humanity and mine" to propose that individuals with different histories may find their own responses echoed in her account and may find comfort in that sharing. She coins the term "concomitant loss" for the lasting damage done to a survivor who finds his or her self radically changed.

The final section, "Working Through," considers processes of mourning and memory. As the psychoanalyst Donna Bassin proposes in this section, "mourning offers generative possibilities as well if the past is not simply ossified and displaced into history but used in the service of transformation."

Patricia Yaeger delves into the question of how we respond to trauma when the "stuff" that remains confounds an ability to distinguish body or flesh from rubble, the difficulty of thinking of the bodies of the dead being cleared away with the debris. She offers five types of responses to this mingling: an impulse to convert the detritus of ground zero into something sacred; a deeply felt nausea; the attribution of an uncanny power to the detritus itself; a corporeality imposed upon the detritus, animating the dead matter; and a recognition of the lost work of production in the "waste." No matter what the response, each remnant, she finds, offers an archive for exploring the lost, a portal into the past. Donna Bassin's insights about mourning also begin with a meditation upon the proximity of the dead and trash, the missing and relics. What do we hold onto? What remains? As a member of a group led by New York City's Department of Mental Health to support bereaved families, Bassin describes some of the feelings of being inside ground zero. She captures a sense of the overwhelming nature of trauma: "I lost all sense of scale, of embodiment, all sense of myself as a human being with resources." Such an understanding of the impact of trauma upon the psyche is echoed by psychoanalyst and Holocaust survivor Dori Laub. According to Laub, trauma can mute the voices of survivors, who feel an uncertainty about the truth of their experiences, and silence often surrounds experiences of genocide. Trauma creates a struggle between the "urge to know" and the "need to deny." September 11 opened old wounds, created a sense of paralysis, and left an absence of narrative, authority, and safety. The process of resuming an internal dialogue that would enable one to take informed action is a difficult one; it involves recognizing the truth of trauma in the struggle against denial. Finally, James Young examines the relation between mourning and memorial. Young proposes that the "New World Trade Center" should embrace rejuvenation and celebrate life rather than be dictated according to the terrorists' sanctification of a culture of death. Regenerate and reinvigorate rather than paralyze with memory, he advises. The new complex should make room for the conflicting agendas of mourners and include both a permanent museum and memorial and an exhibition space that changes over time and lets future generations make it their own. In Young's terms, "let life remember life."

We each remember separately, and yet the shared witnessing of 9/11 invites shared remembering as well. The diversity of these essays reflects the multitude of narratives that come to fill the void created by 9/11. As Gara

LaMarche has written, "When it comes to September 11, everyone is an expert and no one is" (*Nation*, April 2002, 33). The myriad of voices, responses, and "threads thrown out" attests to both the desire to construct meanings and 9/11's resistance to be contained by one image, one unified voice, an easy summation.

Trauma at Home

The Dead of September 11

Toni Morrison

Some have God's words; others have songs of comfort
for the bereaved. If I can pluck courage here, I would
like to speak directly to the dead—the September dead.
Those children of ancestors born in every continent
on the planet: Asia, Europe, Africa, the Americas . . . ;
born of ancestors who wore kilts, obis, saris, gèlès,
wide straw hats, yarmulkes, goatskin, wooden shoes,
feathers and cloths to cover their hair. But I would not say
a word until I could set aside all I know or believe about
nations, wars, leaders, the governed and ungovernable;
all I suspect about armor and entrails. First I would freshen
my tongue, abandon sentences crafted to know evil—wanton
or studied; explosive or quietly sinister; whether born of
a sated appetite or hunger; of vengeance or the simple
compulsion to stand up before falling down. I would purge
my language of hyperbole; of its eagerness to analyze
the levels of wickedness; ranking them; calculating their
higher or lower status among others of its kind.

Speaking to the broken and the dead is too difficult for
a mouth full of blood. Too holy an act for impure thoughts.
Because the dead are free, absolute; they cannot be
seduced by blitz.

To speak to you, the dead of September, I must not claim
false intimacy or summon an overheated heart glazed
just in time for a camera. I must be steady and I must be clear,
knowing all the time that I have nothing to say—no words
stronger than the steel that pressed you into itself; no scripture
older or more elegant than the ancient atoms you
have become.

And I have nothing to give either—except this gesture,
this thread thrown between your humanity and mine:
I want to hold you in my arms and as your soul got shot
of its box of flesh to understand, as you have done, the wit
of eternity: its gift of unhinged release tearing through
the darkness of its knell.

Toni Morrison,
September 13, 2001

1. Impact

On That Day

Geoffrey Hartman

On that day I checked in at LaGuardia for a flight to Logan Airport and a lecture in Boston, a few moments before the first plane struck one of the World Trade Center towers.

On my way from the check-in to the gate, I saw people crowding around a TV monitor at a bar. I noticed but did not give much thought to it. (The second plane may just have hit, since I had stopped at an airport store around 9:00 A.M.) Perhaps ten minutes later the PA system announced that the airport was closed. Only then did I go to the bar and see a replay of the disaster.

I assumed it was an unbelievable accident, until another plane approaching the second tower disappeared, a cloud of smoke and then flares indicating it also had struck. Although alarmed and perplexed, I cannot say that a distinct thought of danger invaded me, until the rumor spread a short time later that the Pentagon and the White House had been bombed. Even as flames issued from the wounded towers, I thought only of how many casualties there might be and in no way anticipated the scope of the disaster to come.

After another interval—it may have been fifteen or twenty minutes—we were asked to leave the terminal and found ourselves outside without transportation: The bridges had been closed. I made my way (in what may have been a gypsy limo) to a subway station near Queensboro Bridge, then, because the subway was not running, streamed with a large crowd to Manhattan, via the pedestrian sidewalk of the bridge. It was a beautiful day; on my left side smoke could be seen near the horizon, which I kept looking at as if it was bound to go away once firefighters had it under control.

I have had several months to think about what happened on that day. What difference did that event make, which put its mark on time as if an epoch had passed, even if one cannot yet fully gauge the hope that was lost or the determination gained? With some reluctance I decided to add this short epilogue to my just completed book, *Scars of the Spirit*.

A rhetoric of specificity, common to temporal markers, is used these days with exquisite precision: We hear that the self-awareness of the United States and the West changed shortly after 8:46 A.M. that clear September morning. On the one hand, the flow of time seems mechanical, as if perpetual and infinitely divisible, a banal matter of record; on the other hand, an emotional stopwatch punctuates life with traumatic or near apocalyptic effect.

The power of a traumatic episode to define an epoch is caught by Freud's essay "On Transience," which expresses the feeling that World War I, then barely a year old, "had robbed the world of its beauties, . . . shattered pride in the achievements of our civilization, our admiration for many philosophers and artists and our hopes of a final triumph over the differences between nations and races."[1] Even Europe, that "Old World," subtly permeated as in Henry James's novels by a sophisticated corruption and ceremonies of complicity, Europe, it seemed, had still an innocence to lose. As for America today, many times in the last few months the figure of the American Adam has surfaced: of a suddenly vanished and already nostalgically haloed fall from innocence and security.

I wonder whether there is not always a wake-up call in the life of individuals or collectives. John Donne describes that "now" moment when he calls falling in love a "good-morrow to our waking souls."[2] Its other side is a decisive disenchantment affecting basic trust. The demystifying incident, one that precipitates a major turning of mood or mind, could itself be deceptive in the sense of crystallizing previous shocks rather than being unique. As the lives of some of the hijackers come into view, we are often told that they seemed normal enough, even bourgeois, until "something" changed them into radical Muslims.

Did the strain of living with an invasive sense of alienation, of the unreality of society, self, or world, feed their contempt of worldliness and particularly of the Western style of life? The yearning for purity, lost or about to be lost, for dedication, for truth that lodges elsewhere— beyond corruption, humiliation, hypocrisy, injustice, materialism, grinding poverty, or poverty of spirit—can lead to the adoption of a transgressive, even outlaw, identity. Instead of impassiveness or trivial pursuit, an exalted, visionary sense of purpose takes over; popular fiction is full of avengers and purifiers of that kind.

A spectacular act can give the illusion of agency or self-identity, even at the cost of unleashing disaster. In Coleridge's famous poem *Rime of the Ancient Mariner*, the consequence (although not the motivation) of the mariner's killing of the albatross is clear: The act opens his eyes to a universe filled with spirits. They demand the perpetrator's punishment yet also make him their focus. Everything turns on his (guilty) presence. His trespass in this Eastern tale, as this kind of story was often called, accrues revelatory power: A hidden legion of supernatural enforcers comes into view. The hijackers, by the light fiction throws on history, may have pursued an aim that seemed to them exalted rather than malignant: something akin to the well-known religious temptation to "hasten the end." Did they also seek to redeem the image of the fatalistic Muslim by making themselves instruments of a fatal action?

The quest for authenticity (intending to restore the true Islam, the true Christian faith, or some other religious way of life) exposes an inflammable identity crisis. Perhaps induced by a "call," a crisis of this kind inheres in every formation of the distinctive individual. The impulse to separate from one community (family, home) leads to a second birth within a chosen community. In extreme cases it creates deodands, self-proclaimed messengers of God, or provokes sacrificial deeds to overcome the vanity, impurity, and emptiness of human life—although it would be sheer hubris to enumerate and typify here all the intellectual and emotional malformations that might ensue. What is clear is that evil can have idealistic as well as cynical roots.

The call may ask believers to change their life and "put away childish things." But what does that mean? What model of maturity or authentic existence is implied? I find it impossible to respect a culture that in fact denies childhood and trains children to grow into warriors or even suicide bombers. Or movements that wound secular time by seeking to end it, inciting the Apocalypse by way of a schism that parts "The man to come . . . as by a gulph / From him who had been" (which is how Wordsworth described certain ideologies accompanying the French Revolution).[3]

Realpolitik, too, as in legal philosopher Carl Schmitt's sheer polarity of friend and foe, is often presented as a spiritual imperative, though it is really a sick outgrowth of the very desire for a paradisal harmony and unity. Genocide, the German philosopher Theodor Adorno remarked, involves the wish for absolute integration.

The ground zero left by the collapse of the Twin Towers is literally a scar of the spirit. It testifies to more than an attempt to shatter icons of capitalism and U.S. power. The smoldering devastation of those ruins creates a new icon, a permanent mental image of how violence can cloak itself as spirituality. Wordsworth discerned the religious or pseudoreligious intensity of the passion leading to such acts when he describes how, in the era of the French Revolution, he became for a time "A Bigot to a New Idolatry / Like a cowled Monk who hath forsworn the world."[4]

When I finally reached Boston in October and gave my lecture, I took in a show by two famous fashion photographers who had worked in Europe and America since the 1930s. Because of TV, my head at that time was filled with images of Afghan women veiled completely in burkas according to the strictures of the Taliban. Nothing of their body was visible. They were shapeless statues. In contrast, the Boston exhibition covering more than thirty years of models and celebrities contained but a single photo of a totally swathed woman, a famous dancer. It was a study of her garments' rhythmic, dynamic flow. It projected the image of a second or more glorious body superimposed on the first, a body more abstract or less patently functional, with lines sculpted as lovingly by photography's liquid gradations of light and shade as the beard and draperies of certain Romanesque figures at Vezelay or the Hellenic "Victory" that greets visitors to the Louvre.

Given our own, intensifying visual culture, it may be hard to understand why Taliban iconoclasm, its fear of images, has gone so far. The key, I think, is not found primarily in the concept of a pure monotheistic religion and its zeal to tame the lust of the eyes. Rather, a normative distrust of appearances turns into a species of Gnosticism, that very old religious heresy resisted by both Judaism and Christianity. Positing a deceiving demiurge who may be the god of this world but is not the true God, it fostered the quest for deliverance from a deceit that could only be destroyed together with the world itself.

The *real presence* of falsity is a terrifying notion. It supports the idea of an evil empire. What comforted us in the past, when we became aware of social suffering, political oppression, or, generally, living in untruth, was that falsity had only an unreal presence. Truth, as the saying goes, is the daughter of time; political, scientific, economic, and medical remedies would surely, in time, alleviate global misery; reality was on the side of progress. In the West, this assumption has suffered a shock. Totalitarianism, two world wars, and a post-Holocaust awareness of continuing genocidal episodes have disclosed the extent to which "organized appearance" backed by terror can create for long and murderous periods a consenting populace.

In the more extremist parts of the Islamic world, very often it is modernity, its technological power of imitation and simulation, that is held to be in the service of a deceitful demiurge. But elsewhere too uneasiness prevails. While augmenting the pleasure of living among beautiful and distracting things, modernity increases almost beyond human discernment the critical burden of distinguishing a merely vicarious from a truly participant and productive form of life.

The sterility of a consumer culture, the difficulty of endowing it with ultimate value, has a multitude of effects, including pernicious ideologies. These do not see a way out of the dominance of the pleasure principle and complicit institutions except by resorting to violence. The devil of technology is turned strategically against the enemy who fathered it. Moreover, when some Muslims pretend to be assimilated Westerners in order to destroy an infidel culture, the fear revives of the *faux semblant,* or enemy within, and threatens a hard-won multiculturalism as well as settled civil liberties.

Democratic institutions cannot afford to self-destruct under such pressure. We have not forgotten what happened in the McCarthy era or the immense tragedy inspired in good part by the Manichean ideology of Nazism, which disenfranchised even assimilated Jews (who were often more German than the Germans in their love of that culture), dooming them to expulsion and destruction. The Nazis could not often profile the assimilated German Jews by discernable marks of difference. Yet the very absence of distinguishing features (except for the disproportionate contribution Jews made to Germany's intellectual and artistic life) was held against that tiny minority and incited a propagandistic caricature viciously exaggerating the slightest physical difference and claiming that assimilation was a deceptive and dangerous mask. Fear of the real presence of falsity created a devil myth once again.

Historical analogies are risky, but they are what we have to go on. Unlike the relatively small number of pre-Holocaust Jews, who at that time had no nation-state in which they were the majority, over a billion Muslims, the predominant majority in several nation-states, now pose a real challenge to the West. Most of Islam has not passed through a significant Reform movement separating church and state, and in its confrontation with secular modernity it is convulsed by a conservative revolution. Whether or not a "clash of civilizations" is now inevitable, the temptation of radicalizing the East-West conflict and profiling differences returns in all its crudeness. Blake's "Human Form Divine," his saving concept of a reconciled, this-worldly humanity, is split apart, wounded by a powerful distrust.

A cause, unfortunately in the guise of a casus belli, has unified Americans, perhaps for the first time since World War II. I have never seen so many show the flag. The struggle against semblance and inauthenticity continues, entering an especially perilous phase.

Notes

1. Sigmund Freud, "On Transience," in *Writing on Art and Literature* (Stanford CA Stanford University Press, 1997), 176–79.

2. John Donne, "The Good Morrow," in *Songs and Sonnets*.

3. William Wordsworth, *The Prelude* (1850), 12:59–60.

4. Wordsworth, 12:77–78.

September 11: Between Memory and History

Richard Stamelman

A Klee painting named "Angelus Novus" shows an angel looking as though he is about to move away from something he is fixedly contemplating. His eyes are staring, his mouth is open, his wings are spread. This is how one pictures the angel of history. His face is turned toward the past. — Walter Benjamin

Several months before his suicide in September 1940 after failing to cross the French-Spanish border, the literary critic and philosopher Walter Benjamin had imagined in one of his allegorical "theses" on the philosophy of history the kinds of landscapes, events, and visions that the angel of history— more witness to than actor in the tragic chronicle of past time—had been compelled by fate to see. From millennium to millennium without surcease, the angel, as Benjamin envisioned him, had been forced to watch a sight (and a site) of unending, irreversible, and devastating "catastrophe."[1] History had not been and could never be otherwise, for in Benjamin's dark imagination it expressed the senseless, disjointed record of barbarism, death, and destruction. Turning toward the past the angel keeps his eyes fixed on the debris mounting before him.

While most people would perceive in the endlessly accumulating ruins the sequential chain of events that a rational, organic, synthetic, and evolutionary concept of history had taught them to see, the angel has an altogether different perspective. Where we look for order and discover a pattern that connects events one to the other, he perceives "one single catastrophe which keeps piling wreckage upon wreckage and hurls it in front of his feet."[2] The catastrophe is explosive, random, and constant. With every passing second, more and more fragments are added to the pile of debris. The effect is cumulative; yet no meaning—outside of the continuous accumulation of blasted fragments of time—emerges. Although "the angel would like to stay, awaken the dead, and make whole what has been smashed," although he would like to heal the wounds and repair the tears opened in the skin of memory and the fabric of history, he lacks the power to do so. "A storm is blowing from Paradise; it has got caught in his wings with such violence that the angel can no longer close them. This storm irresistibly propels him into the future to which his back is turned, while the pile of debris before him grows skyward."[3] The winds of so-called progress install an ever-growing distance between the angel and the debris field from which he is being swept away by the ineluctable march of history.

Through Benjamin's allegorical image of the angel, history self-reflexively examines itself and learns sadly that the downtrodden and the dead cannot be redeemed; that historical continuity, despite the self-delusion of historicism, cannot be reinvented; and that the past, given its continuous movement toward catastrophe, cannot be refashioned into a meaningful configuration. Whatever might be said about the past is immediately contested and undone by the changes perpetually at work in the landscape of disaster. For Benjamin, profoundly sensitive to the rumblings of a debacle that ultimately would swell into a catastrophe of death and genocide even beyond the imagination of his angel of history, the reality of historical time was that of nothingness itself: a perpetual reenactment of negativity and vacuity.[4] As a landscape of wreckage and debris, a field of ruin and decay, a place of loss and mourning, history is, as Benjamin makes so presciently and tragically clear, a ground zero. A scant five years after his death, science and imagination would give to Benjamin's *vision* of catastrophe a nightmarish *actuality* that the newly minted expression "ground zero" would once and for all powerfully represent. Along with the atomic age it announces, the term "ground zero," the *Random House Unabridged Dictionary* reports, makes its appearance in English between 1945 and 1950 as the designation for that "point on the surface of the earth or water directly below, directly above, or at which an atomic or hydrogen bomb explodes." While Benjamin had hoped that theology in general and the mysticism of the Kabbalah in particular might come to the rescue of history—only the Messiah, he declares, can repair the catastrophic history that the angel is powerless to stop—he may have abandoned such hope once confronted by an atomic catastrophe that no reparation—mystic, messianic, or otherwise—could ever set right.

The fact that Benjamin's image of history as "one single catastrophe" continually piling wreckage upon wreckage would become the ground zero of Hiroshima and Nagasaki and the fact that the nuclear devastation signified by the allusion to absolute nothingness in the image of ground zero would then come to express the pulverization of the World Trade Center reveal the coincidence, the nearly literal overlapping, of history and language, of event and word. The resurrection of "ground zero" as a term designating total, unimaginable, and devastating destruction carries with it, as it moves from August 6, 1945, to September 11, 2001, an echo and a resonance that link both events. In using "ground zero" to refer to the attack on the World Trade Center we call to mind, either consciously or unconsciously, those wastelands of total ruination that newsreels and photographs of Hiroshima (and Nagasaki, three days later) have embedded in our visual memories. But the conflation of the atomic event with the terrorist attack, the fusing of August 6 with September 11, changes the symbolic valence of the image of disaster they both share and evoke. "Ground zero" (1945) is on the surface the same expression as "ground zero" (2001), and yet it is very different; the temporal distance separating them has created this difference. The original expression from the end of World War II does not have—how could it?—the same metaphoric meaning or the same charge of symbolic specificity that its latest incarnation has generated.

Ground zero at the World Trade Center refers, it is true, to a specific event that occurred on September 11, 2001; but at that same time the contemporary event it designates is encircled by the aura of atrocity belonging to its avatar; it both calls upon and calls out for symbolic support to the ground zeros at Hiroshima and Nagasaki, as well as to those at Bikini atoll (in the central Pacific) and Yucca Flats (in New Mexico), sites of American atomic and hydrogen bomb tests from 1946 to the end of the 1950s. "Ground zero," therefore, installs Hiroshima (and other nuclear sites) in the heart of Lower Manhattan. It adds to the void at the World Trade Center a series of powerful associations, images, memories, and ideologies that over a sixty-six-year period have enveloped and crystallized around the image of an urban landscape of total emptiness. Having lost its power of metaphor almost immediately after the unprecedented annihilation and unimaginable nothingness of Hiroshima had brutally revealed the extent to which the "zeroness" of the site could never be metaphorical—could never even truly be articulated—"ground zero" as applied to the World Trade Center is reinvested with new analogical power; it becomes the metaphor for that earlier event to whose priority and precedence as the archetype of catastrophe it cannot help but refer. For while the loss of life and property at the World Trade Center and the Pentagon and the horror of the attacks have no equal in American history, ground zero in New York could never, except as metaphor, be said to resemble ground zero at Hiroshima or Nagasaki.

In its original designation as a place of complete and devastating destruction and injury, "ground zero" was site-specific, and that site was atomic and Japanese. But the symbolic valence of the term in its New York reincarnation has increased; it now has more than one singular identity. Out of the historical reference it makes to a place and time of destruction (New York City, September 11, 2001) the historical memory of an earlier site and date (Hiroshima, August 6, 1945) has been developed (in the photographic sense of the word). The image of the earlier disaster lies behind the later event like a ghostly, tragic presence. It is the phantom image behind the image, the invisible writing behind the writing, the dark shadow moving at the bottom of the well of the present. In Benjamin's terms, the wreckage of one catastrophe has yet again been piled atop that of another. The ruins of the two events lie fused together, their fragments intermingled in the same debris field of history.

The fact that ground zero now contains at its very center a remembrance of an earlier event, which it automatically (either intentionally or involuntarily) calls to mind, makes the expression into what French historian Pierre Nora has called a "memory site" (*lieu de mémoire*). Such *lieux de mémoire*, he writes, are "moments of history torn away from the movement of history, then returned; no longer quite life, not yet death, like shells on the shore when the sea of living memory has receded."[5] The sea of history, whose tempestuous, incessant waves create the "single catastrophe" Benjamin had imagined, deposits on the shore of the present the shell of a prior, lost, forgotten, or repressed event. This is a fragment out of time, which the present rediscovers and in which, like the hermit crab, it takes up residence, a shell wherein the muffled echoes of a distant explosion in the past blend with the thunderous detonation of a present disaster.

Usually, it takes time for a *milieu de mémoire* (the very moment of the event itself in the historical here and now) to undergo the sea change that makes it into a *lieu de mémoire*.[6] Battlefields like Gettysburg or Verdun, for example, became memory sites once the actual event had been "replaced" and rearticulated through commemorative monuments that had literally occupied—if not symbolically taken over—the site. Statues, obelisks, cenotaphs, *arc de triomphes*, and memorial events add to the historical site their own history (of design, construction, political debate, public reaction, controversy) as motivated and shaped by the ideologies and symbols inherent to the act of commemoration itself. Interpretation overwhelms event; metaphor replaces history. Spontaneous cries of rebellion, stirring mottoes of resistance, and fervent passwords of solidarity, dramatically associated with the "presentness" of historical events—"Give me liberty or give me death," "Remember the Alamo," "They shall not pass!" come to mind— are, once they pass into collective memory, distanced from the immediacy of their temporal origins, changed by forgetfulness and revisionism into catchall or cliché expressions referring to many different, sometimes contra-dictory, kinds of human activity; thus, they become petrified (like statues) and ossified (like corpses) into sites of memory. In a less stirring but still powerful way, this fossilization has happened to the expression "ground zero" in its movement from 1945 to the present.

The metamorphosis of a locus of history into a site of memory usually requires, Nora argues, the passage of decades, generations, even centuries. What is most interesting about the World Trade Center disaster, however, is not only that it has literally and physically been taken over by a word whose evocation of vacuity truly represents and symbolizes it—the pit at ground zero in place of the once-looming towers, the hole of absence figuring a lost presence—but that the event itself and the landscape of the event have so rapidly been transformed into a memory site. It is as if the sign of disaster, this irrefutable, brutal absence revealed in and at ground zero, demands that "the hole in the real," the term that the French psychoanalyst Jacques Lacan once used to express the sudden apparition of death, not be allowed to remain empty: that it be filled with words, stories, anecdotes, testimonies, biographies, images, photographs, documentaries, objects, mementos, and icons; that it become a site of memory and of remembrance, a place of disaster made meaningful by the representations—personal, collective, commemorative, spontaneous, official—that follow catastrophe, a writing of disaster that is also a *re*-membering (a recalling and a reconstruction) of disaster.

Outside of the absolute desire to recollect, remember, and memorialize the over three thousand victims of September 11 and outside of the absolute need to transform the *nothing* of ground zero into a *something*, why has the ruined World Trade Center become transformed so quickly into a memory site? The metamorphosis has not taken place through years and decades but in a few months. Perhaps this is due to the speed with which objects, events, and persons in the postmodern age of rapid communication, imme-diate globalization, and instantaneous commodification are transformed into symbols and icons. Objects become fetishes, events myths, persons celebrities: and all three, products. Nothing is too great, too catastrophic, too devastating, even too sacred that it cannot be appropriated by forces of consumerism and marketing. Even language has been quick to keep pace with the mainstreaming of disaster and its consequent devaluation. Already the idioms of September 11 have been turned to pedestrian uses. "Ground zero," one newspaper reported, is being used to refer to the "total mess" of a teenager's bedroom.[7] An out-of-fashion hat, dress, or pair of shoes is said to be "very September 10th."[8] Lexicographers, the *New York Times* reported, are already debating what words specific to September 11 will become permanent entries in their dictionaries; "ground zero" will continue, for the time being it seems, to keep its original nuclear signification.[9] Even the use of the term "September 11" or "9/11," with its distinctive virgule—and no hyphen—to express all that happened in New York and Washington, has become a symbol, an abbreviation, a sign, a code word permitting an all too contained and convenient encapsulation of the inexpressible chaos and confusion of that day.

Even more revealing of the commercialization of September 11 are the allusions that advertising has made to it. Conceived and designed in the weeks following the terrorist attacks, these advertisements—the first tremors of ground zero to have been picked up, as it were, on the Richter scale of popular culture—began appearing in mass-circulation fashion magazines a mere three to four months after the event. Abandoning the images of raunchy, overheated sexuality, of cemetery chic, and of baroque excesses of wealth prevalent in many of the fashion layouts of the late 1990s, Seventh Avenue, in a reaction to September 11 so immediate that it seemed to happen in a "New York minute," changed direction. As the *New York Times* observed, the thuggish pouts, the steely cold looks of boredom, the haughty gazes of disdain, the wasted, overdosed faces, and the "ominousness on which fashion advertising has depended" suddenly vanished. " 'The world,' " one fashion executive was quoted as saying, " 'was not ready to see another typical fashion ad.' "[10]

The longing for protection, comfort, and consolation was immediately answered by images of protection, comfort, and consolation offering objects (transitional, surrogate, and fetishized) that would truly give protection, comfort, and consolation. A young couple, for example, lies fully clothed on a bed. The man sleeps. The woman wears a beige blouse over a simple black dress with a thick studded black belt around her waist. She is awake. Her smile and the peaceful expression on her face—the tranquility is made more intense by the soft, out-of-focus light pouring through lightly curtained windows—indicate great well-being and contentment. The woman stares at the screen of a laptop computer on the bed next to her; a hand rests lightly on the keypad. "On September 12," this advertisement for the designer Kenneth Cole informs us, "we used protection in the bedroom, not the mailroom. Today is not a dress rehearsal."[11] Another ad in the series pictures a woman in a black dress languorously lying supine on a rustic, weather-beaten kitchen table, holding a bowl of strawberries in one hand and absentmindedly putting the fruit in her mouth with the other. The ad copy declares that "On September 12, families returned to the dining room table. Today is not a dress rehearsal."[12] A third advertising image in the same vein shows a woman in white pants lost in thought, seated in a leather armchair, legs dangling over the armrest, a telephone close to hand. Below the image a legend proclaims, "On September 12, people who don't speak to their parents forgot why. Today is not a dress rehearsal."[13]

These Kenneth Cole advertisements express, as the *New York Times* reported, the idea of "domestic contentment."[14] The designer, according to his spokesperson, wanted " 'to show a relationship, warmth, humanness— moments most people would actually relate to.' "[15] Moreover, the combining of what some might generously be willing to call a public interest ad with a fashion image is hardly a new phenomenon, especially for Kenneth Cole, who in past years has opened his various fashion images to moral, uplifting, even self-critical slogans and sentiments. "You can change an outfit, you can outfit change, or both," an ad from 1999 proclaimed.[16] What is new in the "Today is not a dress rehearsal" series, however, is the undisguised appropriation of a catastrophic historical event—an event already integrated into memory but not yet archived in history, an event caught in the space between memory and history—for the marketing and publicizing of the products of a name-brand designer. Even though advertising executives might point to the message of comfort and humanness conveyed by these ads and to the image of a restored normalcy that they offer to a traumatized, post-September 11 world evidently in need of the comfort couture offers, the conjunction of the catastrophic and the chic is self-serving and distasteful, especially considering the appearance of these images so quickly after the collapse of the World Trade Center and the attack on the Pentagon.[17]

Are there no events so devastating, so murderous, so painful, so unthinkable, and so off-limits that they cannot be seized for representation by the advertising industry? The idea that *today* in the wake of September 11 we live in a world that can no longer be called a rehearsal—that we can no longer be content (as we once were on September 10 and earlier) to pretend, to dress up, to hide behind costumes, clothes, makeup, and perfume, and that the distinctions between theater and world, rehearsal and life are no longer possible, especially now that, with all performances cancelled, we have come face to face with the "real"—suggests, falsely of course, that September 11 has removed mask, pretence, sham, superficiality, and illusion (but, strangely, not fashion) from our lives. The terrorist event, the ad implies, has done away with everything that is *not* reality.

Whatever this "reality" may be, it is at least, as Kenneth Cole seeks to assure us, "not a dress rehearsal," even when we put on our Kenneth

Cole clothes. For in the post-9/11 world these are not the clothes we wore at earlier rehearsals; these are now "reality clothes." In Kenneth Cole's image of "today," the post-9/11 "today," we get along better with our families, with our parents, and with ourselves. We become more contemplative, more sensitive, and more content with simple things: a bowl of strawberries, a bed, an old table, a companion by our side. Yet, this announcement of the end of life-as-rehearsal and the beginning of life-as-reality also expresses a disingenuously contrary message: namely, that, despite the fine sentiments of the ads, no change has really occurred between September 10 and September 11, because Kenneth Cole is still open for business. His shoes, sweaters, dresses, and accessories are still available for purchase. But now, as we wear these garments and give ourselves the comfort and contentment of his clothes, we must adopt a new attitude. We must recognize, as Kenneth Cole has instructed us to do, that fashion is no longer the rehearsal it once was but reality itself. Fashion now articulates, reiterates, and coincides with the reality effect put in force by September 11 itself. But to turn the event into image—that is, to equate the collapse of the World Trade Center with a new look, a new style, a new fashion attitude—raises serious questions about taste and its relationship to sites of memory and trauma.

There is certainly no need to be naive about the power of advertising to repossess, rearticulate, and recycle the events of history. Many are the battlefields, the monuments, the cultural icons, the architectural spaces, even the killing fields whose image and icons have been transferred to T-shirts, hats, pens, metal souvenirs, coffee cups, and drinking glasses designed to be carried away as souvenirs and mementos. Such a transfer and a transporting of historical sites—miniaturized, of course, in souvenir form—occur once the ground of the historical event has been softened, so to speak, by the passage of time for the easy unearthing of its remains, once it has been readied, as it were, for "translation": the kind of sea change that occurs when an original text is recast in a foreign language or when a body is removed from a grave and moved to a memorial crypt. This translation coincides with the metamorphosis of a historical space into a memory site. The *lieu de mémoire*, torn from its past and set adrift in the direction of an unknown future, is ready to be filled with whatever meaning or ideology or image the present decides to assign to it. It is like an empty bag that can only stand on its own once it is filled with something; it belongs to the future—that tomorrow to come that will create the *lieu de mémoire*—to choose what that something will be. We already have filled the container represented by "September 11," or "9/11," or "ground zero" with new meanings and associations. What new images and forms this memory site will contain, however, in the months and years to come, as the history (and then the myth) of September 11 crystallizes and solidifies and as the forces of commodification seize the event for their own purposes, is anyone's guess. It is clear, though, that if the movement of history is indeed that of catastrophe and its action that of the endless piling up of debris and detritus, as Benjamin fatefully imagined, then the memory of that history, its *lieu de mémoire,* will also involve the endless piling up of incomplete fragments of meaning. For September 11 will occupy that unstable space *between* memory and history, that ground zero where the "truth" of history is perpetually forgotten and the "illusion" of memory perpetually remembered.

NOTES

1. Walter Benjamin, "Theses on the Philosophy of History," *Illuminations,* ed. Hannah Arendt, trans. Harry Zohn (New York: Schocken Books, 1968), 257. For an interesting history and interpretation of the "Theses," see Michael Löwy, *Walter Benjamin: Avertissement d'incendie. Une lecture des thèses "Sur le concept d'histoire"* (Paris: PUF, 2001).

2. Benjamin, 257.

3. Benjamin, 257–58.

4. Benjamin's 1940 "Theses" can be seen as a "fire alarm," an air-raid siren sounding a shrill warning to his contemporaries about "the imminent dangers threatening them and about the new catastrophes gathering on the horizon" (Löwy, 19).

5. Pierre Nora, "Between Memory and History: *Les Lieux de Mémoire,*" trans. Marc Roudebush, *Representations* 26 (spring 1989): 12.

6. Nora, 7.

7. Emily Wax, "In Times of Terror, Teens Talk the Talk," *Washington Post*; rpt., *International Herald Tribune*, Mar. 20, 2002, 1.

8. Patrick Cabasset, "Tellement 10 Septembre," *L'Officiel de la couture et de la mode de Paris*, 863, March 2002, 52.

9. Janny Scott, "Words of 9/11 Go from Coffee Shops to the Dictionaries," *New York Times*, Feb. 24, 2002, A1, 10.

10. Ginia Bellafante, "Sell That Dress: Back to Basics in Spring Advertising," *New York Times*, Feb. 5, 2002, B8.

11. *Vogue*, March 2002.

12. *Harper's Bazaar*, March 2002.

13. *W*, March 2002.

14. Bellafante, 8.

15. Bellafante, 8.

16. *Vogue*, September 1999. This multipage advertisement displays other secondary "good speak" slogans exhorting the consumer to "Carry Protection," "Have a Theme Song," "Designate a Driver," "Donate Your Time," and "Keep Your Head." Another Cole ad informs the reader that "We considered doing a controversial ad about a socially relevant issue. But we decided to remain Clothes-Minded" (*Vogue*, September 2000), a tongue-in-cheek pun that allows Cole to have his cake and eat it too. His self-declared intention is to make a social statement. But as a prisoner in the *closed*-minded world of clothes, he self-critically acknowledges that he is powerless to do anything but design clothes; for this he calls himself to task, as he congratulates himself for being astute, aware, and politically correct. The designer Moschino also likes the ambiguity of double-edged fashion ads that use slogans simultaneously to celebrate and to indict the fashion system. From a 1999 campaign are the following self-contradictory statements: "Fashion Victims of the World, Unite"; "I am not just wearing a dress: I'm fighting illiteracy" (in reference to a dress imprinted with a vertical list of over thirty words); "Fashion: Dictates or Dictatorship?"; "Do Clothes Have the Power to Make You Happy?"; "Will Fashion Be the New Opium of the People?"; and "DON'T $TOP THE FA$HION YTEM," a slogan whose lettering subverts its very message so that one can be both for and against fashion as one literally "buys" into it.

17. One designer who has alluded to the World Trade Center disaster but in a subtle and dignified manner is Donna Karan in an ad for DKNY jeans (*W*, March 2002). A model (who could be male or female) wears a T-shirt imprinted with images of the American flag and a motorcycle. He or she stands in front of an enlarged background created from a collage of New York City sights (the Brooklyn Bridge, the Empire State Building, the Met Life Building, the Statue of Liberty, Grand Central Terminal, the East River). A raised finger wipes a tear from an eye.

Wounded New York

Judith Greenberg

Humpty Dumpty sat on a wall. Humpty Dumpty had a great fall. All the king's horses and all the king's men couldn't put Humpty together again.

Since September 11, a troubling message resonates inside this nursery rhyme that we frequently recite in my two-year-old daughter's classes. Although recited to reassure children with its rhymes, it's actually quite morbid. There's no redemption, no healing, only a fall into irreparable bits and fragments.

The odd condition of childhood innocence, sheltered from not only the dark signification of the nursery rhymes but also (we hope) the knowledge of the violence to which they refer, was especially clear to me on that day. After watching the events on television all morning and realizing that staring at those images might be detrimental to our daughter, my husband and I did the thing we knew how to do when in shock that afternoon—we took her to the neighborhood playground. There, across the street from Ladder Company 25, a firehouse that we would soon learn lost nine men that day, adults wandered about aimlessly with blank stares on their faces or tears in their eyes, as children ran around as carelessly as on any other sunny afternoon. It was the most incongruous of situations—trying to keep children feeling secure in their normal routines while nothing was either normal or routine. There we were as parents, trying to avoid transmitting what we knew was already our "secondary trauma" to our children. How could we keep intact their sense of security and home?

AT HOME

I spent the morning "safe" at home six miles away on the Upper West Side of Manhattan. In addition to my horror in imagining the death toll, I worried about my husband, working in a skyscraper near the Empire State

Building. No one knew what would be hit next. He appeared home after what for him was a surreal walk uptown, and although helicopters circled outside our window, home (our apartment) seemed the safest place to be. As former Texas governor Ann Richards said on *Larry King Live*, she felt the same way in New York on September 11 that she did in Texas on the day of Kennedy's assassination: she just wanted to go *home*. For those of us who have made New York our home, the attacks freshly complicated those terms—"home" and "New York"—and proved anew that they signify not just location but also a relation to identity.

In New York, one's neighborhood can feel as much like home as a cramped apartment. In my neighborhood, the aftermath could be felt viscerally. I encountered seemingly familiar faces on missing person fliers posted on streetlight posts and shop windows. For days (or was it weeks?) I could see a huge gray cloud hovering over the southern end of the city, and when the winds shifted and blew uptown I inhaled the death-infused air. American flags ostensibly claimed their turf but left me feeling even more vulnerable, both because of the violence that produced them and the apparent joy they embraced in their promise of military action to follow. New York felt newly "unhomey."

Two quotes from the Naudet brothers' documentary, *9/11*, which aired on American television six months after the attacks, capture some of the extreme feelings about home that were often expressed. At one extreme is paranoia, a fear that home has disappeared. "There's no way to get home!" cries a woman running from the collapse of the second tower, referring to the stoppage of public transportation and the closure of the bridges and tunnels to and from Manhattan. In a sense, her despair speaks a truth; the fall was irreparable.

At the other extreme we find unity. A fireman reflects upon the events, saying, "what kept it all together was us, as a group, as a body, as a firehouse." The unified house, body, and community "keeps it all together"—holds the broken pieces. This was a sentiment much echoed in the media—they stressed the togetherness and unity of New Yorkers, Americans, and even the "civilized world."

These two extreme feelings—the sense of dislocation and the celebration of unity—are not unrelated. They express responses to a troubling of the concept of home, in the sense of both an internal feeling of security and a national homeland. The ways in which the events troubled a sense of home were, of course, diverse, tied to one's physical location and personal history among other factors. Much as the notion of home turns our attention to the private sphere of family, much of the mourning process, at least in

New York, troubled the concept of home on a public stage. The intimacy produced by the "Portraits of Grief" section in the *New York Times* and the "family album" quality of the missing person fliers publicly attempted to bring the grief of the broken private home to the broken public home. As we reestablish a relation to home both publicly and privately, we must consider the emotional and political layers at work in our responses.

The trauma of September 11 broke a collective protective shield, and "all the king's horses and all the king's men" cannot put us back together again, as we were. Our sense of home must be built anew, and in so doing we must confront what the fragments mean to us. While some memories may appear as clear as the sky on that bright September day, many pieces of our experience remain missing. Cathy Caruth emphasizes the absent and all too present nature of trauma: "its very unassimilated nature—the way it was precisely *not known* in the first instance—returns to haunt the survivor later on."[1] According to such an understanding, trauma is tied to an idea of missing, something that cannot be grasped. As I write this essay six months after the attacks—a time in which some say the images have already lost their shock value—we are only beginning to relate to both what haunts and what remains obscured in our psychic homes.[2]

DISTANCE

How do those of us whose grief is harder to specify address our encounter with violence and death? How do we return to what remains missing, in part, to ourselves? Most New Yorkers I've encountered do not consider themselves victims and frequently explain: "no one close to me died." Such statements appropriately acknowledge the incommensurate grief of the victims' families and loved ones. But these disclaimers also perform a kind of distancing from the grief of secondary trauma. One editorial assistant at a university press told me that the press wasn't interested in this book because "we're just not into that September 11 thing." For some, there was even a shame of claiming a relation to the events, as if such recognition could usurp the trauma of the victims and their loved ones.

Geographical distance also allowed psychological distance. Just as people uptown were less affected than were those downtown, so identification with the victims was more tangential to those outside of New York, whose sense of home remained less troubled or at least the role of the witness was harder to grasp. My friends "safe" across the country could discuss politics and the problems of globalization with a detachment that New Yorkers in the immediate aftermath could not afford. As usually happens, location affected a sense of vulnerability.

Others consciously or unconsciously identified with the aggressors. More explicit were the critiques in the first couple of weeks that asserted that the United States deserved the attacks for arrogance and foreign policy. They almost gleefully cried, "I told you so." Such apparently easy distancing and blatant insensitivity to human loss bespeak denial, aggression, and possibly a counterreaction to the pain of identification. Dr. Rachel Seidel recognizes the symbolic value of the attacks upon diverse psyches: "the powerful images of aggression and annihilation charged our inscapes, evoked traumatic childhood antecedents and spoke directly (for the most part, unconsciously) to the wishes of the terrorist within. Destruction raging in the outer world met and amplified the archaic aggressiveness inhabiting the inside."[3] The tremendous destruction of the Other could trigger all kinds of devouring fantasies.

Both the distancing mechanisms and the acts of identification with the deadly aggressors surfaced as responses to the massive encounter with death, an encounter that exposed the ineffable proximity between the living and the dead. To resist the pull of the dead, one may fervently claim his or her place among the living and even turn away from the impact of the event. The thought "that could've been me" may produce the reassuring afterthought "that wasn't me," possibly followed by "I don't want that to be me" or even "I want no part in (thinking about) that."

September 11 blew apart not just our sense of home but our psychological unity as well. If not literally, then internally, it tore many of us into fragments. There was much talk of the unity created in the aftermath, but in actuality much was ripped asunder. I felt divided from—rather than unified with—both those who could analyze the situation with critical detachment and those who suffered greatly. Anxiety, the psyche's defense from further fright, tore into me. Dreams of plane crashes, bombings, and attacks and fears about the subway (and, for a time, the mail) appeared, as psychoanalysis would put it, to shield me. Although public rhetoric focused on how all Americans suddenly joined the same side, in private, isolation and distance grew on both individual and international levels. The war in Afghanistan provided a unified external projection of fragmented wars within. No matter how many degrees of separation distance us from the dead, the ripple of grief spreads wide. Amnesia, or distance, can make one numb at the very moment it serves as protection against painful memories.

The role of posttraumatic amnesia—a distance from one's own self—was embodied in the story of fireman Kevin Shea, who was the sole survivor from his company after 9/11.[4] Shea cannot remember if he was a hero or, as he fears, a coward. His blank reminds us of the ties between memory and identity and the fragility of both constructions.

The Missing and the Body

New York has a wound—an enormous, smoldering (for a time) hole signifying the missing. The proliferation of missing person fliers and the related fact that so many of the dead were first identified as missing mean that for many there was a phase of literally not knowing whether their loved ones were alive or dead. Even if we didn't know the individuals on the fliers, those of us who encountered these faces went through a process of uncertainty, hoping for their survival, despite all evidence of its impossibility. Mourning needs to heal the wound, to build a scar, but the missing cannot be buried. As I write six months later, bodies continue to be exhumed, and many will never be recovered. It takes time to convert absence into death. Wounds remain open despite the yearning for rapid closure.

Then, of course, there are the missing towers. The towers dwarfed neighboring buildings; they overwhelmed—a point made by both the terrorists and the commentators. The towers now overwhelm in their absence. The proliferation of their photos in windows around the city testifies to a grieving and an attempt to claim that lost home. How do we see absence? The city's memorial of two towers of light projected from the site, visible but not tangible, has dramatized their absent presence. The shafts remind us of where the buildings stood ("Where were they exactly?") and the primary nature of our relation to objects in space. We relate to objects even before we have a concept of identity; we ground ourselves in space. A profound dislocation is created when part of our landscape is missing.

In a different but related landscape, there is the ever-missing Osama bin Laden, who is wanted "dead or alive," as Bush said in a posturing rhetoric that assumed that the possession of his body could close this gap. Bush's inane choice of words may display more than his cowboy mentality and in fact belie an anxiety about the uncertainty about the missing (dead or alive?) in our national home. The abundance of American flags, although different in purpose and tone, seems to enact a similar gesture of trying to fill in the wound and absence with patriotism and symbols.

Perhaps the most wrenching image from the attacks is that of the falling bodies and the accompanying realization that people selected such a gruesome fate over remaining in a horror that we will never see. That image evoked a new sense of bodily horror, true to the original signification of the Greek word *trauma* as a bodily injury.[5] Our first home, of course, is the body—the maternal body and then our own. If home can be interpreted through the body, then the shattering of a sense of a secure national home may evoke feelings about the shattering of a collective body. In place of the psychological and geographical distance, the images of trapped and falling bodies pull one into an immediate confrontation with the dead body of the Other. The collapsing of bodies together into smoke, detritus, or whatever remains introduces a profoundly disturbing distortion of the fusing of infant and mother, Self and Other, animate and inanimate.

I was struck by an especially horrific detail from the film *9/11*. The "rookie" fireman Tony recalls digging out of ground zero the corpse of a "girl" who seemed to be pregnant, an exhuming that had to be abandoned because of unsafe ground. The attacks claimed the maternal body, housing a growing fetus, as victim. If the New York symbolized by the Statue of Liberty offers the hope of a mother welcoming immigrants with open arms, then on September 11 (with the statue in the background) it witnessed a desecration of the maternal body.

A pediatric ENT surgeon related to me an example of how this tragedy has been played out upon the body and in the mind. In the weeks after September 11, he saw five separate adolescent girls all with identical symptoms. Each came to the hospital having lost a tremendous amount of weight in a short period because she was unable to swallow. All five *believed* that some debris or body part from the destruction of the towers had lodged in their throats and *produced* the symptom. Their identification with the scene of witnessing was so strong that it "entered" their bodies. Upon examination, each girl indeed *had* a physical constriction in the throat, but there was nothing, no visible matter, inside to cause it. The girls converted a collective external absence into an internal one, starvation. They expressed hysterically what many of us feel—that the information is too difficult to swallow. What lodges in our throats?

MOURNING AND REPETITION

A New York Historical Society exhibit of 9/11 images taken by the photojournalism collective Magnum helped me to think about my own process of mourning and memory. Among the pieces included in the exhibit was a twenty-five-minute silent video by Evan Fairbanks shot in close proximity to the towers. One of the most unnerving aspects of the video is its ability to transport the viewer to a scene of watching *before* what we now know would occur was known. Like the film *9/11*, it places the viewer back in time and "on location," allowing us to participate in a unique kind of witnessing, vastly different from the experience of watching the clips shown repeatedly on television. It enables a return—repeated returns—to a time of shock, during which we could not linger to absorb traumatic events. In the safety of the museum and at a time of reflection, we can relive our fright, identification, and sympathy (and other responses) during that frozen time of trauma. The video gives us pause to reexperience our relation not only to witnessing but also to knowing—and not knowing—the collective wound.

Fairbanks was at Trinity Church near the World Trade Center at the time the first plane struck and began filming soon after. His video captures the crash of the second plane into Two World Trade Center and documents activity in the area until that tower collapses. Before the second plane hits, the camera records people on the street standing in crowds, staring up in disbelief, transfixed by the enormity of the sight. But its focus is upward, depicting a new way of looking at the sky and at airplanes in particular, a new relation between the sky and the ground. For many, that fear of the skies continues to haunt.

As we watch the events transpire in real time, the video transposes us into its present, and yet we remain far apart in a future that holds knowledge that those in the video cannot predict. A startling sense of calm, enhanced by the video's lack of a soundtrack, prevails as people struggle to witness that which they both cannot avoid and cannot fully see or understand.[6] The shock keeps them frozen. For those of us watching the video, who know what is to follow, there is a sense of dread and a wish to tell the spectators to clear out to safety. We know the dangers ahead, even for the cameraman. (One photographer, Bill Biggart, died while shooting, killed in the collapse of the North Tower.[7]) The video captures firemen heading into the scene, and we realize that this may be the last footage of them alive. When the second plane zooms into the second tower, the video spectators gasp as the actual spectators on screen begin to run. The second plane crash joins the two sets of viewers in an awareness of intention behind the event. The pace then changes dramatically, and the video continues until the second tower, the first tower to implode, collapses. The screen darkens and the viewers in the audience groan. The video ends. As our witnessing stops, we know that the darkness signals the end of life for many. The divide between past and present, life and death, reopens. The video spectators separate from the spectators caught on film and return to a room full of still images and memorials.

I am struck by the need to witness. When the witnesses near the towers do not yet sense a danger to their own lives, they cannot look away. A need

A man walks
away from
ground zero.
Photograph by
Larry Towell,
Courtesy
Magnum
Photos.

to see the destruction, the wound, overwhelms. A similar need exists for the crowd at the museum (or for audiences of the *9/11* documentary and other visual exhibits) that mirrors the spectators on the scene, unable to fathom what's before our eyes and possessed. Despite having seen the impact of the planes countless times, we are drawn to look.

The repetitive witnessing testifies to something that evades. Will we see that which cannot be seen? Perhaps in watching replays like a repetition compulsion we prepare ourselves in ways we could not at the time of the event. One image from the Magnum exhibit taken by photographer Larry Towell captures how, as Freud put it, "the remaining psychical functions are extensively paralysed or reduced."[8] In the photo, a dazed man stares at a sheet of paper, burned around the edges, that he holds in his hands. His hair and shirt disheveled and dusted, he stands alone, motionless, in the middle of a street thick with ash and littered with papers while others walk with heads lowered and mouths covered. He stands upright and stiff like a statue in air thick with soot. His dress, stance, and vacant gaze all convey the paralysis, the stare of trauma.

Retrospectively, we try to understand the role of this stare to ourselves. No matter how many times one repeats the scene of watching, ultimately it confronts us with an absence, an empty skyline, ground zero—the stare of trauma. The familiar landscape of New York, home to many symbolically as well as actually, becomes radically unfamiliar as pieces of steel come crashing down, papers fly and sparkle through the gray air like some strange snow on a distant planet. A doctor I know rushed to ground zero in the immediate aftermath in order to help (although there was little for him to do) and captured this unknowable element when he described to me his journey south. The scene became progressively stranger and then "you get to the moon." The moon. We had never been to this New York. Our home became stranger than we ever imagined. The video pulls us back into that frozen and strange zone, the time that may be missing to ourselves. Not only as New Yorkers but also as witnesses who come to ground zero, like those from around the world, we are trying to reencounter memory in this absent landscape.

New York is now a city of the missing. It is a city with a trauma, a wound that has not yet become a scar, for a scar implies healing. The new wounded New York is related to the old New York, the New York of the Twin Towers and a trust, ignorance, or fantasy we can no longer afford. While there has been much said about the divide crossed on September 11 after which "we will never be the same," the change is not an absolute before and after but a dialectic relation between past and present New Yorks that can be understood in the context of trauma. Ruth Leys articulates the way Freud understood trauma as two times in relation to one another, "constituted by a dialectic between two events, neither of which was intrinsically traumatic, and a temporal delay or latency through which the past was available only by a deferred act of understanding and interpretation."[9] We can no longer understand the New York of the past without relating it to our post-9/11 consciousness, and we cannot understand our new state as New Yorkers as separate from our sense of loss, the missing, and our vulnerability.

In a *New York Times* review of the MOMA photography exhibit "Life of the City," Sarah Boxer discusses the anonymous snapshots in the show, poised between classic photos of the city and monitors displaying images from "Here Is New York" (a gathering of photographs of the disaster). She perceives these snapshots to be "a kind of buffer zone between the New York that existed before Sept 11: a strange place to fear, loathe, strive for and be raucous in, and the New York of today: a strange place to mourn, worship, respect and be silent in."[10] Calling both pre- and post-9/11 New Yorks "strange," or, as we might add, *unheimlich*, she assumes a trajectory that moves from extremes to redemption. First came the exceptionally rough, fashionable, sinister, rich, and poor New York, and then came the quasi-religious New York of silence, meditation, and connection. The snapshots, she observes, act as a kind of purgatory or limbo between the two clearly defined eras in the city's history.

While I agree that shock has forced us to pause, I am not sure what the relations of the two New Yorks will be or whether a transcendent trajectory really exists. The reviewer's use of the word "strange" for both periods acknowledges how this "home" promises both belonging and estrangement and the difficulty of defining either period according to a monolithic vision. Furthermore, I wonder how reflective or mournful we are when we step outside the museum space. We are not only a group of respectful worshipers, or, perhaps more accurately, what we worship is not so clear. We remain diverse individuals, and how we absorb the trauma remains to be seen. Perhaps for the present many of us remain in the limbo of the snapshot, facing a new distance from ourselves.

We know that one of the hardest aspects of trauma is how survivors may unwillingly repeat the scene. What has not and cannot be assimilated can possess us and reenact itself. For our collective trauma, we too are at risk of repetitions. It is not clear that we will remain a city, a nation, or a world of respectful mourners working through the trauma. We risk repeating behaviors, identifying with the aggressors, or otherwise enacting scenes we could not know. I was stunned to hear many people willing to abandon

A toddler stands
by a wall of
missing fliers,
September 2001.
Photograph
courtesy
Mark Seliger.

civil liberties in order to "secure" a new tightly enforced home rather than examine the very meaning of this home. I fear for victims of future violence that emerges as some outgrowth of these events. Our trauma may lie in the future as the new New York reshapes itself in relation to the old New York.

FUTURE HOMES

The last time I was at the World Trade Center was in the late summer of 2001. I had recently discovered a wonderful playground in Battery Park, and my husband, daughter, and I spent the afternoon there, walking around the neighborhood and marveling at the towers. As I watched their destruction weeks later, I thought of our time playing safely in their shadows with other families. If I situate myself in relation to September 11, then I return to the space of the home, the family, and my role as a maternal body, that is, in relation to my daughter and all of the children growing up in a world of dangers. Rather than see this sense of identity as perpetuating gendered stereotypes, I consider it one aspect of my identity that crosses national boundaries. How will homes around the world provide safety? Will the attacks cause us to widen our conceptions of home or to build tighter "gated communities"? It is inevitable that to some degree our wounds will be transmitted to our children. I hope that they will not find their homes altered by violence more radically tomorrow. But after September 11, as soon as I entertain that hope, I hear the disturbing echo of "All the king's horses and all the king's men couldn't put Humpty together again."

NOTES

1. Cathy Caruth, *Unclaimed Experience: Trauma, Narrative, and History* (Baltimore and London: Johns Hopkins University Press, 1996), 4.

2. "Although it has been only six months since the World Trade Center was attacked, already it seems as if we can't be shocked by those events anymore" (Caryn James, "Experiencing the Cataclysm from the Inside," *New York Times*, Mar. 6, 2002, E1).

3. Dr. Rachel Seidel, *Psychotherapy Forum* 8, no. 2 (winter 2002): 1. Boston Psychoanalytic Institute.

4. See David Grann, "Which Way Did He Run?" *New York Times Magazine*, Jan. 13, 2002, 32.

5. See Caruth, *Unclaimed Experience*, 3.

6. There is a different sense of response when the soundtrack of screams and sirens can be heard, as in the HBO film *In Memoriam: New York City, 9/11/01.*

7. For the story of Bill Biggart, see *American Photo* 13, no. 1 (Jan./Feb. 2002): 42.

8. Sigmund Freud, *Beyond the Pleasure Principle* (New York: Norton, 1961), 34.

9. Ruth Leys, *Trauma: A Genealogy* (Chicago and London: University of Chicago Press, 2000), 20.

10. Sarah Boxer, "Prayerfully and Powerfully, New York City Before and After," *New York Times,* Mar. 6, 2002, EI, 3.

2. REPORTING

Reporting the Disaster

Nancy K. Miller

On December 31, 2001, the *New York Times* printed the last of the daily portraits it had been publishing since September 15. The end of the year also saw the last installment of "A Nation Challenged," the special section dedicated to reporting the "War against Terror" in which the portraits had appeared. The stand-alone section was deemed no longer necessary because the traumatic effects of September 11 had "been woven into all aspects of national and international life" (Dec. 31, 2001, B1). As of 2002, portraits would be published as further discoveries were made or as more families were willing to reveal their loss in print.

On September 16, when thirty-nine bodies had been identified, Katie Stern, whose husband, Andrew, was identified in the official body count, was quoted as saying she was relieved to know that he was no longer among the missing, even though that knowledge also meant that he was dead: "I'm so happy that I have his body, and that we have closure. I pray to God that he gives them their loved ones so that they, too, can have closure" (A9). This desire for closure that can be satisfied only by the return of the body (or its identification through DNA) in many, many cases remains unfulfilled.

A hardcover book containing the portraits from 2001 printed in the *New York Times* will be published by Times Books. No doubt the book version, superseding both the daily newspaper installments and the Internet archive, also will be said to provide closure (Katie Stern's word and the mantra of the aftermath) to the events of September 11 that destroyed a staggering number of lives and shattered the consciousness of survivors, whether first-degree witnesses or simply those whose knowledge of the event arrived through the highly mediated narratives of television reporting.

Almost immediately after the disaster, the frantic search for missing persons took the form of fliers that had spontaneously materialized with the news reports and appeared pasted onto walls, mailboxes, lampposts, and phone booths. In addition to detailed descriptions of what people were wearing (Timberland shoes, Izod polo shirt, ruby ring), the fliers usually included photographs of the loved ones (almost always smiling). The text of the fliers included height, weight, eye color, hair (balding, light brown), birthmarks, moles, scars (even a Caesarean), and tattoos. But the key piece of information was location—not only where the missing worked and the name of the firm but the floor of the building (Sept. 13, 2001, A3). As the hope of finding survivors faded, the distinction between the missing and the dead began to blur. It's perhaps for this reason that on September 13 the original title of the series "Among the Missing" dropped the word "missing"—with its promise of finding—to become "Portraits of Grief."[1] The emphasis moved at the same time from those who had perished to those who remained alive, those who began to mourn their loss, as the mourners became biographers.

Consciously or unconsciously, the journalists borrowed from the model put in place by the fliers, which not only provided visual clues that could help identify a missing person but also sketched the personality of the dead. One that stood out on the crowded wall at St. Vincent's Hospital (the fliers and photos protected from the elements by a ledge overhanging the wall) featured the photograph of a tall, dark-haired woman in a bathing suit standing on a dock, proudly displaying a fish she had caught; the handwritten description gave the phone number to call, should someone see her (there was also a snapshot of the same woman in street clothes—in case you weren't likely to recognize Cynthia (Cindy) Giugliano in a swimsuit). Her name has not yet appeared on the list, and when I went to look at the wall a few weeks after writing this essay, the photograph had been removed, her absence from the world now a blank on the wall.

In the "Portraits of Grief" series, the fliers and the portraits were juxtaposed on the same page, almost as though we were meant to perceive continuity between the modes of portrayal. As part of the coverage, the newspaper also began supplying a list of the names and numbers of those confirmed dead, as well as the names of the reporters responsible for the mini-profiles. The daily updated numbers of the totals appeared in the index to "A Nation Challenged." On December 29, two days before the elimination of the section, there was the following breakdown: "At the World Trade Center, 2,937 dead or missing, with 147 dead on two hijacked planes; 380 missing; 585 death certificates issued by medical examiner's office; 1,972 death certificates issued at request of families. At the Pentagon, 184 dead or missing, with 59 dead on hijacked plane; in Pennsylvania 40 dead on hijacked plane" (B2). (The nineteen hijackers are not included in the total either of the dead or the missing.) In a ghostly recall, the numbers bring to mind the television reporting during the Vietnam War, when the number of dead and wounded would appear in the lower right-hand corner of the screen as the grim reporting unfolded above. The numbers are a way of reckoning loss and tracking the faceless in the face of unremitting disaster.

Given their spontaneous and multiple origins, the makeshift fliers varied widely in size, style, and presentation: snapshots, head shots, in color or black and white; couples, a father and daughter, at restaurants, in the country, at work, in uniform, holding infants, wearing a strapless gown; handwritten, scrawled in marker, neatly typed, photocopied, torn, taped, illustrated. The newsprint portraits of necessity became more uniform (if equally improvised at the beginning), the photographs—and captions— more like a yearbook. Everyone was given equal space and equal treatment. The coverage aimed at minimizing social differences: a maintenance worker took up as much room as did a financial trader, a fireman, a corporate vice president. (These differences would emerge sharply with the question of economic compensation.)

Andrew Stern's portrait appeared on September 17. As told by his wife, theirs was a love story. Andrew and Katie met in front of the copy machine in Two World Trade Center. She was a sales assistant, he was a trader. The courtship led to marriage, children, a house on Long Island, and a promotion. Andrew became a broker at Cantor Fitzgerald with an office on the 104th floor. (It was hard not to notice the ironic inversion of Manhattan real estate values: now, the higher the floor, the greater the chance of fatality.) The anecdote that closes Andrew's profile, entitled "A Circle of Life," returns to the theme of true love. On the weekend before the disaster, the couple attended a wedding in Manhattan and spent the night in the Roosevelt Hotel—"I'm so glad to have a memory of that romantic evening," Katie is quoted as saying (A10). As they strolled down Fifth Avenue they could see the towers of the World Trade Center.

On October 14, the one-month anniversary of the profiles, an editorial titled "Among the Missing" analyzed their attempt to master the trauma of unaccountability. Faced with the massive numbers of victims, how were these profiles to get at what is singular about each one within the constraints of the form?: "each profile is only a snapshot, a single still frame lifted from the unrecountable complexity of a lived life" (A12). In an earlier framing, the metaphor of photography also figured—perhaps as a self-conscious carry-over from the fliers: "Snapshots of Their Lives, with Family and at Work" (Sept. 15, A11)—but the language of the visual portrait gives way to the literary and the linguistic. Making these anonymous people recognizable to us, the readers, sometimes requires an act of translation. This movement between lives from victim to reader takes place through storytelling—anecdotes elicited from the survivors and reshaped by journalists through the filter of "archetypes." These stories touch us because they follow archetypal plots made familiar by songs, novels, and movies: courtship, marriage, aspiration, family, success. A mirror of the American dream. Lives just like ours—"really our own stories." We see ourselves in them, them in us, but with a crucial difference, of course. *Their* plots were interrupted by the catastrophe; we still have ours to live. Continuing the theme of interruption—all that will remain unfinished, not brought to term—the editorial concludes that the portraits supply an interlocking set of maps: a "map of loss" but also a "map of fulfillment," commitment to family and community. Through this geography of trauma, then, the group portrait of lives attached to the World Trade Center offers a purchase on an America beyond the towers—a Bush-like America of goodness and compassion.[2]

By all accounts (as reported by the *New York Times*) the "Portraits of Grief" were hugely popular. Hundreds of e-mail messages poured in from readers testifying to their importance. Some found the stories "uplifting, a guide how to live a better life." Susan Sontag, the writer, said in an e-mail message, "I read the 'Portraits of Grief,' every last word, every single day. I was tremendously moved. I had tears in my eyes every morning'" (Dec. 31, B6). (A cynical reader might wonder whether this response was meant to counter the bad press generated by her earlier remarks in the *New Yorker* [Dec. 21] in response to the attacks on the World Trade Center about the courage of the hijackers.) The novelist Paul Auster is quoted too: "We weren't mourning an anonymous mass of people, we were mourning thousands of individuals. And the more we knew about them, the more we could wrestle with our own grief" (Dec. 31, B6).

But are we mourning the loved ones who died—mourning *for* them? What about the survivors doing the mourning? What's really their story? If the portraits aimed at capturing individuals, could they also render the grief of those who remained to mourn their loss—the loss of the identified dead or the human remains waiting for identification through a DNA profile? The profile of George DiPasquale, from Ladder Company 2 in Manhattan, begins with a plea for silence: "Melissa DiPasquale has told enough stories about her firefighter husband, cried enough tears before strangers. Now she wants peace and privacy. Another article about George DiPasquale? His wife begs a reporter to use what has already been said about him in his local newspaper, the *Staten Island Advance*" (Nov. 28, B10). The rest of the portrait quotes from that article. It is not possible to know how many widows (and given the fact that 1,270 men died, compared to 340 women, there are many widows) like Melissa DiPasquale refused to put their sorrow into the language that will fit the published portrait or to bring their loss to words at all.[3] Perhaps the widow was waiting for the right interlocutor to tell her story; perhaps she could not bear to bare the wound one more time. In a piece about the families who learned that the samples they offered with the hope of producing a DNA match were useless, another widow, Stacey Staub, said to a reporter, "It's like opening the wound that's just been sewn over and over and over again" (Feb. 9, B4).

In the aftermath of the aftermath that is now under way, the loving ones have stories of their own that are just beginning to be told, though many will remain as buried as the unnamed remain—until another event revives the trauma. These stories emerge individually and in groups. The government's plan for compensation has produced a significant protest that messes up both the maps of loss and the maps of fulfillment. For if the families (and who is family presents serious problems of entitlement, particularly if the person left behind—again, usually a woman—was only engaged, not married, to the victim) felt themselves to be equally wounded, it turned out that in calculating the value of a human life it was not enough to have been a wonderful person unjustly struck down in youth or the prime of life. The democratic scrim of the portraits notwithstanding, beyond a commonly shared pain and suffering, the lives of a security guard and a securities trader are not of equal monetary worth. Such issues as who should decide how the benefits fund is distributed or what is an appropriate memorial to the catastrophic loss of life are under passionate debate.

The story that has most disturbed me in this liminal moment where the effects of loss begin to work through individual paths is one reported with the following headline: "Widow of Sept. 11 Victim Kills Herself in Their Just-Finished Dream House." Here is a case where we can contrast the obituary/portrait published on November 29 with the report of the effects of loss two weeks later on December 13. The portrait of Joseph Waldken Flounders in many ways typifies the World Trade Center model of work. He would rise at 3:30 A.M. (the earliest in a group of early risers) to make it to his desk by 8:30. The couple both felt that this commute, which entailed driving from the Poconos to a train station in New Jersey and from there to the World Trade Center, was well worth the trade-off since it meant living in their dream house. (Patricia Flounders's health had led them to leave Brooklyn for a "better quality of life" and the house in the country that she described to reporters as her husband's "sanctuary.")

Joseph Flounders was a money-market broker on the eighty-fourth floor of Two World Trade Center. Slightly older than the average man in finance (he was fifty-one, while the average age was thirty-eight), and unsmiling in his photo, Flounders had a brutal schedule that resembled those of the successful younger men who worked in the towers, lived in the suburbs with their wife and children, and also rose at dawn. The poignancy of his death was sharpened by the fact that after three years the couple had finally finished renovating the house he would not live to enjoy (Nov. 29, B10).

Friends and family described Patricia Flounders as a woman who no longer wanted to live "without her husband of 21 years, and she went to join him" (Dec. 13, B1). Patricia Flounders found it "painful" to "discuss with others the events of Sept. 11," in which he died trying to help a co-worker "who was hysterical and in shock" rather than just heading down the stairs immediately and saving himself (B8). At the funeral service for her husband Patricia Flounders seemed composed, but clearly she was not. " 'I had hoped that the service would bring her some peace and closure,' said her brother, . . . 'but it didn't happen that way' " (B8). The article tells the story of their courtship (a staple of the portraits that often read like the marriage announcements in the Sunday "Styles" section) and how her husband helped her survive cancer. In the photograph accompanying the article the couple looks as though they had found the peace they sought. Mr. Flounders is wearing a red plaid shirt and holding a small dog.

Closure.

Closure represents the opposite of trauma's pathways, which by defini-tion are understood by their afterlife, persistence, and reoccurrence, even if a goal for victims of traumatic experience is to find a narrative that can integrate the event (which, of course, is not always possible). But we live in a culture whose rhythms push us to wish for the pain to end so that we can, as they say, move on. Closure implies another beginning—the door closes to reopen on another scene. Enough grief already. Patricia Flounders didn't see it that way. Surely she is not alone among the grieving to prefer death to mourning, but her response is not the preferred one to the disaster in which one lives with the memories. "Closing a Scrapbook Full of Life and Sorrow," the article written about the last installment of "A Nation Challenged," expresses this sentiment. Always a form of memorialization constructed from ephemera, the scrapbook seems an apt metaphor for the portraits project as a whole. The scrapbook of September 11's dead and disappeared becomes a collective history of life before the disaster.

Like the snapshot and the anecdote, which in the "Portraits of Grief" stand in for a life narrative, the scrap, by definition, is a part of something larger, a fragment, an excerpt. The scrap calls up what's missing. In the aftermath of a death, the survivors often find themselves at odds over the most minute possession of the person they loved. Nothing is too small to covet, to cherish, to wish to hold onto, to make ours. To own the part feels like a way of remaining attached to the vanished whole. The widows regretted having relinquished items belonging to their husbands in the hope—disappointed—that they would produce the longed for DNA grail. People who have lost loved ones believe in their rights to these items: sometimes their ownership is subject to debate.

The story "After a Father's Death, Bitterness over a Scrap of His Other Life" (Feb. 10, 2002, A33) describes a struggle over a leather motorcycle vest. The vest belonged to a forty-nine-year-old father of grown daughters and a member of a New Jersey–based "all-police Harley Davidson club." To whom does the vest belong? To the club, their rules give them ownership. To the daughters, "the vest is the last shred of the father who often left them behind for part of his life they didn't share." And then there is the girlfriend. But despite the intensity of their four-year relationship, the "stunning" girlfriend is entitled to nothing before the law. Left with a photograph of her "Wild Pig" boyfriend posed on his bike, she takes consolation in paying for his cell phone (which the daughters had disconnected) so that she can dial several times a day and listen to his voice saying hello on tape. Shreds of a lost conversation. One victim, many stories: "There was no body, but pointedly separate funerals."[4]

In *Between the Acts*, Virginia Woolf's last novel, the author uses the phrase "*scraps, orts and fragments*" (188–89) to represent the disaster for civilization the war had brought. Is that, she wonders, what we are, torn asunder, bewildered: ourselves? But at the same time, paradoxically, the fragments suggest to the writer that "we are members one of another. Each is part of the whole. . . . We act different parts; but are the same" (192).[5] This glimpse of wholeness was belied in life; Woolf committed suicide before the book appeared. September 11 was a brutal demonstration of that twin sense of human connectedness and fragility. The portraits were a group biography that embodied both. The World Trade Center disaster was a reminder of vulnerability, an almost apocalyptic memento mori that sent many (even young people) to make their wills (Dec. 13, 2002). I too finally made mine.

Stacks of newspaper clippings from the *New York Times* clutter my study. I began by saving the front-page headline news on September 12, 2001—"U.S. Attacked." When the *New York Times* started publishing the "Portraits of Grief," I found myself collecting them as well. Of course, for a while now the portraits have been available on the Web, and I could jettison my dusty piles. But since I read the *New York Times* "on paper" (not on-line, as a student recently characterized my retrograde tendencies), I felt that I had to stare at the newsprint, spread it out like the morning news, and dirty my hands in order to figure out the place the portraits occupied both in the newspaper ("my" newspaper as a native New Yorker) and in my mind.

I can't say I cried reading the portraits. On the contrary, I often experienced a powerful sense of disbelief. Here are typical examples from February 10, a day I was working on this essay: Was it possible that no one who died in the attack on the World Trade Center was ever depressed ("They were always giggling"); self-centered ("Despite a hectic work schedule [he] took pains to put his family first," "She wanted to make sure everyone was happy"); without a passion ("He was also crazy about pop music from the 1950's and 60's"); had a career that seemed stalled ("He dreamed of becoming a recording engineer"); or sometimes found life not worth living ("He lived life to the fullest")? Even the small number of older victims, closer to my age, took their place on the map of fulfillment. I could not perform the translation, identify with these lives from which all traces of unhappiness were banished. But the fact that I can't stop collecting, that I know I will buy the book, that I can't stop reading about these interrupted lives and the people left behind, means that, having lost no one close to me on September 11, I'm no less located on the map of loss it produced—a map of trauma whose borders are still missing.[6]

Notes

1. In "Talk of the Town: Grief Desk" (*New Yorker,* Jan. 14, 2002, 30–31), Mark Singer gives a helpful account of how the portraits evolved.

2. In "Naming the Dead" (*London Review of Books*, Nov. 15, 2001, 3–7), David Simpson analyzes the rhetoric and politics of commemoration in the language of the *New York Times*.

3. I'm grateful to Liisa Korpivaara for the statistical and thematic analysis of the portraits she performed and for bringing this particular portrait to my attention.

4. There is also a general silence, with very few exceptions, about the losses of those whose partners were gay. See about Mark Bingham in Evelyn Nieves's article, "Passenger on Jet: Gay Hero or Hero Who Was Gay?" *New York Times*, Jan. 16, 2002, A12.

5. Virginia Woolf, *Between the Acts* (New York and London: Harcourt, Brace, and Co., 1941).

6. Interviewed near the World Trade Center as events were unfolding, Mayor Giuliani urged people in the area to leave the site of the disaster and "go north." For

many of us living uptown who witnessed the events of television, it almost felt as though we were inhabitants of another city. But a young woman who lived in my building and who had served on the co-op board died on September 11. Although I did not know Karen Klitzman (who by all accounts was a remarkable person), I attended along with neighbors a memorial service in celebration of her life that her family had organized at a local synagogue; it seemed a small, if inadequate, gesture toward sharing in the communal grief. I found it strange and poignant to see her face for the first time when her portrait was published in the newspaper shortly after the service. Like most of the victims, in the snapshot that accompanied the portrait Karen Klitzman was smiling.

If You Have Tears

Peter Brooks

The morning of September 11 swept those of us old enough to remember back to the November afternoon in 1963 when John F. Kennedy was shot. In both cases the sense of loss and grief was coupled with an intense anxiety. The world suddenly seemed a much more treacherous place. But for the presidential assassination there were rules and forms and traditions that kicked into action almost at once: a successor designated by the Constitution, a ritual of mourning sponsored by the state, a solemn demonstration of American power at the moment of its wounding. Whereas on September 11 our sense of wounding and outrage had no appropriate ceremonies to manifest continuity and reflective strength. We felt flayed, vulnerable, naked to any coming insult, inept to protect ourselves.

When people say that nothing will ever be the same post-September 11, I think it is above all this sense of vulnerability that they mean to evoke. We have lost some prior sense of our place in the world, our firm footing, our balance. It seemed to me, in the immediate aftermath, that one good could possibly arise from this disorientation—something along the lines of this: America, welcome to the world. It's not that one wants to find anything positive in terrorism and mass destruction but that precisely our new vulnerability to them might alert us to how much they are part of the daily experience of much of the world. This was a moment for American "exceptionalism" to understand its limitations, for isolationist mentalities to be discarded, for the citizens of this land so largely exempt from the tread of invading armies to understand that the time of exemption was over.

"The complex of melancholia behaves like an open wound, drawing to itself cathectic energies . . . from all directions, and emptying the ego until it is totally impoverished"—thus Freud, on the pathological form of mourning that becomes melancholia.[1] The open wound is still there, at ground zero, and in our psychic lives as well. But for me its drawing of investments of energy into itself, its impoverishing of our egos, derives not merely from the horror of the attack itself but also from the failure of our mourning. I mean the *political* failure of our mourning and thus its failure to bring us the right, sobering lessons about our global responsibilities. I believe that our mourning was hijacked by a simplistically militaristic response, a knee-jerk jingoism that substituted for any reflective policy. As I write, more than half a year later, I find I am now distressed by the stars and stripes that continue to fly ostentatiously from taxicabs and highway overpasses. Those flags were moving at first. Now they seem to me to signal a refusal to grow up, the worst aspects of American innocence. There was an end to innocence on September 11, I want to say to the flag-wavers. Grow up. Get over it. Face the new reality.

The rhetoric of "evil" reiteratively used by our president does not promote maturity or clarity. It rather masks the perceptions of large sectors of the globe. I won't debate whether war in Afghanistan was the most effective response to terrorism: the alternatives to war never were clarified, and the results of war, beyond the rout of the Taliban—no tears to shed there—are still unclear. But look at what else we have been offered as a response to September 11: a proposed massive increase in the military budget, one that smuggles the funding of all sorts of expensive (and probably useless) weapons systems unrelated to antiterrorism under the cover of fighting terrorism. Coupled to this grand new expenditure we find not the tax increase one might expect in order to pay for it but rather a new tax cut that would further relieve the wealthiest Americans of their social responsibilities and would compensate for the loss of revenue (now ascribed to the terrorist attacks, not to the administration's fiscal fecklessness) by further reducing benefits for the poorest sectors of society, while delaying indefinitely any reform in our health care nonsystem. We are also offered an "energy plan"—a rampage through national forests and the Arctic National Wildlife Refuge—now mantled in the excuse of independence from oil imports, at the same time all efforts at energy conservation are thwarted. This administration has also managed to refuse to classify prisoners of war as such, to invent military tribunals that violate fundamental values of American justice, and to retreat from more forward-looking global engagements such as the world criminal court.

Declaring war on terrorism to be the key to world politics, our administration has given cover to the repression of dissidence in a number of countries and has blinded itself to how the repression of terror can itself be terrorist. As I write, the conflagration of the Middle East has begun to force the recognition that you can't pursue the dream of war on Iraq—

which may turn out to be what was really mantled in the folds of the Afghan war—without some attempt to see things from the perspective of the Arab countries. The rhetoric of virtue versus evil becomes our perceptual liability.

While we have been mourning, then, our political leadership has not been idle. It has used the cover of our mourning to forward its highly partisan political agenda. Whether self-blinded or cynical, it has promoted September 11 as an excuse for policies that are ideologically motivated rather than any reasoned response to terror. I don't suppose for a moment that this is the first time in history that the mantle of mourning has been used to conceal political maneuver. Shakespeare, of course, creates the classic instance in Mark Antony's funeral oration for Caesar.

It is the very mantle of Caesar's body—sliced through by the knives of Cassius, Casca, Brutus—that Antony uses at the key moment of his oration, descending from upper to lower stage and unveiling the body.

> If you have tears, prepare to shed them now.
> You all do know this mantle: I remember
> The first time ever Caesar put it on;
> 'Twas on a summer's evening, in his tent,
> That day he overcame the Nervii.
> Look, in this place ran Cassius' dagger through
> (*Julius Caesar* III, ii, 174–79)

Antony, recall, has in his earlier soliloquy over the fallen Caesar called on his wounds to speak and to cry for havoc:

> Over thy wounds now do I prophesy,—
> Which like dumb mouths do ope their ruby lips,
> To beg the voice and utterance of my tongue,—
> A curse shall light upon the limbs of men;
> Domestic fury and fierce civil strife
> Shall cumber all the parts of Italy
> (III, i, 259–64)

> And Caesar's spirit, ranging for revenge,
> With Ate by his side come hot from hell,
> Shall in these confines with a monarch's voice
> Cry 'Havoc!' and let slip the dogs of war
> (III, i, 270–73)

Mourning becomes the giving voice to a message of vengeance, civil strife, and personal ambition. By the end of the funeral oration, it is done:

Now let it work: mischief, thou art afoot;
Take thou what course thou wilt!
(III, ii, 2265–66)

Thus is political mischief wrought from mourning.

Trauma, mourning, and melancholia: I believe they can leave a nation, as much as an individual, in a weakened, depressive condition, that "open wound" having absorbed all emotional energies. This leaves a large opportunity for the nation's leaders to pursue the agenda to which they are committed and to pass it off as the response to the time's hard necessity. In our self-absorption over the wound of September 11, we have given our leaders a nearly blank check to do their mischief.

Freud's brilliant essay "Mourning and Melancholia" suggests how that can happen and how the individual needs to recover from the pathological, narcissistic form of mourning. It may be partly because I have spent considerable time since September 11 abroad that I find myself becoming impatient with my fellow Americans. It's time to get over it, to look up from the wound, and to see what's happening in the world—the rest of the world, where hatred of the United States seemingly increases daily. Blindness to this hatred and its causes is not an effective way to put an end to terrorism exercised on the United States.

In the German original of Freud's essay, the word for mourning is *Trauer*. That word reappears as one of the components of the German term for tragedy, *Trauerspiel*. I think we have become victims of the *Spiel* concocted by those governing us, and it's about as authentic as Mark Antony's. It is time to wake from mourning and melancholy and to assert a saner interpretation of the world that should be brought into sharper and soberer focus by September 11.

NOTE

1. Sigmund Freud, "Mourning and Melancholia," in *Standard Edition of the Complete Psychological Writings of Sigmund Freud* (London: Hogarth Press, 1957), 14:253.

"There's No Backhand to This"

James Berger

Theories of trauma are immensely appealing. They presume to provide a logic to the most radically unredeemable, unassimilable, unsymbolizable phenomena. I would argue that in literary studies trauma theories actually offer a poetics. They theorize trauma as a secular apocalyptic moment: shattering, obliterating, but also revelatory. It is the nuclear, blinding flash that stands at the center, yet not at the center, rather, just beyond the horizon, and defining the horizon, of contemporary culture.

There is something morally, intellectually, and aesthetically satisfying in these directions of thought. They suggest levels of experience deeper than language and consciousness, and this is comforting because it confirms what we feel. There is no language for that moment of pain and dissolution; but gradually language forms around it. I am struck in much writing about trauma by the use of the word "precisely" when the relation being described is not precise at all.[1] An enormous, inconceivable, visceral condition is rendered algebraic by means of a terminology. The argument itself indicates that precision is impossible, and yet the language *is* precise: it is precise *as language*. This precision about the inconceivable is why I refer to trauma theory as a sort of poetics. It is about making, about the creative acts—combining conscious and unconscious motives and powers—that arise out of horror and confusion. Trauma theory is itself one of those creative acts. It is precise in the way all powerful and rigorous acts of the imagination are precise, even though it describes nothing very precisely.

Those buildings couldn't fall. Look at them, I said to my wife, in the bedroom, watching (on television); the second plane had hit. The buildings were burning. It was unbelievable. Those are some solid buildings, I said. A plane hits them like that and they're still standing. As they fell, they couldn't be falling. As the first one fell, it couldn't be falling. It might as well have been rising, freed from gravity; it might as well have taken off and flown to the moon.

Nothing to say at that point.

The World Trade Center didn't exist anymore. I had just watched thousands of people die in a few seconds of time. I never thought I would see such a thing. We sat on the bed and watched. I touched Jennifer, lightly, on her back or shoulder. I thought, we're watching this together. She was more affected than I was. All those people, she was saying, crying. *You* didn't think they'd fall, she said, in a strange tone, as if she knew all along. I don't think she felt my hand.

I felt the beginning of a tremendous isolation.

It lasted several months.

School nurses reported an "increase in stomach aches and other physical ailments" (Mulligan 17). There has been an increase since 9/11 in depression and anxiety disorders ("September 11 and Anxiety"); a Pew Poll in October reported that 70 percent of Americans felt depressed, and one-third reported sleep problems (Arehart-Treichel 4). Sales for insomnia medication rose 12 percent (Lamberg 10). Moreover, the trauma of September 11 triggered the recurrence of older problems. There was a return of insomnia in previously stabilized patients (Lamberg 10). According to Dr. David Schonfeld of the Yale University School of Medicine, "the stress surrounding a crisis such as that of September 11 tends to cause children (and adults) to disclose other unresolved personal crises," and doctors can help patients deal with the current events "by addressing these unrelated issues" (Wyckoff 239). Even *Psychology Today*, as number four in its top ten list of "expectable reactions" to September 11, reported "Resurgence of Memories: New pain triggers pain from past trauma" (Scurfield 50).

Mental health clinicians themselves are not exempt from personal post-traumatic responses. One psychiatrist, in mid-September, noted that his patients' hands were shaking. Only after seeing several patients did he realize that it was not their hands that were shaking but his own (Rosack 13).[2]

As for me, I couldn't make love. In fact, I couldn't love. My little tower . . . my sense of connection . . . Everything hurt me. I had collapsed.

Things came back to me that I thought I'd thoroughly worked out: my two mentally retarded sisters and my failures to save them, my absolute helplessness. What did my sisters have to do with the World Trade Center? Well, why didn't I protect them? How could they suffer such damage and

I was their brother? And why couldn't I help Jennifer? She had injured her shoulder, very painfully, and I couldn't heal her. Her publisher was giving her a hard time, and her department, and I couldn't help her. I wanted to punch their faces in.

What happened? What is it called? September 11, 9/11, 911, the events of September 11, the trauma of 9/11, the catastrophe, the tragedy, the attack, the terrorist attack, attack on America, the horrors of September 11, the terrible events, the disaster, the terrorism of September 11, the cataclysmic events, the World Trade Center attack, recent events, the national tragedies, these horrible events, appalling events, massive crimes.

When the planes hit the towers and the towers fell, it wasn't clear what word to use. It was unclear what had happened—that is, what it meant—and so what name could designate it; or what name could designate it and give it a meaning that could be believed and lived with. At that moment, it had no meaning. Something happened, was happening, was happening over and over—in memory and on television and in memory and on television—awful beyond imagining, without scare quotes or exclamation points ("awful beyond imagining!!!!") because it really was. Nothing adequate, nothing corresponding in language could stand in for it. No metaphor could carry language across to it.[3] There was nothing to call it because it had taken over reality entirely.

But almost immediately, people began to name it. We were no longer entirely immersed in it. The media, of course, had to call it something, as did political leaders. Linguistic control of the event was a sign of social and political stability. At first, for the most part, the names were rather general: "catastrophe," "tragedy," and, most broadly, "event," or simply the date, 9/11. The word "attack" was used in these early days and weeks but markedly less often than the other, more general, terms.

By October 11, however, the "event" had become the "attack." What is the difference? An attack requires a particular kind of response: a counterattack. To use the name "attack" is to determine also what will follow. Once the destruction of the World Trade Center had been definitely named a terrorist attack, the paralyzed, nameless agony of that event, that thing that happened for which every attempt at meaning was inadequate, was converted into the beginning of a war. The event now had a meaning and a vocabulary. We could now speak of evil, justice, troop deployments, alliances, daily briefings, smart weapons, Al Qaeda, Taliban, Kandahar, the caves of Tora Bora. The traumatic impact, the "eventness" of the destruction, though not forgotten, was no longer in the foreground.

The destruction of the World Trade Center and the damage to the Pentagon were, of course, as we soon learned, the results of a murderous terrorist attack. The use of these terms is not inaccurate. Yet it is incomplete. To call the fall of the towers a terrorist attack and nothing more narrows the range of possible responses. Loss and horror are subsumed in our new military obligations. "Terrorist attack" is accurate, and yet it also is a form of denial. While it does not claim that pain and loss did not happen, it makes these experiences secondary to the war and to patriotic fervor. It is a term that curtails mourning, a premature closure to a wound that will not heal for many years.

Another strange movement of language in the aftermath of trauma has been the transformation of overwhelming loss into a kind of victory. The media soon spoke more about the heroes of September 11 than of the dead. Or the dead were spoken of now as heroes. In the *New York Times,* the daily page of victims' short obituaries performed such a great service, I think, because it reminded readers every day that these particular lives had been extinguished, so many of them; each day they were still dead, each day more of them were still dead, no matter how many bombs were dropped, no matter how many heroes were celebrated. But it was astonishing to me how quickly the media's focus was on triumph: of the nation's spirit, New York's spirit, our resolve, our community, our political system, the president's oratory, our policies, our strategies, our weapons, our soldiers, our way of life. Francis Fukuyama informed readers of the *Financial Times* that "adversity can have many positive effects. Enduring national character is shaped by shared trauma" (in Willis 11). And many commentators from across the political spectrum expressed satisfaction that the attack and its wartime aftermath would purge American culture of its trivialities. Again, I think, we see denial in a specifically psychoanalytic sense: not a repression of the trauma or a claim that it didn't happen but a claim that the trauma's consequences will not be traumatic; that it will not have symptoms but, rather, only beneficial lessons and varieties of redemption.

When this essay is published, about a year from now, much will have changed. But today, March 7, 2002, I support the war in Afghanistan. I have no problem with taking out the Taliban and Al Qaeda. At the same time, this war on terrorism has got to be accompanied by real reform of the way the world's wealth is produced and distributed, and I'm not optimistic about that effort.[4]

It is too soon to know what symptomatic aftershocks and shifts in attitudes, in culture, and in politics September 11 will produce. A terrorist might smuggle an atomic bomb onto a cargo ship, blow up an entire city, and September 11 will become merely the prelude to what we will know as this century's *real* traumas. Or, let's hope, the events of September 11 will not be equaled in horror for a very long time, though I fear that may be hoping for too much. And it needs to be said that events of comparable and greater devastation in terms of loss of life happen in other parts of the world quite regularly.

Just after the destruction, people spoke in apocalyptic terms. "This is the start of a new era," said Daniel Shorr. We now live in "a different world," said Anthony Lewis. There was a sense of some unbreachable rupture with the past, a fissure whose visible emblem was the horrifying, smoking absence at the southern tip of Manhattan. We heard about the end of irony, the end of postmodernism. And, as in most apocalyptic scenarios, the world was now said to be clarified and simplified—a struggle of good versus evil, civilization versus barbarism, or, from the other side, faith versus godlessness, virtue versus decadence, good versus evil. Apocalypse is the end of ambiguity and doubt. Trauma brings a shattering of certainties, and apocalypse provides a way to restore them. Catastrophe acquires significance and value as the first chapter of a final reckoning. It is a revelation of where we are, who we are, and who is against us. If not for the traumatic apocalyptic event, such enormous, value-laden concepts tend to be difficult to determine, and so the apocalyptic (or postapocalyptic, coming after the revelatory event) sensibility can be politically useful. As Condoleezza Rice put it, "September 11 was one of those great earthquakes that clarify and sharpen. Events are in much sharper relief" (in Lemann 44).

Are you with us or against us?

Traumas of the 1950s return in the fear of alien attack and subversion. Thousands of people are detained, based on no evidence, charged with no crime. We determine to arm ourselves against every threat, whether conceivable or inconceivable. There are real dangers—September 11 made that clear—but many of our responses have been excessive and symptomatic. Other responses have been simply self-serving political opportunism—the renewed plans for oil drilling in Alaskan protected areas and more tax breaks for corporations and the wealthy. The Bush administration's cynicism is evident: six months after 9/11, a White House official responding to setbacks to Bush's domestic agenda said, "The post-attack glow is fading" (Sanger 1).

In its official historical unconscious, the United States remains the City on the Hill, the New Jerusalem, a new world conceived in innocence and perfection and getting better ever since. In this fantasy, America contains no flaw (that has not been corrected), no wound (that has not healed stronger than before), no loss (that has not been redeemed many times over): in short, no trauma—for trauma is that wound, or crime, that persists and returns, that must be faced, experienced, and reexperienced, whose only healing narrative is, ultimately, the truth, which must be continually reimagined so that the truth of the (changing) present is understood in terms of the truth of the past, which will also change as it is reimagined, reunderstood.

"There's no backhand to this, it just hits you straight on," said one of the salvage workers at the World Trade Center ruins ("At the Edge of Ground Zero"). The tennis metaphor doesn't quite work, but I know what he means. Trauma is what is absolutely there. But to describe it in metaphor is already to be partly outside it, running to hit a backhand shot of a ball that has been hit back and forth already numerous times. The man's comment is brilliant; its skewed metaphor encompasses both the initial obliterating force and the subsequent reverberations in which memory and language return, though changed and damaged.[5]

NOTES

1. See, for instance, Elaine Scarry: "Physical pain—unlike any other state of consciousness—has no referential content. It is not *of* or *for* anything. It is precisely because it takes no object that it, more than any other phenomenon, resists objectification in language" (4, 5); Cathy Caruth: "History, like trauma, is never simply one's own. . . . History is precisely the way we are implicated in each other's trauma" (24); Shoshona Felman: "To testify from inside Otherness is thus . . . to speak from within the Other's tongue insofar precisely as the tongue of the other is by definition the very tongue we do not speak" (231).

2. See also Sarah Kershaw's article in the *New York Times:* A New York psychotherapist tells her, "we may have underestimated the number of people who were going to have a later onset of the effects. The residue of this experience is going to last a lot longer than we anticipated" (B1). Other clinicians to whom she spoke reported significant increases of recurrences of conditions previously under control.

3. Some recent research suggests that the disconnection between trauma and language may have a neurological basis. The overwhelming experiences we characterize as traumatic, according to Bessel van der Kolk, are processed by the thalamus and amygdala rather than by the hippocampus and prefrontal cortex, which are associated with language use.

4. Now doing final revisions, on April 2, 2002, this is the situation: war in the Middle East, a seder bombed, Israeli troops in Ramallah, Arafat trapped in his office with a dead cell phone. Sharon borrows Bush's language about destroying terrorist infrastructures and shares his avoidance of any other political, economic, or psychological realities. These leaders show almost, and I don't say this glibly, a *love* of terrorism, for it gives them the privilege and pleasure of using righteous force and of avoiding the terrifying complexity of real situations.

5. I realize I may just have misread this comment, thinking of tennis when the man meant a blow with the back of the hand, which would be less damaging than a straight punch with a closed fist. He might also have meant a backhanded deal, which would require gradual unraveling, as opposed to a direct assault. Or maybe he meant a backhanded insult, cousin to the backhanded compliment. In any event, he tried to articulate the violent, physical, unmediated quality of his experience of the site; and he articulates it as a negation: it was *not* this more complex, inverse, interpretable experience. This gesture is itself a rhetorical backhand. But the experience is both. After the straight on, forehand experience, the backhand follows.

Works Cited

Arehart-Treichel, Joan. "Thousands Will Need Postdisaster Mental Health Care, Psychiatrists Tell Congress." *Psychiatric News* 36, no. 20 (Oct. 19, 2001): 4–6.

"At the Edge of Ground Zero." *Soundprint.* National Public Radio, Mar. 9, 2002.

Caruth, Cathy. *Unclaimed Experience: Trauma, Narrative, and History.* Baltimore: Johns Hopkins University Press, 1996.

Felman, Shoshona, and Dori Laub. *Testimony: Crises of Witnessing in Literature, Psychoanalysis, and History.* New York: Routledge, 1992.

Kershaw, Sarah. "Even 6 Months Later, 'Get Over It' Just Isn't an Option." *New York Times*, Mar. 11, 2002, B1.

Lamberg, Lynne. "Sleepless in America: Terrorist Attacks Boost Insomnia, Nightmares." *Psychiatric News* 36, no. 23 (Dec. 7, 2001): 10–12.

Lemann, Nicholas. "The Next World Order: The Bush Administration and Foreign Policy." *New Yorker*, April 1, 2002, 42–48.

Lewis, Anthony. "A Different World." *New York Times*, Sept. 12, 2001, A27.

Mulligan, Kate. "D.C. Psychiatrists Gear Up for Long-Term Response." *Psychiatric News* 36, no. 19 (Oct. 5, 2001): 17–18.

Rosack, Jim. "Terrorism Leaving Its Mark on Psychiatrists' Practices." *Psychiatric News* 36, no. 22 (Nov. 16, 2001): 13–14.

Sanger, David E. "Bush Is Still Winning War There, but Begins to Lose Battles Here." *New York Times*, Mar. 9, 2002, A1.

Scarry, Elaine. *The Body in Pain: The Making and Unmaking of the World.* New York: Oxford University Press, 1985.

Scurfield, Ray Monsour. "The Normal Abnormal." *Psychology Today*, Jan./Feb. 2002, 50.

"September 11 and Anxiety." *http://www.heartsandminds.org/selfhelp.*

Shorr, Daniel. Interview. *The Diane Rheem Show.* National Public Radio, Sept. 14, 2001.

van der Kolk, Bessel. "The Body Keeps the Score: Approaches to the Psychobiology of Posttraumatic Stress Disorder." In *Traumatic Stress: The Effects of Overwhelming Experience on Mind, Body, and Society*, ed. Bessel van der Kolk, Alexander McFarlane, and Lars Weisaeth. New York, Guilford, 1996.

Willis, Ellen. "Dreaming of War." *Nation*, Nov. 15, 2001, 11–13.

Wyckoff, Alyson Sulaski. "Pediatricians Advised on How to Assess, Refer Children Troubled by Sept. 11 Attacks." *AAP News* (American Academy of Pediatrics) 19, no. 6 (Dec. 2001): 239–40.

Trauma Ongoing

Ann Cvetkovich

On September 11, I was in the midst of finishing a book about trauma. Focusing on the intersections of queer theory and trauma studies, the book views the construction of national trauma with some suspicion, given the way that sexual traumas ranging from incest to AIDS have often failed to make a mark on the national imaginary because they are not considered important enough or public enough in their impact.[1] I'm also interested in the widespread effects of trauma across time and space, the way that it is felt in the textures of experience of everyday life and not just as a cataclysmic shock. Moreover, I have a strong investment in seeing trauma depathologized and demedicalized in favor of cultural responses that can address it as a collective, and not just individual, phenomenon. The events of September 11 and their aftermath have not changed what I know about trauma; they have confirmed it.

In the immediate aftermath of September 11, my greatest urgency as a speaker and writer was to create forums for public feelings, to make room for the emotional complexity of people's responses, which included fear, grief, anger, numbness, helplessness, ambivalence, and more, often in contradictory and confusing combinations. I was especially eager to prevent these emotions from being channeled into forms of patriotism and militarism that offer reassuring and simplified solutions. Although there have been enormous spectacles of public mourning in the wake of September 11, there has been little room for connecting grief with expressions of dissent from the actions of the U.S. government. I take inspiration, though, from the forms of queer mourning created by AIDS activists, who forged new rituals of grief, including activist ones, in the face of overwhelming public neglect and indifference. AIDS activist and theorist Douglas Crimp has argued, for example, that mourning and militancy must be brought together.[2] Activism ignores mourning at its own peril, and it cannot simply displace mourning with militancy or fail to address the ways that anger is also motivated by loss. Queer perspectives on sexuality teach us to depathologize the nonnormative, and I would like to acknowledge and embrace the queer or nonnormative dimensions of our emotional responses and to see them as a resource for public cultures of feeling that can challenge violent retribution and narrow or exclusionary patriotisms.

Moreover, the primary affect of left critique seems to be righteous indignation and anger, in its own way a relative of the anger that has been mobilized into militarism. For those of us who also feel grief, fear, compassion, and just plain confusion, other public forums of statement are necessary. To that end, I take inspiration from Amber Hollibaugh's call for a politics of sexuality that embraces "dangerous desires," that acknowledges the riskiness and unpredictability of feelings.[3] It is short-sighted to dismiss those who are affected by the losses in the United States as distracted by sentiment from the real issues across the globe. It is important to consider these feelings of terror and grief as evidence that people have been touched by systemic forces and to start from there.

This approach is especially urgent for the task of building cultural memory around September 11 and of resisting the momentum of the culture industry, which is eager to tell a story that glorifies heroes and stresses national unity. In the United States, September 11 has already joined the pantheon of great national traumas, and I fear that its many and heterogeneous meanings (including the fact that it is a transnational trauma) will be displaced by a more singular and celebratory story. In my own work on trauma and lesbian cultures, I have been wary of the mechanisms by which certain forms of suffering are deemed worthy of national public attention, while others are left to individuals or minority groups to tend to on their own.

In the months since September 11, New York City has mustered its considerable popular and institutional resources to produce cultural memory at a staggering rate and volume. Two exhibitions in particular stand out: "Here Is New York: A Democracy of Photographs," an installation of photographs by anyone who wants to contribute one, and the New York Historical Society's "Missing: Streetscape of a City in Mourning," a display of the public memorials that appeared around the city after September 11. Both exhibitions begin from the populist premise that everyone's experience of September 11 counts, bringing the people's response from the home and local neighborhood into the public space of exhibition. The "democracy of photographs" displayed in "Here Is New York" makes graphically clear how many people were "eyewitnesses" to the burning and falling of the

World Trade Center from rooftops, balconies, streets, and neighborhoods far beyond Lower Manhattan. The image of a woman on the phone framed by her balcony doorway with the view of the burning buildings beyond captures the traumatic incommensurability of the destruction of the towers and domestic life elsewhere.

"Missing," sponsored by Manhattan's folklore organization City Lore, preserves the physical memorials that sprang up all over the city: the posters of missing people; the butcher-block paper and candles of Union Square; the neighborhood street altars; and the artists' responses. Martha Cooper's documentary photography offers shrewd context and commentary; her photographs of other public memorials in the city that commemorate the deaths of Princess Di, John F. Kennedy Jr., and neighborhood children underscore the ongoing urban traditions of which the memorials to September 11 are a part. The material culture left in the wake of September 11 offers testimony to the ways in which people took action by transforming the space around them. In the process of displaying the documents that represent people's feelings, these exhibitions also make public space for mourning. The "Missing" exhibit does so by focusing explicitly on mourning, but the display of the traumatic images in "Here Is New York" also provides a way to revisit what happened in order to make sense of it. At least as important as the materials themselves are the publics that they enable. Both exhibitions gesture toward and seek to create affect that invests images and objects with meaning independently of their content. They confirm my investment in the vicinity of trauma rather than its center, moving away from the moment of impact to the ongoing work of response and from the World Trade Center to the surrounding neighborhoods in which people live with its loss.

The value of these exhibitions was underscored for me when I found myself, through an accident of circumstance, at CBS's *Upfront* show, a multimedia spectacular at Carnegie Hall, where the network announces its fall season to potential advertisers. After appearances by David Letterman, Mary Tyler Moore, Celine Dion, and other stars, the show closed with clips from the *9/11* special that CBS broadcast in March. The audience gave a standing ovation to Jules and Gedeon Naudet, the filmmakers, and to the firemen they documented. Although members of the audience were ostensibly clapping for the heroic firemen, it also seemed like they were clapping for CBS's heroism in broadcasting the film. It's frightening to see how easily the image of September 11 can be attached to a commercial enterprise in order to boost its credibility. It seems all the more urgent to find ways of documenting September 11 that don't feed the machines of the culture industry.

One of the memorials I have found most moving is a display included in the "Missing" exhibition and assembled by Hilary North, an Aon employee who didn't go to work on September 11. As she frantically made phone calls to track the whereabouts and welfare of her coworkers, she kept notes on a pad with the Aon logo. There are lists of names with notes about whether people are safe and accounted for; too many of the names say "dead" or "missing" beside them. Other notes that detail the experiences of those who survived suggest that North couldn't take the information in and had to write it down as a memory aid. And there are doodles from the nervous energy of not knowing or of being on hold. North decided that this record of her time was important enough that she framed the sheets of paper and then contacted the organizers about including her piece in the exhibit. Her notepad is part of history, and the experience of being on the phone that it documents is one version of how trauma is lived. The doodles tell the story. They belong in the "archive of feelings," my fantasy of a collection that documents emotional life as part of history.

Having worked on oral histories of AIDS activists in order to create an archive of feelings, I am especially curious to see how oral testimony will be a resource for remembering September 11. Feminism has inspired my interest in legitimating personal memory as historical record and in exploring the emotional dynamics of the interview. I note with interest that New York City firemen resisted having their oral histories recorded by the fire department's internal affairs personnel because it made the process resemble a criminal investigation. I wonder what kind of sympathetic listening will elicit the stories that need to be told and who will be best equipped to do this work. It helps that testimony as a concept has significant popular appeal, and I would credit the increasing visibility of Holocaust testimony with raising public awareness of the importance of oral history for documenting trauma. Like the exhibitions of photographs and public memorials, oral history is a popular medium that presumes that everyone has a story to tell. In fact, the "Here Is New York" and "Missing" exhibits both incorporated oral histories; "Missing" included excerpts from "Tell Us Your Story," an impromptu interview project that was set up in a variety of public places, and "Here Is New York" created the "Listening Booth" project to allow visitors to record their stories, some of which emerged in response to viewing the photographs. The widespread effects of September 11 have produced many witnesses, and it will be important to think critically as well as creatively about including as many of them as possible in the historical record.

I am hopeful about "The September 11, 2001 Oral History Narrative and Memory Project" sponsored by Columbia University's Oral History

Research Office, because it casts a wide net in order to find those whose experiences are not adequately documented in the mainstream media, including Afghan and Pakistani Americans, activists, artists, and non-U.S. citizens.[4] Out of a desire to remain sensitive to the ways in which the interview process itself might be invasive or retraumatizing, the project has not immediately sought out those who lost family members or were part of the rescue efforts (although there are a number of interviews by such people in the collection). By collecting the stories of those who might be considered on the periphery of September 11 but who are also affected by it, the oral history collection will reframe the conception of a witness.

Given the huge numbers of September 11 stories, the decision by the organizers of Columbia's September 11 oral history project to focus on certain groups is both strategic and suggestive. The interviews with Afghan and Pakistani Americans, many of them Muslims, reveal that many people experienced the double trauma of not only being affected by September 11 but then being subject to racist backlash and constructed as the enemy. Mexican immigrants talk about the inequities in access to aid for undocumented workers and the heightened stakes, for those without proper citizenship documentation, of deciding whether to stay or leave the United States. For artists, who make it their business to think about the world around them, September 11 forces them to reflect on their creative process, sometimes inspiring new work and sometimes bringing it to a halt.

Conducting interviews so soon after September 11 has raised a host of methodological questions about how to work both ethically and effectively in relation to trauma. The interviewers themselves have their own experiences of September 11 and thus have to contend with their emotional responses to the interview process. There are decisions to be made about how to return transcripts to people in a way that will not be unduly disturbing. The plans for the project include interviewing people again to see whether their stories are affected by the passage of time. Although it has been suggested that contributing their oral histories might be helpful to people because it makes their experiences historical and publicly significant, there are many delicate decisions to be made to ensure that this potential is realized. The Columbia oral history project is working in conjunction with experts on trauma to explore these procedural challenges more fully.

Having conducted oral histories myself, I'm especially interested in how they get used. A collection such as Columbia's September 11 project is driven in part by an affective desire to preserve the past, and the concept of an oral history collection can be as significant to people as its content. I have been struck by how vivid and important everyone's story is, regardless of their position, both literal and social, in relation to September 11. Because those being interviewed were invited to place their experiences of September 11 in the context of the rest of their lives, the stories are long and detailed. The oral history interview is thus very different from journalistic documentation because there is no demand for the brevity of the sound bite. For the reader or listener, however, it is slow going to absorb each interview in its entirety. The archive thus contains a potential overload of information, and it is likely that scholars will find themselves excerpting and condensing the interviews when they present their research.

In considering how September 11 oral histories will be made public, it is important to keep in mind that the collection will serve a memorial, and not just documentary, function and that it must be available not only for scholarly purposes but for a larger community. The oral histories are themselves microcosms of the larger process whereby September 11 ideally becomes knitted into the fabric of the future, through forms of mourning that can also give rise to hopefulness.[5] It is important that the archive of September 11 become something more than the reification of the traumatic moment, something more than an endless video loop or repeated image of the planes hitting the buildings. Oral history can help break out of that potentially obsessive focus because it documents the process of people making meaning out of a rift in their lives. It is too soon to tell what exhibition strategies will work best, but I hope to see oral histories combined with other media to facilitate public forums about how September 11 continues to affect the present.

Feminists have focused on how trauma is linked to everyday life, emphasizing that it takes root because it is connected to ongoing violence and systemic structures of oppression. I'd like to see an oral history of September 11 open out onto the range of global and local histories that are constellated around the traumatic events. This is a cultural story that goes beyond the immediacy of dead bodies and the spectacular sensation of falling buildings. I resist the idea that, after September 11, everything has changed and nothing will be the same again. The need to connect cataclysmic moments to our everyday life persists; I'm interested not just in what happened on one day in September but also in how that shock is absorbed into the textures of our ongoing lives.

Notes

1. Ann Cvetkovich, *An Archive of Feelings: Trauma, Sexuality, and Lesbian Public Cultures* (Durham: Duke University Press, 2003).

2. Douglas Crimp, "Mourning and Militancy," *October* 51 (winter 1989): 3–18.

3. Amber Hollibaugh, *My Dangerous Desires: A Queer Girl Dreaming Her Way Home* (Durham: Duke University Press, 2000).

4. For more on the project, see Mary Marshall Clark, "The September 11, 2001 Oral History Narrative and Memory Project: A First Report," *American Journal of History* 89 (fall 2002): 569–79. I thank Clark for sharing this work with me, as well as for our conversations about the September 11 oral history project, which have provided the background for this article.

5. For more on mourning as open-ended and productive, see David L. Eng and David Kazanjian, eds., *Loss* (Berkeley: University of California Press, 2002).

3. Photographing

I Took Pictures: September 2001 and Beyond

Marianne Hirsch

Giuliani said not to. The policeman yelled at people, "Put your cameras away, show some respect. This is a graveyard, not a place to come and gawk." "Put your cameras away," shouted the policewoman. "Keep the line moving." "This is a crime scene, no pictures," yelled a third. I did not have my camera with me on that day (September 29), but I had already taken pictures the previous week when people were first allowed to walk to the area around ground zero. On my first visit, I walked down Broadway in a crowded line of people who were tearful, stunned, angry, even defiant. But each person had a camera pointed toward what used to be the World Trade Center towers, to take pictures of distant and hard to see smoke and rubble, peeking around trucks, guardrails, and workers who were blocking the view.

The week before (on September 14) I had gone from the Upper West Side, where I have been living, to St. Vincent's Hospital to be closer to where it happened. I also went to a candlelight vigil at Union Square that had been announced informally on various flyers and Internet sites. I had not known whether it was appropriate to go to the hospital area where some of the injured had been taken and where families were still looking for the missing. Certainly I had not felt comfortable bringing a camera along. But, as soon as I got there, I bought a disposable camera and took pictures of the signs, of people holding them, of streets blocked, of the silent crowds at the vigil. I took pictures of pictures, of people looking at pictures, of people taking pictures. All the while I wondered about what I was doing—what was I after? What did this desire to snap the shutter—as uncomfortable as it was uncontrollable—mean?

Commentators have agreed that the September 11 attacks were "the most photographed disaster in history."[1] Well-known photographers and photojournalists and ordinary snapshot takers like me have all been pho-

People taking pictures at ground zero. Photograph courtesy Diana Taylor

tographing. Within the first four minutes of the first impact, the *New York Times* had dispatched four photographers on assignment. One hundred people eventually submitted images for the front page of September 12. The event marked us visually at the time, as people watched live, and then in unremitting replay, planes hitting towers, towers falling, people jumping, running, screaming. Even as we watched, we wanted to record everything ourselves—however grainy, small, amateurish—on home videos, digital or analog cameras. I have even gotten together with friends to compare the snapshots we each took, snapshots that require narratives and explanations because, ultimately, not much is visible on them or, better said, because what we experience as utterly extraordinary appears just too ordinary on our snapshots. Web sites have been created to collect the images of amateurs and professionals, galleries have invited people to submit their images for public viewing, images are being sold for benefit purposes, exhibitions have opened around the country, magazines and newspapers continue to publish and republish professional and amateur photographs. "It's caused a sea change," reported the front-page photo editor of the *New York Times*, Philip Gefter, at a panel I attended at New York University's Tisch School of the Arts. The paper's editors decided that people want to see as much as they want to read, and thus in the *New York Times* there are more photographs, they are bigger and generally in color, and they are more creatively laid out on the pages of the newspaper. In Gefter's words, "words are cerebral, but pictures are visceral."

Certainly, still photography has emerged as the most responsive medium in our attempts to deal with the aftermath of September 11. But what does it mean to take pictures at the sites of trauma? Is it disrespectful, voyeuristic, a form of gawking? Or is it our own contemporary form of witnessing or even mourning? I started thinking about these issues specifically in response to the ban on photographs—a very short-lived ban, as it turned out, since later a viewing platform seemed actually to invite photography, but one that seemed to say something important about the relationship of photography to trauma. How, on the one hand, has photography affected the public and private process of mourning and memory and what, on the other hand, can the photographic acts of the fall of 2001 tell us about the testimonial functions of photography? How has photography inflected the ethics and the politics of grief?

THE TEMPORALITY OF THE SNAPSHOT

If still photography is the visual genre that best captures the trauma and loss associated with September 2001—the sense of monumental, irrevocable change that we feel we have experienced—it is due to the photograph's temporality. Photography interrupts, actually stops time, freezes a moment: it is inherently elegiac. The feeling that time stopped around 9:00 A.M. on September 11 has created an immeasurable gulf between the before and the after. Ironically, what makes us feel that time stopped is precisely the fact that the unfolding of events could not in fact be stopped. The towers, once hit, crumbled in front of everyone's eyes, even as rescue efforts were in full force. The fires did not stop burning; other buildings followed. Those who were caught in them could not get out in time. Photographic images can somehow convey a sense of this unforgiving temporality and the basic human impulse to stop it. The *instantanné,* the snapshot, has become the genre of the moment.

But to be able to stop time is also to be able to hold on to the trauma and outrage when everything conspires to forget and to go back to normal. Every picture of the devastation, however grainy or imperfect, stops this gradual normalization for an instant, recalling the extraordinary that befell us, making it visible even as it is in the process of disappearing like the towers have. This becomes clear for me when I see a number of pictures of quite literal *still lives*—interiors covered in thick layers of dust, like Edward Keating's beautiful image of a teapot and cups. The picture can show the dust, but the apartment will soon be cleaned, the cups reused. And in the image it looks like our Pompeii—we can imagine being able to assess the shock of an interrupted life by looking at this one image alone.

A third element of the photograph's temporality needs to be added to these two ways of stopping time. To photograph, we might say, is to look in a different way—to look without understanding. Understanding is deferred until we see the developed image. This deferral is as inherent to photography as it is to trauma, enabling photography to help us understand the traumatic events of September 11. Thus, for example, one photographer injured during the collapse was surprised to see the images he had taken of the explosion after the first plane hit printed in the *New York Daily News* with his byline. He could not remember taking the picture. Another Associated Press photographer reported on the *Charlie Rose* interview program on October 31, 2001, that the lab technician developing his picture called to ask him if he knew what was visible in one of his pictures of the exploding tower— a person holding on to a piece of the falling building. He had not seen that as he was shooting. This is an example of what Walter Benjamin calls the camera's "optical unconscious"—the technologies of sight reveal more than we can see through the eye, but the realization of that supplemental revelation is deferred, as is the experience of trauma.[2]

Thus time and space work the same way in the photograph; they expand, allowing distance and deferral. For Benjamin, the now of the image is composed of layers of interconnected moments, and this is nowhere as apparent as in the images of what we call September 11—a moment that has expanded backward and forward into durational time.

THE TIME OF MOURNING

Almost immediately after the attacks, the images of destruction were not the dominant images seen around New York City and in the press; they were superseded by the innumerable homemade posters of the missing, posters pasted up on walls, cars, lampposts, bulletin boards; worn on bodies; and walked around the city. As images from another moment were placed into the context of this disaster, they came to clarify what John Berger calls the "shock of discontinuity" that photography makes visible, the gulf separating the moment the picture was taken from the moment we are looking at it.[3] They came to clarify the connection between photography and death. For weeks, the faces on the posters were the only smiling faces in the city. The smiles were traces of another time—a vacation on the beach or on a boat, a barbecue on the patio, a wedding, a moment of familial intimacy. These are images of people looking toward a future they were never to have. They were intended to be placed in school yearbooks, collected in family albums, or circulated among friends, not to be displayed in public as they came to be. Violently yanked out of one context and inserted into another, totally incongruous one, they exemplify what Roland Barthes describes as the retrospective irony of looking at photographs—the viewer possesses the deadly knowledge that the subject of the image ignores.[4]

The walls of posters themselves changed from day to day. Initially hopeful calls for information—containing detailed descriptions of the missing person, down to clothing, moles, tattoos, and other markings, and inscribed with names of friends, relatives, and phone numbers to contact—they soon became memorials to the dead. The hopes of finding anyone alive changed to the hopes of finding a body, or a part of a body, to bury. Of course, this shift made the smiling faces and the familial scenes in which they were photographed all the more poignant and touching, the knowledge of the ways in which they died all the more devastating. More haunting still was the next phase—when the images faded and washed out, when they disappeared to be collected and classified in the archives that were created for this purpose, or when they were covered in plastic to serve as a more lasting memorial to a moment that is as transient as it seems eternal. Later

"Give blood." Photograph courtesy Lorie Novak. © Lorie Novak 2001.

Wedding anniversary. Photograph courtesy Lorie Novak. © Lorie Novak 2001.

photographs of the memorials became the basis for exhibits about this act of memorialization.

The power of these images and posters lies in their confrontation of past and present, but here in a private and protected familial context, a context that is familiar and shared. Violated by the attacks, the familial scene stands as a measure for the loss and devastation with which any of us can identify. These familiar family pictures engage us in the "affiliative looking" that characterizes ordinary family photographs. We all have pictures like these in our own albums, and thus we invest them with a form of looking that is broadly shared across our culture. In this way, precisely, they become markers of loss: the loss of our children's childhood, the loss of a time before, the imagined loss of a mother, or father, or friend. They mark the ordinariness, the familiality, the domesticity that for so many was interrupted by the attacks. And, at the same time, their haunting presence brings that past life back in spectral form.

Hudson River Park near the Winter Garden, November 2001. Donated teddy bears provided the backdrop for memorials (such as photographs, poems, eulogies, flowers, candles, and gifts) for those lost in the World Trade Center. Photograph courtesy Lorie Novak. © Lorie Novak 2001.

Flat Death

As I look at the pictures I took both near ground zero and around the city, I am frustrated at how little is visible on them. Everything everyone experienced and felt—the gravity, the enormity, the loss, the smell of smoke, the energy of the cleanup activity—none of this can be shown. I am conscious of what that policeman was trying to convey—that this is a graveyard, that every particle of dust contains human remains. None of this is even remotely visible in the pictures.

Roland Barthes's sense of photography as a form of "flat death"—flat in the sense of "plat," platitudinous—may well be appropriate to think about here. It is this ordinariness, this platitude that I find frustrating in the pictures. I look at them and I seek out the monumentality I feel. I wonder how, through these photographs, others who are not here might be able to share in the dimensions of these deaths, their grandeur.

But perhaps the flatness of the images is precisely what we need. The photographs might enable us to look at an indescribable event, to make it manageable, frame it, bring it home, show it to friends, make it small enough to fit into our living rooms or even our pockets. Flattening and miniaturizing death is a coping strategy—we look at the remains of the towers, at the missing people, through the viewfinder rather than straight on. We need to place a camera between us and the sight—to use it as a form of protection and distancing: "When I couldn't photograph, I really had to look," says the photographer Lorie Novak of her thwarted effort to take pictures of the search/memorial walls located at the center set up for families of the missing. The pictures she took from a distance inscribe a long barrier separating her from the sight—a barrier is a figure for the inherently distancing camera.

We contain and circumscribe the enormity of the event, but even as we stare at the small square print, we know that it is only a fragment, and that, in itself, brings us back to all that cannot be contained by the frame. Around the edges of the image we catch a glimpse of something huge and incomprehensible except as it is broken into small and painful stories and snapshots. The framing and the flatness of photographs give a sense of the fragmentariness of our knowledge, the inability we feel to take in the magnitude of the event and the losses it engendered.

It is for this reason that the snapshot has provided a metaphor with which to describe the profiles published daily in the *New York Times* about the victims of September 11: "Each profile is only a snapshot, a single still frame lifted from the unrecountable complexity of a lived life, and there

Seeing absence: ground zero. Photograph Marianne Hirsch.

is a world more to know about each of these victims, as their survivors understand only too well."[5]

And yet, with all that photographs cannot convey, there is one thing that the small print and the square frame, the two-dimensionality of the photographic image, cannot disguise—and that is my presence at the scene. Through photography I can become a witness in my own right, a witness not so much of the event as of its aftermath, a witness to the other acts of witness all around me. In circulating my images, I can invite others to become my

co-witnesses. The proliferation of books, photographic displays, and exhibitions allows everyone to share in this act of witnessing and working through.
The most interesting to me is "Here Is New York," a photography exhibit
that opened in an empty Soho gallery on September 28 and has now opened
in another New York location and in several other cities. These are, as the
brochure says, "Images from the Frontline of History." Subtitled "A Democracy of Photographs," the exhibition includes all photographs, amateur or
professional, that are donated in response to the organizers' broad-based
invitation to create an activist memorial that would benefit a 9/11 charity.

TOUCHING TRACES

One image from this show illustrates with particular force the various
qualities of photography that I have raised here. The tattooed drawing
emblematizes the profound bodily effect of the event we have come to call
September 11 and the ways in which—for this artist and subject—the nation
has been materially wounded by it, has had its memory carved onto its skin,
as it were. The flag marks the tattooed body as a subject of the state, the
state that was attacked and injured, and thus it inscribes the state's injury
onto the skin of the citizen. The tattoo shows both the moment of injury
and the act of perpetration. Highly technological, the syringe is like an
airplane, or like a bomb, at the moment of impact (note the angle). At the
same time, the drawing on the skin shows the citizen's defiant appropriation
and flaunting of the attack displayed for all to see and, more important,
to feel. The waving flag recalls the words of the national anthem—the flag
may be tattered, bloody, but it is *still there,* waving above the sunrise. The
visual display of the very act of wounding elicits spectatorial identification
on a physical, bodily level—for me a squirm or shudder in response to the
prick of the needle with which I identify. I would say that this may be as
close as one can come in communicating physical pain visually. At the same
time, by invoking well-known icons, the drawing evokes a familiar scenario
and thus attempts to elicit predictable emotional responses such as anger,
defiance, patriotism. In its close cropping and physical intimacy it seems to
me to thwart or foreclose more distant, critical, intellectual responses, thus
showing both the power and the appropriability of the visual that lacks a
label or narrative frame.

This photograph illustrates for me some of the qualities through which
photography can communicate the bodily wounding that is trauma and the
sense memory of it. If photography can even attempt to evoke the material
inscription of memory unto the body, it is because of the continuing popular

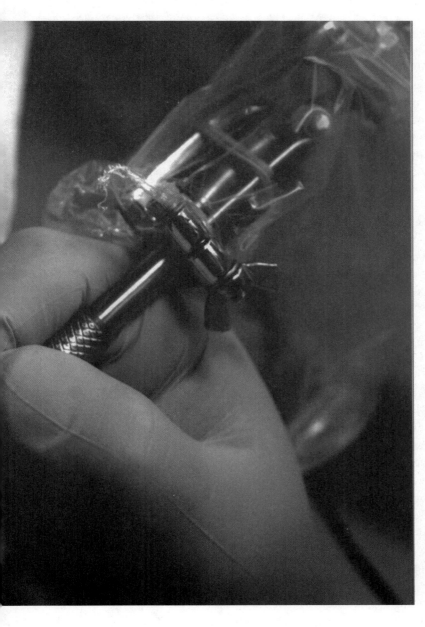

Tattoo.
Photograph
courtesy
Tony Savino.

perception of the material link between the photographic image and the object photographed. Semioticians have defined the photograph as an index based on a relationship of contiguity, of cause and effect, like a footprint or a trace. In his *Camera Lucida*, Roland Barthes argues that the material touch of the photographic image is as painful as a tattoo: something in each photograph "shoots out of it and pierces me," he says. "The photograph's *punctum* is that accident which pricks me (but also bruises me, is poignant to me).[6] Through the punctum, photography can be the medium for the communicability of trauma: just as the tattoo artist's needle pricks the skin, the photograph's material connection to the real can pierce the layer of consciousness that protects us from traumatic reenactment.

The art historian Jill Bennett has argued that images do more than *represent* scenes and experiences of the past: they can communicate an emotional or bodily experience to us by evoking our own emotional and bodily memories. They *produce* affect in the viewer, speaking *from* the body's sensations rather than speaking of or representing the past: "It is no coincidence that the image of ruptured skin recurs throughout the work of artists dealing with sense memory. . . . It is precisely through the breached boundaries of skin in such imagery that memory continues to be felt as a wound rather than seen as contained other. . . . it is here in sense memory that past seeps back into the present, becoming sensation rather than representation."[7]

But photographic images are also flat and two-dimensional, moments frozen in time and mere surfaces—*photo-graphy* is literally written on the *skin* of the paper. This double-sided quality of photography can perhaps best be seen in the white gloves covering the hand in the image and the plastic encasing the syringe. The tattoo artist's skin is tightly covered—impermeable. On one level, the white plastic illustrates yet another aspect of the September 11 events—the fear of "infection" and the careful attempts in New York to contain it in a delimited part of the city. Even the term "ground zero" suggests this effort at containment. But as the tears, or droplets, on the image show, things spill over and containment is ultimately impossible. On another level, the white plastic and the white gloves can be read as visual echoes of the white frame of the image that contains its impact by signaling that it is not the act of wounding but its representation.

PHANTOMS

As I took photos at the ground zero site, I began to realize that, after all, it is the absence of the towers that I have been trying to show, and that absence, by nature, is not easily visualized. But although they have physically disappeared, the towers are actually still present all over the city: framed black and white photographs, postcards, T-shirts, and key chains featuring the trade towers are available on every street corner. In drawings, poems, and reconstructions people are evoking presence where there is only absence. Photography as a medium can well confront the shocking absence with phantasmatic presence. The photographs of the towers are touched by the towers, and looking at them enables viewers to be touched by that touch. There is an intimacy of looking at images that makes that touch gentle, domestic—the pictures are, after all, miniaturized versions of enormous buildings that could only be fully seen from a great distance.

Images printed onto paper by way of light are ghosts that haunt. This is as true for the pictures on the posters of the missing as it is for the pictures of the towers themselves. Art Spiegelman understood this from the first week, when he created the black on black *New Yorker* cover. In the discussions about the memorialization of the event, focusing on whether the towers should or should not be rebuilt, two artists came up with the same idea: temporarily create life-size neon projections of the towers' outline so that they would not have disappeared. Many say that they still see their outlines, that they are haunted by them. Rick Burns, director of a documentary on New York City that was broadcast on PBS, called them "our phantom limb." "You feel it but it's not there; you look to where you feel it should be."[8] Photographs can convey this haunting.

THE AESTHETICS OF TRAUMA AND THE POLITICS OF GRIEF

Aesthetic questions and aspirations might well seem frivolous or inappropriate at a time of mourning. And yet aesthetic and ethical questions help us understand how our perceptions are affected and structured by public catastrophes such as this one. More than just evocative and representational power, images also quickly assume symbolic power, Barbie Zelizer has argued: "the photo's significance . . . evolved from the ability not only to depict a real-life event but to position that depiction within a broader interpretive framework."[9] Thus photos that are initially documentary assume a commemorative or symbolic role. Angel Franco, a photographer for the *New York Times* reporting on his work on September 11 at a panel at the Tisch School of the Arts, says he quickly realized that this is no longer journalism but history. "These are like the images I grew up watching in television documentaries," he said. But, for Zelizer, photos are "markers of both truth-value and symbolism," and thus the images of the attacks

Brooklyn Heights promenade, October 2001. The promenade has a clear view of the World Trade Center towers and has been a pilgrimage site to view the loss, to leave memorials, and to be photographed against the new skyline. Photograph courtesy Lorie Novak. © Lorie Novak 2001.

have come to signify nothing less than a modern apocalypse.[10] But which photographs? Is it really, as the "Here Is New York" exhibition implies, a democratic process in which any image is as powerful as any other, or do certain images have elements that make them immediately iconic? "Our intention," write the organizers of "Here Is New York" in their exhibit flyer, "is to display the widest possible variety of pictures from the widest possible variety of sources, believing as we do that the World Trade Center disaster and its aftermath has ushered in a new period in our history, one which demands that we look at and think about images in a new and unconventional way." This is the effort also to look at and think about what has happened in totally new ways. But is that really possible?

Every major historical event has bequeathed a limited number of photographs that have become emblematic for it, such as the picture of the little boy with his hands up in the Warsaw ghetto or prisoners in stripe uniforms for the Holocaust; the naked girl running down the road after a napalm attack for the Vietnam War; the birds in an oil spill for the Gulf War. Which will be the icons for September 11? What elements determine this process of reduction and iconicization? And in what ways will this process be in fact determined by aesthetic factors? It was fascinating to me that the four photographers interviewed on the *Charlie Rose* program agreed that the icon would be the picture of the three firemen raising the flag on top of the rubble because it echoes the famous prize-winning photograph of American GI's raising the flag at Iwo Jima. In their search for the one lasting iconic image, they were looking for the conventional, the coded, not the new. Is this familiarity reassuring, inscribing this event into a known visual register and thus a known history? And does it thus perhaps shield us from the shock of the suddenness and unexpectedness of the devastation? In the aftermath of an event as monumental as this one, we may need, eventually, to reduce the number of available images to just a few lasting ones that will structure our cultural memory. But we are not yet at that point.

As I consider the many images I have seen, I think about the many that were never taken and the many that have not yet come to public view. What they contain we can only imagine. Thus I was at the "Here Is New York" gallery when a rescue worker came to donate two hundred images he had taken during the three weeks of working there. "All the guys there have cameras with them," he reported. Initially hesitant to take pictures, he said that he was convinced by others who said that "you have to remember." The picture he felt most embarrassed about, he said, was one of four rescue workers, hugging and smiling for the camera, smoking cigars (for the smell, he said). He thought this would be controversial, but there they all were, together in this other world—what else could they do but smile for the camera in their togetherness? When these and all the other pictures taken "down there" in this "other world" get developed and disseminated, what else will we get to see? How will these pictures be used? And what images have we not yet seen or will we never get to see? The debates about what is and is not appropriate to show to a public in mourning are as instructive as the images themselves.

NOTES

Earlier versions of this article appeared in the *Chronicle of Higher Education Review* and in the *Brown Alumni Magazine*. I would like to thank Barbara Kirshenblatt-Gimblett, Temma Kaplan, Lorie Novak, Leo Spitzer, Diana Taylor, and Barbie Zelizer for sharing their images and their thoughts about photography and memory with me.

1. Barbara Kirshenblatt-Gimblett, "Kodak Moments, Flashbulb Memories," paper delivered at the Council for American Jewish Museums, Cincinnati, Ohio, Jan. 26–30, 2002.

2. Walter Benjamin, "The Work of Art in the Age of Mechanical Reproduction," in *Illuminations* (New York: Schocken, 1969), 236–37.

3. John Berger and Jean Mohr, *Another Way of Telling* (London: Writers and Readers, 1982), 86.

4. Roland Barthes, *Camera Lucida: Reflections on Photography*, trans. Richard Howard (New York: Hill and Wang, 1981).

5. Editorial, *New York Times*, Oct. 14, 2001, 12.

6. Barthes, *Camera Lucida*, 26, 27.

7. Jill Bennett, "The Aesthetics of Sense-Memory: Theorising Trauma through the Visual Arts," in *Trauma und Erinnerung/Trauma and Memory: Crosscultural Perspectives*, ed. Franz Kaltenbeck and Peter Weibel (Vienna: Passagen Verlag, 2000), 92.

8. Peter Markus, *New York Times*, Oct. 24, 2001, 1.

9. Barbie Zelizer, *Remembering to Forget: Holocaust Memory through the Camera's Lens* (Chicago: University of Chicago Press, 1998), 8.

10. Zelizer, *Remembering to Forget*, 10.

Photographs
Lorie Novak

Union Square memorial, September 17, 2001. © Lorie Novak 2001.

MISSING

JAMES MARCEL CARTIER
LOCAL 3 ELECTRICIAN
BORN 6/22/75, 5'9 185 LBS
LAST LOCATION: 105TH FLOOR 2 WTC
OO RIGHT ARM, SCAR ON FOREHEAD
MATION CALL:
69-6023/ (347)581-5135/ (917)572-9432

UNTIL WE ARE
TOGETHER AGAIN JAMES...
MAY GOD HOLD YOU IN THE
PALM OF HIS HAND

Outside Bellevue Hospital, September 2001; Hudson River Park, November 2001. The missing poster for James was posted on many of the walls throughout the city. When I found the memorial the family had made for him at Hudson River Park, it was as if I knew him. © Lorie Novak 2001.

Outside Bellevue Hospital, September 2001. Which woman has the mint-green toenails and light pink and white hand nails? It looks as if there are the remains of a circle around the shorter woman. Rain has caused the ink to smudge, so we can no longer see her face. Is she the one missing, or is it the taller woman whose direct gaze haunts us? © 2001 Lorie Novak.

Hudson River Park, November 2001. © 2001 Lorie Novak.

Outside Bellevue Hospital, September 2001. I was extremely moved by the display of the actual snapshots both on the "missing walls" outside the hospitals and at the impromptu memorial site near the Winter Garden in Hudson River Park near the World Trade Center site. To my surprise, the public display of this handmade poster struck a deeper emotional chord for me than did the computer-generated printouts. © 2001 Lorie Novak.

Hudson River Park, November 2001. Many of the photographs and memorials at the Hudson River Park behind the World Trade Center site contained messages written to deceased loved ones. Placed near the site as public memorials, the photographs also become portals to speak to the dead. I came across several images like this one where messages to the deceased that have been added by family and friends make private messages public. © 2001 Lorie Novak.

Hudson River Park, November 2001. © 2001 Lorie Novak.

A Camera and a Catastrophe:
Reflections on Trauma and the Twin Towers

E. Ann Kaplan

SEPTEMBER 11 AND AFTER

In the shocked days after the Twin Towers collapsed and thousands of people died in unimaginable ways, I wandered around my neighborhood between Union Square and Soho, trying to absorb what had happened. My camera was my only companion. I snapped (sometimes feeling guilty— was I invading people's privacy?) in an attempt, I think, to make real what I could barely comprehend. My immediate physical world had changed dramatically with the disappearance of the Twin Towers from my daily visual landscape at the end of Broadway and their reduction to a mountain of smoking wreckage sending acrid air into our bedroom. My relation to the public sphere was also changed since New York City and the United States as a nation both were destabilized. But my inner world was even more changed: Not only did the catastrophe jump-start my old traumatic symptoms from World War II England, but it also brought about surprising new crises having to do with my political identifications—or rather with my political *identity*. This resulted in unexpected ruptures with colleagues I had always agreed with before.

Other certainties were threatened as well, for example, my certainty, as a film scholar, that I could easily analyze media manipulations. At first, that was not the case. I would be swept up in certain live reporting, such as the national service of mourning or George Bush's speech to the entire assembled Congress. It was only as I wandered about Union Square and the streets around my apartment with my camera that I was gradually able to attain a perspective on the media reporting and to distinguish the different levels through which I was experiencing this catastrophe.

LEVEL OF THE STREET AND LOCAL COLLECTIVE TRAUMA

There was, first, the street level: Looking through the pictures I took brings those days back as if they were now. The first pictures are of the memorials in Union Square and of the posters stuck all over the streets near me, especially along Tenth and Twelfth Streets, outside the New School and the various fire and police stations in the area. These rows of images of lost people overwhelmed me. They hung there as appeals, as desires that the one imaged not be dead, that he or she turn up having escaped. They made visible the need for closure, the awfulness of not knowing whether a loved one is dead, and, if dead, whether one would ever have a body to mourn over.

I hardly dared move further downtown for weeks. But there is a second group of photos from ground zero, when finally I felt brave enough to go and look as closely as people were allowed to. Civilian guard soldiers in their khakis stood at the barriers, their gear reminding me of the war. The crush of people pressing around me made me feel as claustrophobic as did the crowds jamming into the underground shelters in London during my childhood. We all reached over the ground zero barriers to take photos. The smoke from the long-smoldering buildings still snarled insistently into the air and is captured in my photos. The carcass of one tower loomed in ghostly fashion through the smoke. Huge chunks of twisted metal jutted out from buildings still standing. I tried to snap the shop windows with objects inside covered in layers of ash. Buildings we passed were still covered in ash. Ground zero was a huge crematorium.

A final batch of photos was taken later, when I was getting used to the changed worlds. I found myself snapping all the odd places flags popped up: We had grown used to the flags on cars, especially those flying from radio antennas. But they were also squeezed into shop doorframes or added into window displays in creative ways, such as in a Radio Shack store that juxtaposed three carefully arranged flags in the window on one side with an image of lovers (selling a cell phone) on the other. But sitting in the doorway itself was a homeless man covered by an umbrella and cardboard boxes, while trash sat on the pavement awaiting pick up. That is, response to 9/11 was added onto normal New York life. A flag perched high up on the scaffolding of New York University's new student union was perhaps most eye-catching of all.

But what did all this flag flying really mean? Certainly, on one level the flags represented a newly engaged patriotism (a patriotism increasingly problematic for me), echoing sentiments written on memorials in the park, on the walls, and around fire stations and police precincts, such as "United We Stand: God Bless America," "We Love America," and so on. But (at least in the area of New York where the catastrophe happened) the flags were also a way to indicate empathy for those who had lost people and a shared trauma about the shock to the United States. The inconspicuous nature of the displays supports this view. Some messages in Union Square suggested the same sentiments as the flag displays, such as "The terrorists thought that they can tear us apart. But it brought us together"; "We Are Not Broken"; or "Aimez Votre Frères Parce-Que Demain Matin Ils ne Seront Pas" (Love your brothers because tomorrow they'll be gone). Messages about peace—such as "2001 Years of Violence: What Have We Learned?" or "United We Stand: Violence Creates Violence" or even just "Love One Another"—were more common than saber-rattling.

Perhaps because I had not lost anyone I knew personally, wandering around I began to understand in ways I had only theorized before what collective trauma felt like. Everyone was in shock: people did not laugh out loud in the streets or in the square; voices were muted. People's expressions were somber. I felt a connection to strangers that I had never felt before. On the subway, too, we looked at each other as if understanding what we all were facing, for at any moment, it seemed, another attack could take place, the subway could blow up, gas might fill the tunnels. Nowhere was safe, just as nothing had been safe in wartime England. And we were in this together.

I felt the togetherness especially walking around Union Square, which instantly became a huge, makeshift memorial and also a site for posting images of people still lost. On those bright, sunny September afternoons, the square was crowded with mourners and with people like myself needing to share in the grief and loss we all experienced, even if some had not personally lost a loved one. I snapped pictures of a diverse array of spontaneous, rough drawings and writings. I watched as a huge roll of paper was brought into the square, gradually unfurling as more and more people knelt down to draw or write on the spur of the moment. It became one vast communal outpouring of emotion and thought. The candles and the flowers took on many different forms, reminding one partly of the 1960s protest culture, partly of memorials produced when Princess Diana died. And yet this was so different: this was personal and political in new ways. Different religions were represented. But despite all the differences in perspective that the artifacts showed, an apparent commonality reigned in the form of a respect for differences within a whole (the events) that we shared.

The gap where the Twin Towers had stood in the weeks that followed became a space full of horror but also of heroism. Their visual absence was traumatic; that is, it was impossible to comprehend that they were gone—that I no longer found the towers in their place. Psychoanalytically, this gap or lack can be read in many ways—as Lacan's *petit objet* 'a', castration (the towers were huge, phallic), the infant's loss of the mother, a loss standing in for death, abandonment, abjection. But while these underlying infantile emotions may be unconsciously evoked, the gap is phenomenological as well as symbolic.

On the other hand, the gap was filled with other images—of burning people jumping out of the towers, of firemen rushing up to rescue people and being crushed when the buildings collapsed on them, of the huge cloud of smoke pursuing fleeing people like a cement roller or like the giant marshmallow of the movie *Ghostbusters*. People tried to fill in or recover the absence of the towers by creating images of them. Art Spiegelman created an unforgettable cover for the *New Yorker* that was totally black, but within whose dim darkness one could glimpse shadows or the ghosts of the towers, haunting the city. One or two art stores in Greenwich Village filled their windows with different sizes of beautiful framed color photographs of the towers in the city landscape.

Did we hope that pictures of the towers would undo the trauma of their collapse or that they would write over the haunting, unforgettable scenes of the plane driving straight into the second tower and of the bright flames bursting forth into the pure blue sky—scenes that have returned again and again in nightmares? The images were part of the traumatic symptom already evident in the media's constant repetition of the tower being struck: Given trauma's peculiar visuality as a psychic disorder, this event seemed to feed trauma by being so highly visible in its happening. The images haunted one waking and dreaming. U.S. culture was visually haunted.

LEVEL OF THE MEDIA AND DISCURSIVE FORMATIONS

It was through wandering around the streets with my camera that I began to understand the differences between the media's reporting of more or less national (or at least "official") positions and what I was witnessing myself. The media had to tread a difficult line: In the shaky days following the attacks, reporters presumably felt they had to stick to what U.S. and other leaders were doing and saying as they tried to calm and to unify the nation while desperately figuring out how to respond. The world was watching. Osama bin Laden and Al Qaeda were watching. The media aided the attempt to present a united front. But this was a fiction—a construction of a consensus in a Eurocentric and largely masculine form. On the streets, I experienced the multiple, spontaneous activities from multiple perspectives, genders, races, and religions, or nonreligions. Things were not shaped for a specific effect or apparently controlled by one entity. By contrast with what I witnessed locally, the male leaders on TV presented a stiff, rigid, controlling, and increasingly revengeful response—a response I only gradually understood as actually about humiliation. While a "disciplining" of response was at work through the media, on the streets something fluid, personal, and varied was taking place.

LEVEL OF POLITICAL IDENTITY AND RUPTURES

One of the unexpected aspects of the catastrophe was the rupture in my political persona: Since the 1960s, I have always (if loosely) identified with liberal positions, which I shared with my colleagues and friends. But after 9/11 I found myself with different positions than my colleagues or friends regarding the attacks. I don't want to debate the politics of the U.S. response here. Let me only say that I have always been critical—very critical—of U.S. policies internationally, of the United States as the latest imperial nation, of its insidious role in postmodern, postcolonial global capitalism. But to my mind these past actions did not so clearly "cause" the attacks or justify them, as some colleagues argued. America has gotten what it deserves, they said. But the United States was attacked: The attack was a separate event—in the here and now—that needed to be dealt with in its specificity. Linking the attacks simply to the United States' past crimes was to collapse incommensurable levels of happenings and thought. It reminds me of a colleague who, when I arrived at work at the university on September 11 about three hours after the attacks, said: "What about Hiroshima? Didn't we do that?" Yes, indeed, but to evoke Hiroshima at this moment indicated an intellectualizing of present, highly emotional happenings, a distancing and displacement characteristic of many political scholars. As leftists and political people, can't we also live in the present and relate to emotions?

The problem lies in people's different standpoints vis-à-vis the attacks and their literal closeness or distance from ground zero. Some European scholars immediately took a very abstract and theoretical approach. A typical example of the broad generalizations that arrived promptly via the Internet is Slavoj Žižek's e-mail posting, "Welcome to the Desert of the Real."[1] Looking at the event from a distant intellectual perspective, Žižek in his article overstated the political/psychic symbolism of the attacks. On some level, I agree that the attacks broke through an illusory haze in which many Americans may have been living. I appreciate his argument that in some ways the United States had already anticipated the event in the many movies about uncannily similar catastrophes—as if unconsciously aware of the illusion they were living as repressed knowledge of danger emerged in film fantasies. But this thesis does not exhaust or actually get close to the specificity of the event for those of us living close by. It is possible that the Twin Towers represented to the terrorists (perhaps schooled in U.S. movies) postmodernity, technology, the city, architectural brilliance, urban landscape, the future high-tech, globalized world. But for those nearby, the towers functioned phenomenologically as part of people's spatial universe, in and of themselves, not standing in particularly for American capitalism or American might. The discourse of the United States and "the desert of the real" is orthogonal to the experience of those of us close to the attacks. Both levels need to be taken into account.

The different standpoints of some European and U.S. scholars were evident in a heated debate in the letters section of the *London Review*. It's not that we didn't have our own writers—such as Susan Sontag— taking strong positions. Like Žižek, Sontag saw the event as "a monstrous dose of reality" and the public response as "self-righteous drivel being peddled by public figures and TV commentators." She claimed that politics was being replaced by psychotherapy (*New Yorker*, September 24, 2001, 32). But was the therapy discourse really that inappropriate? Might not therapy talk be viewed as useful in public discourse in times like this? It is true that the media found it easier to relate to the events through a therapy discourse (I have a large number of clippings about the attacks and posttraumatic stress disorder), but isn't it interesting to see psychological issues being taken seriously by a U.S. press that has traditionally scorned such perspectives? While it's true that political public discussion of 9/11 has been, and still is, very inadequate because of the limits set on what can and cannot be debated (something I don't approve of), when does the United States ever have adequate political public discourse? In addition, why must confrontational, thorough, and critical political discourse be opposed to a discourse of empathy for those who suffer, for those who have lost loved ones, for pain, trauma, hurt? Is it really impossible to have a solid, left-leaning political analysis, highly critical of the United States' actions in the past and today, and yet welcome public discourse about trauma, posttraumatic stress disorder, vicarious traumatization, and ways to help those suffering these disorders?

The United States has been humiliated by the brilliance of the terrorists' imaginations and their ability to make concrete what they had imagined (and perhaps what we had imagined also, if we take our movies to heart). And yet, as I said at the outset, once the event happened as lived experience it still felt "unimaginable." It was also humiliating that the terrorists produced the seemingly impossible by using the United States' own open society. The deep humiliation of the United States is another way of framing the current

scene rather than forming theories about the country's descent into the abyss
of the Real.

MARCH II AND AFTER

The March 11 deadline for this volume arrived, and I had still not written
my essay. I had made notes and taken pictures, but I had intended to do so
much more. I have collected piles and piles of newspaper clippings. I have
obsessively saved every article about 9/11 that came my way, every mention
in the newspapers of all kinds—an activity I now see as partly a symptom
of the trauma, as perhaps was also my obsessive taking of photographs.
Then all the books began to appear. The array of 9/11 texts was daunting.
I selected several to buy. I was going to synthesize all of this for my essay.
But the deadline arrived, and I promised to write what I could in the short
time I had.

Part of the problem in writing about 9/11 at this (relatively) late date is
that so much has been written, so many books published, so much visual
art produced (such as the remarkable video documentaries from people
who were at ground zero at the time of the collapse of the towers and the
magnificent Magnum photos shown at the New York Historical Society),
so many dramas, speeches, psychological studies, and endless debates in
magazines that one is exhausted simply attending to these things. What
new could there possibly be to say, I thought?

I was worried that so much had been said, written, and shown: Were
people indeed beginning to exploit the event as traumatic effects waned?
Was the event being fixed within certain patriotic and male heroism tropes
that with distance begin to pall? Was its realness being gelled into stock
images, stock forms that would forever limit its meanings? Hearing that
the scroll of paper that finally wound its way around Union Square was to be
displayed in an upcoming museum exhibition, I felt conflicted. How could
that scroll on display in a museum mean what it had meant when people
spontaneously wrote on it on those warm September evenings in the days
after the attacks? New York University's La Maison Française held a one-day
symposium entitled "Rupture de l'Ordre Symbolique" (with Paul Ricoeur
and Jacques Rancière, among others), taking up Žižek's earlier point about
the United States' being plummeted finally into the Real from an illusory
(exceptional) security. How could we keep the event open, fluid, specific?

I also understood, of course, that we really had not been "together," as
my notes from the time of the attacks assumed. Many Arab and Muslim
individuals have been unfairly arrested or interrogated. There is an entire
spectrum of responses to the attacks, a diversity of interpretations. It has

become its own phenomenon, with circles spreading out like those from a stone thrown into a pond. I sometimes no longer know what "my" response really is. So I was happy to return to the photos I took at the time and the notes I wrote immediately following the catastrophe and to forget any (which, in any case, is impossible) "synthesis."

March 11 was a difficult day. It brought back vivid memories of September 11. I watched the ground zero memorial service for the families of the victims and was moved. America has learned to mourn and to respect mourning, and that's a good thing. I like the twin towers of light that were turned on that day: They seemed a gesture that was strong yet peaceful, against the violence that has inevitably characterized much of the U.S. response. Watching the huge blue beams of light from Fifth Avenue (Broadway is too well lit for the beams to show up), I felt something restored to my visual landscape where the gap had been—or at least there was something there that could not be knocked down. I recalled my last view of the Twin Towers from the Long Island Railroad on my way to work that day: Once out of the tunnel, I turned and saw the two towers still standing, but with great swaths of black smoke pouring from both. The smoke was like an enormous black roll, spreading miles along the sky, following the train to Long Island.

I still have all the front pages of the *New York Times'* special section on the event, "A Nation Challenged" (I appreciated this term, which was much more helpful than CNN's hysterical "America under Attack" and later, even worse, "America at War"). Our nation really was and still is challenged by the attacks. They are a challenge to us in the sense that the United States has had to respond, to deal with the situation. And it has done so with little tradition to rely on, since these attacks are only the second of their kind in the short history of the United States. At first I thought we had learned from Vietnam, but as time went on that did not seem to be the case. As I write at the end of March 2002, it looks less and less possible that our leaders will rise to the occasion rather than lapsing into isolationist or "go it alone" tactics. What will March 2003 bring?

CODA

My previous question prompts another: What will I think of the words I have written here, and the state of consciousness it represents, in a year from now? Already, reading over my text, I find myself distancing from its sensibility, if not its politics. The return to a focus on male heroism and the heightened patriotism the event has produced now come to the fore. Did I succumb to a phenomenological perspective I have always resisted? Here is another problem with September 11: namely, how my own interpretations of the events have changed over time and how they continue to change. The main point in keeping my earlier reflections (and photos captured at the time) is to preserve "readings" produced close to the time of the event—to have a record of the emotions and interpretations of the moment. It is just such records that historians rarely have in hand and that we strive to reconstruct imaginatively without concrete data. What I perhaps have recorded as "my" responses may in fact be responses produced culturally in the place where I was at the time. This complicated question about how emotions are produced in specific contexts, about individual and collective trauma and their interpretations and reinterpretations over time, remains to be explored in another context.

NOTE

1. Žižek's e-mail posting later appeared as a short volume, *Welcome to the Desert of the Real* (New York: Wooster Press, 2002).

4. Imagining

Uncanny Sights: The Anticipation
of the Abomination

Claire Kahane

*Déjà vu: A plane crashes into a massive skyscraper and leaves a black
hole outlining the shape of its penetration. Flames lick the windows of
a towering inferno; black smoke billows out of a dark gash in its side;
tiny figures leap from high ledges into space, falling, falling. The tallest
buildings crumple and collapse like sandcastles, while incredulous millions
watch helplessly. We have been here before.*

On September 11, 2001, we sat glued to the screen of our television sets
for most of the day, watching a rerun over and over again in numb
disorientation. Many had watched the original event as it happened, in
real time. But even in real time, knowing that we were watching a unique
act of devastation, the scenes before our eyes seemed familiar and unreal.
For even as this historical event unfolded, it was quickly recognized, placed
in a familiar category, and given a local habitation and a name: "it's just
like a movie," the newscasters blurted out, a remark echoed repeatedly
that morning; "it's just like *Independence Day*"; "it's like *Towering Inferno*."
Even King Kong scrambling up the Empire State Building after having
devastated midtown Manhattan entered the chain of association. Thus the
actual reality before our eyes was almost immediately transformed into and
by the virtual reality of Hollywood and made familiar, déjà vu. In this
assimilation, as we turned to the movies to orient us to the real disaster,
the historical was confused with the fictional, and the event of 9/11 itself—
familiar and unfamiliar, real and unreal—took on an uncanny ambiguity.

Indeed, our response to 9/11 made disturbingly clear how much our
perceptual experience as well as our psychic life is filtered and managed
through films we have seen, even experienced *as* films we have seen. But
these associations to films also pointed to a set of preexisting anxieties
reflected in the films that were released by the trauma of the day. In *King
Kong* (1933), for example, the Empire State Building had stood as an icon

of the cultural power of New York, the empire state, which in spite of the Depression could withstand and ultimately overcome the primal forces of rage and desire embodied in the giant ape—though barely. Fifty years later the status of the Empire State Building and its symbolic significance had been displaced by the World Trade Center. Now it was not New York but the United States that was the empire state, its imperial power and outreach signified through the new euphemism, globalism. And its phallic icon, the World Trade Center, arguably the biggest erection in the Western world, was uncannily doubled by *twin* towers, ensuring its indestructibility. Like the Gothic cathedrals of past centuries, this addition to the skyline of New York stretching heavenward seemed to confirm our privileged relation to omnipotence. (For this reason alone, how could the World Trade Center not be a target of rage and envy for those outside its arena of dispensation?)

Americans have long believed themselves the chosen people, a nation founded in, and protected by, its innocence and its godliness. Puritan dogma had initially propagated the belief that economic success was the sign of one's chosenness, and while that belief had been tested a number of times since the Founding Fathers declared that we deserved to pursue happiness, in the twentieth century only Vietnam seriously punctured our idealized self-image. (It was no accident that Vietnam elicited a new name for what Freud had called "the war neuroses": posttraumatic stress disorder remained widespread in part as a correlative of our collective disillusion and its effects on returning veterans.) By the end of the twentieth century, those war wounds seemed to have healed; our virtue seemed to be increasingly confirmed by world events—perhaps nowhere more clearly than in the defeat of our archrival, the Soviet Union, the last evil empire—and the subsequent explosion of domestic wealth on Wall Street. As the century drew to a close, we were riding the crest of a new wave of illusion, a childlike faith in a well-stocked and bountiful future that we had earned and that the World Trade Center symbolized. Narcissistically confident in our unchallenged position (even though the stock market rumbled a bit as we moved toward the millennium), we were alone at the top of the world. "I made it, Ma, top of the world!" James Cagney cried out from the top of a skyscraper in *White Heat* (1949) before the reality principle shattered his delusion. Was there not something analogous in our situation in the 1990s?

Slavoj Žižek points out that the most deeply unsettling traumas are not those that are entirely unexpected but those that are anticipated in fantasy, those in which one has a libidinal investment.[1] Wasn't the World Trade Center disaster such an event? Was there not from the beginning of its ascent an anxious anticipation of downfall, of a plunge equal in intensity to the reach? Was there not something of that anxiety already hovering over its observation deck—where the visitor who peered vertiginously over the edge was rewarded and terrified by its awesome prospect? Surely, a similar anxious exhilaration must have hovered around visitors to the observation deck of the Empire State Building in midcentury, when it was *that* structure that towered over the city as its sublime embodiment. Yet after World War II we were relatively innocent in our relations to the world; the horrors of Hiroshima were still buried under the justification of its having shortened the war and saved Allied lives; the Holocaust was something that happened in Europe and could never happen here; our version of apartheid was still excluded from national scrutiny. On the surface, we still shared a pervasive sense of apple-pie goodness and still heard as our destiny the ringing rhetoric of a "God Blessed America."

We are less innocent today; we know that the discourse of foundational innocence on which Americans had established their public identity had hidden a more rapacious reality. Although America in the nineteenth century saw itself figured as the new Adam, the multiculturalist ethos of the late twentieth century insistently uncovered behind that figure of innocence guilty acts of aggression—especially toward the Native Americans, who like the European Jews a century later were almost decimated as a cultural entity, and toward the Africans, on whose back an economy grew without reparations. Given the rapidly expanding international gap between the culture of plenty and the culture of poverty in our own time, would it be surprising if many of us unconsciously anticipated envious acts of retaliation from the margin, from unknown antagonists "over there"? After several decades of globally exporting media images of American prosperity to those struggling for economic and cultural survival elsewhere, did we not perhaps in some corner of our minds expect the fiery flights that were propelled from the Middle East, expect that after all the sunshine of the past decade a sandstorm might blow into the United States from another center of energy, where our ceremonies of innocence are engulfed in outrage? Only our hubris kept us blind. And then came 9/11.

What were we seeing when we saw the black gash in the side of the first tower? What did we imagine was happening inside that dark hole spewing flames? What confirmation did we dread when we saw that wound repeated like an exclamation point as another plane blasted into the companion behemoth, now both spewing flame and ash? The blasted side of American narcissism? A castration? A deserved punishment for some unacknowledged guilt? Or some apprehension of even greater catastrophe?

Clearly, the sight of the World Trade Center buckling, collapsing into a heap of rubble, was a trauma to our national identity as well as a real disaster to thousands who lost their family and friends. Especially for those who identified with New York's skyline, those for whom the World Trade Center was a self-object as well as those for whom it served as a symbolic bulwark against undefined external dangers, the collapse of the towers was unthinkable and at the same time the very image of what was thought. The rubble—itself a powerful metonymy for the invisible incineration of the thousands who were trapped inside—marked our fall, our entrance into the culture of a globalized political violence with no safe boundaries. After years of prelapsarian security, we were falling into a new knowledge. This was not, however, the fortunate fall of Adam and Eve, our myth of origins; through that fall, we are born into the human world, precipitated into a symbolic universe of discourse that can contain our erotic and aggressive energies and displace our terrors. The traumatic fall of the World Trade Center precipitated us into a more primitive anxiety of obliteration; it shattered our symbolic certainties, forcing us to acknowledge the reality of disintegration and annihilation through the very materiality of the ash and debris raining down on Lower Manhattan and, more uncannily, through the *absence* that it left behind, the sheer space a powerful reminder of the event.

And we were forced to acknowledge this reality through something even more disquieting: there were actual people falling along with the ash and debris; some were even jumping, forced from the fire into the abyss *as we watched*, already anticipating their certain deaths seconds later. Significantly, these images were withdrawn from the reruns in the United States, as if too much to re-present as spectacle. (In a recent CBS screening of the documentary *9/11*, a French photographer filming the firefighters inside the North Tower captured the off-screen sound of bodies hitting the ground outside, a sound reflected on the faces of the firemen who winced with each awful thud. And the viewer winced with them. Thus a visceral core of the traumatic scene that had been foreclosed on American television was played out on the TV screen months later for those who had watched the falling bodies but had not heard them hit the ground.)

Eleanor Kaufman observes the link between trauma and falling in an entire strain of post–World War II literature in England; falling, she points out, is a marker of the abysslike structure of trauma.[2] Falling: *losing ground, having the rug pulled out from under you, being pushed over the edge, catch me I'm falling.* My own free-fall thoughts suggest that archaic memory traces of infantile experiences must inhabit the metaphor, signifier of the ultimate loss of control, of loss of agency, of loss of boundaries. Compounded by a host of cultural associations, the fear of falling in all likelihood must be part of our neurobiological makeup, contributing to our survival.

But there is more to the fear of falling than the fear of falling; falling evokes not just memory but fantasy, contaminating both memory and desire with perverse wishes that push us past our limits, urge us toward risk, even toward death itself. Romantic writers especially were on familiar terms with this fascination, no one more so than Edgar Allen Poe:

> We stand upon the brink of a precipice. We peer into the abyss— we grow sick and dizzy. Our first impulse is to shrink from the danger. Unaccountably, we remain. By slow degrees our sickness, and dizziness, and horror, become mired in a cloud of unnamable feeling. By gradations, still more imperceptible, this cloud assumes shape. . . . But out of this our cloud upon the precipice's edge, there grows into palpability, a shape, far more terrible than any genius, or any demon of a tale, and yet it is but a thought, although a fearful one, and one which chills the very marrow of our bones with the fierceness of the delight of its horror. It is merely the idea of what would be our sensations during the sweeping precipitancy of a fall from such a height. And this fall—this rushing annihilation—for the very reason that it involves that one most ghastly and loathsome of all the most ghastly and loathsome images of death and suffering which have ever presented themselves to our imagination—for this very cause do we now most vividly desire it.[3]

No wonder that the response of witnesses to the realization that it was not just debris but people who were leaping from the windows produced sheer terror; it was the terror of a radical ambivalence about life itself that was being experienced as we identified with those images on the screen. Was this one reason they were so quickly suppressed? Certainly to make a spectacle of those forced to jump is ethically repugnant, but it is also beyond the limits of what we can bear to see. The images of live people becoming falling bodies were too real, opening the viewer to a mimetic identification with trauma that was intolerable.

In fiction, however, we are permitted to flirt with the abyss. Alfred Hitchcock, a master of uncanny effects, mined the fear of falling in *Vertigo* (1957), in which the acrophobia of Scottie, Hitchcock's protagonist, and his compulsion to repeat the past in narcissistic pursuit of an impossible ideal point to his own perverse drive toward death. *Vertigo* ends with an uncanny repetition of the scene that has controlled the story from its beginning, the fall from a high tower. Similarly, E. T. A. Hoffman's "The Sand-Man," Freud's exemplary text of the uncanny, ends with its protagonist, Nathaniel, hurling himself from a tower.[4] In the way that death haunts life, both scenes of falling haunt their respective tales; both illustrate aspects of the uncanny that I am suggesting haunted our perception even as we watched the traumatic collapse of the World Trade Center into itself—falling not once but twice. An uncanny repetition, the doubling externalized our inchoate apprehensions, made the phantasmatic real.

Freud described the uncanny as occurring when archaic beliefs we thought we had surmounted suddenly confront us in the world of ordinary reality; among the most common are dread of the evil eye, of confusing the living and the dead, of being buried alive or pushed over the edge. In "The Sand-Man," Freud pointed out, Nathaniel had been threatened as a child with a fearsome punishment for wanting to stay up and spy out his father's secrets: the Sand-Man would come in the night and throw sand into his eyes, blinding him. Freud interpreted that punishment as a form of castration for oedipal wishes and described how the story traces the hallucinatory repeated return of the persecutory Sandman at significant junctures in Nathaniel's adult life. At the tale's climax, Nathaniel, having climbed a tower with his fiancée, spies the Sandman below and, crazed by the sight, leaps to his death. Looking, seeing too much, can be suicidal.

Freud used the Oedipus myth as an explanatory narrative, giving meaningful causal structure to seemingly random acts and events, transforming experiences into metaphors. Traditionally, this has been the task of literature: to provide us with narratives that can articulate the inchoate, that can give us metaphors to contain the unspeakable as it assaults us from within and without. A century ago, Gothic fiction provided dramatic metaphors for the fears of the age: ruined castles, labyrinthine interiors, cliffs, and abysses. These were the formal images that contained and conveyed the apprehensions of an increasingly labile society reconfiguring its boundaries. Indeed, language, metaphor, aesthetic forms generally serve to bind libidinal and aggressive energies to representations that in turn reenergize the culture at large.

Today, Hollywood is the prime producer of popular images for our psycho-cultural life, but the stakes have been raised. Gothic castles may be gone, but their secret interiors are now illuminated and projected onto the screen: what had been taboo is now overtly offered for our voyeuristic delectation. But if sex and violence have become the open subject of our specular play, the more recent blockbuster success of the disaster film speaks to something more: to a heightened and pervasive sense of imminent catastrophe, of a massive global trauma waiting to happen. Indeed, it speaks to our anticipation of a trauma to the species itself, our extinction foreshadowed through realistic fears of nuclear proliferation, pollution, and global warming.

It is therefore not surprising that trauma is the currency of contemporary metaphors and narratives that organize our experience: rape and child abuse, mass murder within the home, genocide, the Holocaust—all have become grist for the mill of popular titillation as well as the subject of historical curiosity. Witness the recent proliferation of Holocaust representations: the media resurrection of visual images of the starving Jews of the ghettos and concentration camps, of bodies being shoveled into mass graves, of corpses piled like dung on a heap to be buried or burned—corporeal trauma, hard to look at, harder to acknowledge as a version of the human, of the self, yet we seek it out.

Documentaries have become fictional docudramas that exploit images of abjection that we watch as if at a Roman circus, not cheering but gasping. Brutally realistic films capitalize on the historical traumas of the past through new digital film technology, such that veterans of the Normandy Invasion seeing *Saving Private Ryan* described themselves as retraumatized by the realism of the filmic representation. Perhaps the most vulgar of such circus acts is reality TV, in which survival is a sport and humiliation a gratification to the viewer. Cumulatively assaulted by images of violence from around the globe and from within the American dream machines, we seemed already to have been preparing ourselves for apocalypse and to have been fascinated by the prospect.

And then came 9/11.

Many of us sat frozen before the images on the screen, our own compulsion to see repeatedly mirrored on the screen, as again and again we were shown, as again and again we watched, what could not be actually happening. Yet we could not not watch. What does it mean to be so fascinated?[5]

"Fascination of the abomination," Joseph Conrad called it in *Heart of Darkness*, pointing to the perverse seduction exerted by images of human degradation on the one hand, transgression on the other.[6] Within the novella, Conrad plays with the image of the Congo River as a primordial fascinating object, a snake winding its way through the still blank center of the map of Africa. It compels him to make his journey into the heart of Africa, an unknown interior where, without the usual boundary marks, he confronts the multiple faces of abomination. Tormented and emaciated African workers, the human detritus of the European rape of the Congo, lie around dying, while the manicured managers plot their own advantage; shrunken heads surround the house of Kurtz, the European idealist who had gone into the interior to bring enlightenment but ended by scrawling "Exterminate the brutes" (66). And the ultimate abomination is that Kurtz himself, the fascinating object of Marlow's quest, in the pursuit of an ideal, has lost all restraints. "He had kicked the earth to pieces" (83), Conrad writes, admiring the sheer destructive narcissism of this overreacher but also horrified by the implications of such absolute power. The analogies to the Holocaust are startling. Doesn't Kurtz foreshadow Hitler, his delusion of omnipotence and his blind pursuit of an idea leading, like the Nazi leader, to "the horror, the horror"? And isn't there something of this horror in the absolutist drama of good and evil to which we became committed on 9/11?

Conrad gave voice to the fascination of the abomination at the end of the nineteenth century, at the height of a barbarous European imperialism in Africa. A century later, when we are the only imperial power left, that fascination has returned in the form of our fascination with spectacles of death and dying, with a voyeuristic relation to the Real. The events of 9/11 were hyperreal but also surreal in their evocation of the uncanny. We saw death that day in the only way that we could see it and live, as a dark hole in the side of a superstructure, the site of the disappearance of the object, which nevertheless left the trace of its impact in space. For a day we looked at what we couldn't see and lost our bearings. We became frozen in time, and time became frozen in us: 9/11, a zero state—ground zero of the psyche.

But watching that disintegration on the screen, we also recognized with shame and guilt the relief of being safe, of experiencing the shudder of the real as a specular event. On the evening of the disaster, on the news program *Nightline*, Jonathan Franzen characterized 9/11 as having a terrible beauty, taking the phrase from Yeats's "Easter, 1916." Coming too soon, that characterization must have unsettled many viewers who were looking for another kind of comfort. And yet Franzen was not wrong. On that severely bright and clear morning in September, a set of compositional elements came together—downward from the sky and upward from the earth—in a material interaction that had its own aesthetic, moving from form to formlessness through a shattering of form, the very image of trauma, into which we entered.

It is this experience of titillation and terror, numbing depression and the fullness of the moment, disgust and the recognition of a certain beauty in the formal image of devastation, feelings that seemed to be not uncommon during the first few days following the disaster, that made it such a complex psychic as well as social and political phenomenon. On that day we had our fall. We watched the enactment of a multidimensional set of primal fears uncannily become history: the invasion of our invulnerable boundaries, the failure of the law of civilization and the collapse of social guarantees that are enforced by its prohibitions, and an apprehension that we too will be pulled from civilization with all its discontents into a dark hole, into what what actualization of the unspeakable in our blind pursuit of justice. "Exterminate the brutes"? Perhaps because we live with a post-Holocaust consciousness, soaked through with images of death and disaster both virtual and real, 9/11 stirred up the terrors of our political and social condition and infused them with echoes of archaic psychic history. And as is our collective habit, we turned to the security of the movies.

Jonathan Hensleigh, who wrote *Armageddon* (1998), a Disney movie about an asteroid hitting Earth, remarked that he hadn't really worried much about the effects of the scenes of devastation in his film, which included computerized images of smoldering twin towers. "When we made 'Armageddon,' we all of us certainly didn't think we were going to be seeing any of those images in real life. . . . When it actually does happen and you're watching it on CNN, frankly, it gives you the creeps."[7] It certainly does.

NOTES

1. Slavoj Žižek, "Welcome to the Desert of the Real," Internet posting, Sept. 14, 2001. This work later appeared as a short volume, *Welcome to the Desert of the Real* (New York: Wooster Press, 2002).

2. Eleanor Kaufman, "Falling from the Sky," *Diacritics* 28, no. 4 (winter 1999): 44–53.

3. Edgar Allen Poe, "Imp of the Perverse" (1845), in *The Complete Tales and Poems of Edgar Allen Poe* (New York: Modern Library, 1938), 238.

4. E. T. A. Hoffman's "The Sand-Man," from *Nachtstücken*, in *Samtliche Werke*, Grisebach Edition 3, is cited and discussed by Freud in "The 'Uncanny'" (1919), *Standard Edition of the Complete Psychological Works of Sigmund Freud*, trans. James Strachey (London: Hogarth Press, 1978), 17:227–33. As Strachey notes, "A translation of 'The Sand-Man' is included in *Eight Tales of Hoffman*, translated by J. M. Cohen, London, Pan Books, 1952" (227 n).

5. One recalls that the Latin *fascinum* was a phallic amulet worn around the neck that gave the wearer the power to freeze whoever looked at it. The eye of the snake fascinates its prey in a similar manner, rendering the object of its gaze motionless and vulnerable.

6. Joseph Conrad, *Heart of Darkness*, in *Case Studies in Contemporary Criticism*,

ed. Ross C. Murfin, 2d ed. (Boston and New York: Bedford Books of St. Martin's Press, 1996), 21. Subsequent page references in the text are to this edition.

7. Jonathan Hensleigh, quoted as epigraph in Nitin Govil, "The Metropolis and Mental Strife," *The City as Spectacle and Performance, Sarai Reader,* 2002. *http://www.sarai.net/journal/02PDF/04spectacle.*

The War of the Fathers:
Trauma, Fantasy, and September 11

Susannah Radstone

In designating experiences "traumatic," the meanings of those experiences are understood to be elusive or impossible to grasp. According to current understandings of trauma, it is the "anomalous" nature of certain events, their "resistance to categories and conventions for assigning them meanings," that renders them traumatic.[1] On this account, experiences that elude sense making and the assignment of meaning cannot be integrated into memory, but neither can they be forgotten. This is an understanding of trauma that contests earlier (Freudian) psychoanalytic understandings of psychical disturbance and unease. While contemporary trauma theory emphasizes the impact of shocking events in the production of psychic disturbance, Freudian-inspired psychoanalysis emphasized (and continues to emphasize), rather, the part played by the conflict that arises from unconscious *fantasy*—perhaps, but not necessarily, prompted by an event—in the emergence of symptoms.[2] The events of September 11 were terrible for those who experienced them and for those who witnessed them. In the discussion that follows, it is not my intention to suggest otherwise. However, in this essay I do want to propose that, in designating such events as traumatic, they are, in fact and paradoxically, being *assigned* particular meanings— meanings that follow from their designation *as* traumatic. In this essay, then, I want to contest the meaning-making process that follows from designating September 11 and its aftermath traumatic by suggesting, instead, that cultural analysis attend to the fantasies in play in the construction of the meanings of September 11.

Well before the attacks on the World Trade Center and the Pentagon, it was already commonplace to suggest that the twentieth century would be "remembered as the century of historical trauma"—a century marked by events of previously unimaginable "nature, scope and implications."[3] The ascription of trauma to events of recent history such as the two world wars and the Great Depression rests on their unprecedentedly overwhelming and unimaginable nature: on this account, their range, their lack of boundaries, and their far-reaching implications combine to stymie the capacity to make meaning.[4] From the perspective of trauma theory, such events short-circuit the mind's and the culture's (defensive) sense-making capacities. Instead of passing through processes of narrativization and memory making, they pierce those defenses, lodging in the mind or in the culture as the shrapnel of traumatic symptomatology.

This view is contestable on two grounds: on the claims it makes for the unprecedented impact of events of the recent past and on the theory of trauma that it associates with the impact of catastrophic events. The contestability of this view of recent and now contemporary history as unprecedentedly *traumatic* is belied, however, by the ubiquitousness with which the turn to trauma has come to color discussions of the personal and the political. The "increasing salience of memory in the public domain" has been matched by a cultural fascination with trauma.[5] Now, as the events of September 11 emerge as auguries that diminish hopes for a "new" millennium, the "turn to trauma" appears to be deepening. The turn to trauma is more usually criticized for its tendency to debase the value of the concept by applying it too liberally to both major historical catastrophes *and* personal life events.[6] In this essay, however, I want to suggest that trauma may be of only limited value in aiding understanding of the impact of large-scale events such as those of September 11. The questions I wish to raise concern the stakes for discussing recent history—and now September 11—in the context of theories of traumatic memory. What does it mean to say that the recent past, including, now, these most recent events, will be remembered as historical trauma? And are there alternative approaches that need to be set besides what has become a popular academic script? In what follows, I want to suggest that the trauma perspective may obscure from view aspects of September 11's potential meanings in cultural memory that might be illuminated by other approaches.

To speak of September 11 in the context of trauma prompts analyses of the hidden wounds etched on cultural memory by these attacks. On this account, the shocking impact of the events leaves its mark as a gap or absence where memory should be. Though this gap can never be made good, a belated acknowledgment of that which has not been fully experienced and remembered remains a possibility. This is a theory that proposes a passive, acted-upon victim or culture. The traumatized individual or group has played no part in shaping their experience; they have simply been overwhelmed by the unexperienced happened, and it is their psychical wounds that become the focus of attention. According to trauma theory, the impact of catastrophic events closes down free association: that creative process through which experience, memory, and fantasy are woven into the texture of a life—or a culture.

Moments after the first plane flew into the first tower, news of the events of September 11 was broadcast electronically, on radio, and, most spectacularly, on TV. It might be suggested that the continuous replay on TV of images of the planes hitting the Twin Towers of the World Trade Center signified not the beginning of meaning making but a cultural equivalent of the traumatic symptom of the flashback. As Thomas Elsaesser has suggested, "the recurrent repetitive aspect of the media's treatment of (historic, public, shocking) events" might be related to "the obsessive time of (subjective) trauma memory."[7] Yet the alignment of the media's response with the processes of subjective trauma memory belies the preexistence of meaning-making paradigms into which these events, shocking as they were, could tentatively be located. That is, events do not impact onto a tabula rasa. Watching the events unfold on TV, one screenwriter, Lawrence Wright, remarked that "this looks like a movie—my movie," while Steve de Souza, director of the movie *Die Hard*, commented that "the image of the terrorist attacks 'looked like a movie poster, like one of my movie posters.' "[8] These comments were broadcast during a fascinating edition of the British television current affairs program *Panorama*, in which it was also suggested that "as millions of people watched the horrific spectacle of the Twin Towers collapsing after the September 11th terrorist attacks, many eye-witnesses and survivors compared the dramatic images to a Hollywood movie."[9]

This is interesting for what it suggests about the ways in which one might begin to understand how the experience of September 11 began to enter cultural memory. Trauma theory suggests that the shocking nature of the events produced a cultural response similar to that of subjective traumatization—incomprehension, flashbacks, and the like. For trauma theory, it is the unanticipated, unimagined quality of certain events that renders them so shocking. The mind has not prepared itself for an event that traumatizes—it has not been able to shield itself in advance. Yet the *Panorama* program arguably suggests that, in the case of September 11, U.S. culture had anticipated events of this nature: indeed, not only had the movies anticipated such events but filmmakers had made movies based on similar occurrences.[10] Indeed, one CIA case officer, Robert Baer, commented that Hollywood's anticipatory representations of terrorist attacks on the United States came closer to realism than did the Pentagon's pre-September

11 views of the likelihood of such events: "The way I look at Hollywood is it has more imagination than the government. The government is made out of bureaucrats. Hollywood takes the facts as they see them in life and turns them into these scenarios that are very close to reality in a certain sense. The only difference between Hollywood and reality is Hollywood has a happy ending, and there's a hero."[11] Though Baer sees little difference between real life and the movies, he acknowledges, nevertheless, the place of the imagination in the cinema. Much has been written on the ways in which the cinema draws on, speaks to, or provokes fantasies that are already circulating, albeit unconsciously, among spectators and in cultures.[12] Contra this CIA officer, I would want to place greater stress on the relation between film and the imagination or fantasy. Whether or not witnesses, survivors, and journalists had memories of actual films to draw on, their sense making of September 11 will have been shaped, in part, by that reservoir of fantasy scenes that also informed the movies that uncannily predicted September 11. This cultural process that weaves events into preexisting fantasy scenes, which shape the sense made of lives, is a process that trauma theory cannot address.

The approach I want to advocate here would acknowledge the shocking impact of September 11 while contending that trauma and fantasy need not be sharply counterposed.[13] An event may prove traumatic, indeed, not because of its inherently shocking nature but due to the unbearable or forbidden fantasies that it prompts. Or, conversely, an event's traumatic impact may be linked to its *puncturing* of a fantasy that has previously sustained a sense of identity—national as well as individual. How might an attention to fantasy illuminate processes of cultural memory after September 11? I want to propose that fantasy scenarios underpin the formation of those dominant cultural memories, which testify to the transformation of events into meaningful experience. Psychoanalysis suggests that the world of fantasy (of whatever kind) is inextricably connected with sexual difference and with desire. Psychoanalytically informed feminist analysis (of many hues) has long advocated modes of analysis attentive to fantasy's traces in order that the hidden dynamics of sexual difference might be articulated. At times of national crisis, such as September 11, these fantasy scenarios emerge starkly. In what follows, I want to suggest that an analysis of the fantasy scenes emerging post-September 11 might pay attention, in particular, to those fantasies' imbrication with the dynamics and politics of sexual difference.

It is possible to discern a range of fantasy "scenes" beneath themes that have emerged in commentary on September 11. The first fantasy upon which I want to focus is that of impregnability or invincibility. Though the scale of devastation wreaked by these events is not unprecedented on any world scale, in recent commentary the attacks of September 11 emerge as "unimaginable." What needs to be acknowledged here is the cultural specificity of this response. What rendered these attacks unimaginable was precisely what *had previously been* imagined. The dominant cultural imaginary of the United States has been shaped, in part, by *fantasies* of impregnability and invincibility, and, dreadful as the events themselves were, it was also the puncturing of these fantasies that contributed to the shock of September 11. Though fantasies of invulnerability are associated with narcissism, they are hardly gender neutral, since, as feminists have repeatedly argued, under patriarchy, male narcissism defends itself by projecting its vulnerability onto women.

Second, in the "wanted dead or alive" Western rhetoric of the war against terrorism, "justified," "measured" violence pits itself against a force represented as perverse, evil, excessive. Here, a battle between the sons of two fathers can arguably be glimpsed, as those expressing loyalty to the chastened but powerful "good" patriarchal father encounter the corrupt potency of those representing the "bad" archaic father of the primal horde. In this Manichean fantasy can be glimpsed the continuing battle between competing versions of masculinity. This Manicheanism arguably projects disavowed aspects of masculinity onto the attackers, while revealing, too, perhaps, that fantasies of disorder and transgression, such as those mobilized by some Westerns, undergird the sustenance of social order. What requires further analysis within this scenario is, first, the (hidden) place of women and, second, the complex places of religious and ethnic difference within this "battle of the fathers."

The notion that after September 11 nothing would ever be the same again needs reevaluating in light of the fantasy scenarios glimpsed here. If the nation constitutes an "imagined community," the reimaginings of gender prompted by September 11 appear anything but new.[14] Fantasies of invulnerability and of a battle between different orders of paternal power appear to leave women on the margins of a war that is at once political, psychical, and cultural. This is, however, a situation that might be challenged.

Events do not come out of nowhere, and neither do they leave their mark on a previously blank page. The "problem" with trauma is that the subject it proposes—the victim—is too absolutely passive. One might argue, indeed, that trauma theory feminizes its subject. Trauma suggests an unreadable scar that might, with difficulty, be accorded some meaning. Fantasy, on the other hand, shifts attention to the activities of the fantasizing subject or nation and to the processes of meaning making (albeit unconscious) that give rise to scenarios that shape minds, cultures, and events.

NOTES

1. Hayden White, "The Modernist Event," in *The Persistence of History: Cinema, Television, and the Modern Event,* ed. Vivian Sobchack (New York and London: Routledge, 1996), 21.

2. For a longer discussion of the debates concerning trauma, events, and fantasy, see Susannah Radstone, "Screening Trauma: *Forrest Gump*, Film, and Memory," in *Memory and Methodology,* ed. Susannah Radstone (New York and Oxford: Berg, 2000).

3. Suzette A. Henke, *Shattered Subjects: Trauma and Testimony in Women's Life Writing* (Houndsmills: Macmillan, 1998), xi; White, "The Modernist Event," 20.

4. The examples of recent historical events are taken from White, "The Modernist Event."

5. Paul Antze and Michael Lambek, *Tense Past: Cultural Essays in Trauma and Memory* (New York and London: Routledge, 1996), xiii. Antze and Lambek have noted the central place given to trauma in contemporary memories of the past (xii–xiii). For an argument that suggests that the attainment of "full" historical subjectivity may now be inextricably tied to an encounter with "trauma," see Lauren Berlant, "Trauma and Ineloquence," *Cultural Values* 5, no. 1 (January 2001): 41–58; and Lauren Berlant, "The Subject of True Feeling: Pain, Privacy and Politics," in *Cultural Studies and Political Theory*, ed. Jodi Dean (Ithaca NY: Cornell University Press, 2000), 42–62.

6. In her book *Trauma: A Genealogy* (Chicago and London: University of Chicago Press, 2000), Ruth Leys proposes that the ubiquitous deployment of the concept of trauma in relation both to large-scale catastrophes and to the arguably less catastrophic experiences of individuals may be debasing its value (2).

7. Thomas Elsaesser, "Postmodernism as Mourning Work," in "Special Debate, Trauma, and Screen Studies" (special edition edited by Susannah Radstone), *Screen* 42, no. 2 (summer 2001): 197.

8.   *http://news.bbc.co.uk/hi/english/audiovideo/programmes/panorama/news.d-18 75000/1875186.stm.*

9. "September 11th: A Warning from Hollywood," *Panorama*, BBC1, March 24, 2002; *http://news.bbc.co.uk/hi/english/audiovideo/programmes/panorama/news.d-1875000/1875186.stm.*

10.   *http://news.bbc.co.uk/hi/english/audiovideo/programmes/panorama/news.d-18 75000/1875186.stm.*

11. *http://news.bbc.co.uk/h:/english/static/audiovideo/programmes/panorama/transcripts/transcript-24–03-02.txt.*

12. For a useful introduction to cinepsychoanalysis and the place of fantasy in film studies, see Robert Lapsley and Michael Westlake, *Film Theory: An Introduction* (Manchester: Manchester University Press, 1988), esp. 90–95.

13. This is an argument that I flesh out more fully in Radstone, "Screening Trauma."

14. Benedict Anderson, *Imagined Communities: Reflections on the Origins and Spread of Nationalism* (London: Verso, 1983).

Masked Power: An Encounter
with the Social Body in the Flesh
Orly Lubin

"The events of September 11, 2001, were so overwhelming, so devastating in their impact, that more than four months after the fact, we are still struggling to explain and comprehend their meaning." So opens the brochure accompanying the exhibit "Aftermath: Photography in the Wake of September 11" at the International Center of Photography.[1] The word "LEARN," written at the memorial site in Washington Square Park, caught the eye of Sylvia Molloy, current president of the Modern Language Association: "It's attraction resided in its very opaqueness, an injunction without a specific object or practical resolution."[2] Colleges across America have developed courses relating in one way or another to the events of September 11 and their aftermath, catering, apparently, to the need to understand and to give meaning.[3] And Susan Buck-Morss argues that Americans have had to come to a "conscious acceptance of realities . . . that have been in front of our eyes and ears for decades, but that the code of American self-understanding with its master signifier of innocence has effectively blocked out as meaningless."[4]

It seems at times as if the function of the mourning following the terror attack was to maintain that innocence, namely, the innocence of the victim suffering an unjust injury inflicted on her for reasons that she can grasp but are beyond her control. She mourns from the bottom of her heart and in the very act of mourning proves herself to be the good person she always knew she was, that we all were.

But mourning, even when it does not need to have a meaning, does need to be framed. This framing became "the community"; and the notion of the community seems to be a prism through which one can view the trauma, as community becomes the tool of the containment of the trauma.

After 9/11 "community" became the magic word. The sense of community born at the very moment of the event has become, already, an object of nostalgic lament. Very quickly people began to reminisce nostalgically about both the shock and the sense of togetherness; the terrible sense of vulnerability and the birth of new friendships; the feeling of isolation and the ability to rely on others for company and help. It is this construction of the near sacredness of the community, though, that also enabled a discourse of revenge, military action, violations of civil rights, and "the post 9/11 hush," as Hilary Russ labels the lack of civic activism.[5] The community also determines both the structure and the content of the testimonies of the traumatic event so that they will cater to the needs of the community. That is to say, it reaffirms its own coming to be, its norms and morals, and its function as a collective supplying a site for the individual. Thus the *New York Times* "Portraits of Grief" section converted short obituaries of the victims into personal memories as much as images of the collective memory. Along the same lines, on the March 11 broadcast of *Nightline*, Ted Koppel visited the site of the collected personal effects of the victims, most of them badges, company cards, credit cards, all organized alphabetically but also communally—that is, according to ethnicity, gender, and work place. The sense and existence of the individual were kept intact through the private name and the particular, unique biography. However, that very evidence was testimony also to the fact that there was a community that cared and that could be defined along various axes of identity other than the uniquely named individual.

One of the best examples of the constitution of this sense of community without "neglect" of the individual is the amazing documentary *9/11*, made by the brothers Jules and Gedeon Naudet and screened on CBS on March 10. Begun as a film documenting a fire station through the nine-month probation of a rookie, it became a haunting record of the terror attack on the World Trade Center from both inside and out, from the perspective of onlookers and rescue workers, stunned spectators gazing paralyzed at the unfolding drama and stunned officials (who seemed to have little sense of what was going on other than a haunting awareness of the thud of the desperate as they leapt from the upper floors and landed, with grim regularity, just outside the lobby of the North Tower). In the editing room, though, the documentary took on the structure of a Hollywood film, with a narrative, a protagonist replete with a distinct character and view on life, as well as the obligatory happy ending. Structured as testimony, it was more careful to answer to the needs of its audience—that is, with regard to narrative conventions and to the desire for a community—than it was to using (or even filming) footage that might be more "real" but less "useful." Thus, before the documentary was aired, both CBS officials and journalists assured viewers there were "no graphic depictions of deaths on screen," and

Jules Naudet kept telling the press how he saw in the lobby two people on fire and "chose not to film them, thinking no one should see such a thing."[6] Perhaps the most alarming thing of all is the way the events, which no one controlled, lent themselves to this kind of structuring of a story: Here is our protagonist, the rookie in a documentary about "how a boy becomes a man," as the soundtrack announces, selected from a group of trainees, whose auditions we see on screen, assuring us it was not retroactively manipulated. Here is our setting, the station coincidentally close to the World Trade Center. Here is the buildup of expectations, through the impatient wait for a real fire to happen and through the absence of the protagonist from the line of retroactively contemplating talking heads. Here is the action, the initial rush to the towers after the first plane hit. Here is the complication, the disappearance of our young, unseasoned hero, who finally gets to the site of action. And here is the resolution, when he returns to the station after the collapse of the buildings—after a masterfully built suspense during which all firefighters are back at the station, worrying about him—like an urban cowboy, appearing alone from the cloudy, dust-covered horizon. We are relieved to learn the company has lost no one. All the Hollywood conventions are there: the reliable storyteller, the linear bildungsroman and the rite of passage, the birth of a hero, and the happy ending.

As impossible as it might seem, this manufacturing of a happy ending turns out to be the major component of the structure of this testimonial narrative: the creation of a community. As it is, when the rookie first joins the station he finds there an already well-organized community, down to the daily cooking details, gastronomic rituals of an army-style fraternity based on mutual dependency. It is an environment replete with a self-irony that disarms homosocial threats built into the communal closeness. But this proximity and its constant visibility are the necessary, most precious components of the testimony, even more so than the creation of heroism. It is exactly what the spectators need, namely, the testimony of those people who witnessed the community that constitutes the source of bravery.

Being the intended addressee of the testimonies, the listener is their constructor, in the sense that the story is created for her, for her need to believe in the power of community. At some point the community takes over the testimony. As the trapped firefighters are trying to find their way out of the lobby among the rubble, the camera, always rolling, becomes a source of light in the darkness, functioning as a lantern, saving rather than documenting the group. The witnessing apparatus itself becomes a tool for the unification of, and at the service of, the community. It is now a community of which the spectator imagines himself or herself to be a member.

However, this is a community that is presented also as vulnerable and fragile. This is the mark of a society that cannot contain inner fissures and cracks and is constantly aware of the presumed fragility of its social order. Such a society senses the threat of the total breakdown of its social order whenever it encounters a strong contest to its morals, narratives, and, most important, self-perceptions. A kind of puritanism sets in, and the community then becomes the major policing apparatus. When the hegemonic moral boundaries are not flexible enough to contain all kinds of behavior, from revolution through dissent down to juvenile rebellion, the tenacity to hold on to a rigid, unchanging structured communal social order becomes a major concern. Symbols such as a flag, a national hymn, as well as ethnic and religious purity become the hallmarks of the "community," as is the case in so many other threatened communities that find nationality and nationalism to be the most accessible unifiers. The lack of discourse that might provide alternative kinds of communities, possible in the age of global communication and global threats and interests, based on mutual commonalities or interests other than ethnic or religious or national, makes these symbols the most obvious representation of the interests of the community.

The community is also functional in containing the trauma, thanks to the ability to construct it itself, making it a community that is imagined, in this case through the necessary imagining of the meaning of its strength in times of evident fragility. For some, the realization of the United States' dominance in the world became an easily digestible explanation of the hatred directed at it. For others, the lack of total power spelled a kind of vulnerability that can never be corrected. Yet for others, this strength meant economic or moral responsibility, at times even the right to impose the "correct" morals of democracy and equality on the rest of the world. And the process of securing power has resulted in the untenable position of a state becoming at once a lover of power and a proselytizer of power sharing, democracy, and the tenet of nondiscrimination between the powerful and powerless, overlooking the problems inherent in shoring up power, in owning the gaze, and the huge investment in making sure the steps taken to retain power are occluded.

September 11 created a traumatic shock not so much in the realization of actually having power but in the realization of the horror of being in power. Students of culture, of colonialism and postcolonialism, of feminism and queer studies, have been theorizing and demonstrating in the last two decades the position of the victim of the gaze. They have studied the gaze as a hierarchical relationship, in which the passive party "lowers her eyes" and is, as Laura Mulvey put it, situated in the position of to-be-looked-at-ness; and they have studied closely the various possible reactions to this passive positioning—the acts of subversion, revolt, disturbance, and disruption.[7]

But not much has been done so far to learn how to get rid of power. Being in power, being the owner of gaze, implies a horrible positioning and the terrible responsibility to act. In his article "The white stuff (political aspect of whiteness)," Homi K. Bhabha demands an action that, as academic as it sounds, has strong pragmatic consequences. He writes: "The subversive move is to reveal within the very integument of 'whiteness' the agonistic elements that make it the unsettled, disturbed form of authority that it is—the incommensurable 'differences' that it must surmount; the histories of trauma and terror that it must perpetrate and from which it must protect itself; the amnesia it imposes on itself; the violence it inflicts in the process of becoming a transparent and transcendent force of authority."[8] Thus the owner of power, the owner of the gaze, has to encounter herself as a source of violence, inherent in her status, which she, more often than not, has not chosen, to confront her own positioning, which she cannot change. Her only way out, her only option to get rid of the objectifying power or gaze, is to move—metaphorically, when the literal move to "the other side" is impossible—to the side of the Other. To "move" metaphorically would mean to follow Bhabha's list of needed revelations. It would also mean to LEARN—not, as Molloy suggests, as "a new awareness of this society's others, an awareness more demanding, more urgent, more disquieting but, one hopes, better informed than our often short-sighted critical musings on alterity have been until now," but an altogether different understanding of the very notion of Otherness, of how to get rid of power and the gaze by defying the "demand" to have an Other in order to maintain one's identity, by never gazing long enough so as to objectify the gazed at, never standing long enough in one identity positioning so as to have to create an Other for that positioning to imagine itself as a position.[9]

As abstract as it sounds, this is the task that the shock of recognition of power brings. It requires one to be on the move constantly, never being "one" long enough for the creation of an Other.

This is, of course, another component of the trauma that calls for the help of the constructed community, for in a community one is never moving, one is always static, one is always part of something, which is by definition an Other of an Other. If the realization of the horror of being powerful, the horror of being always an instigator of violence by virtue of being powerful, necessarily leads to the demand to act—to acknowledge and to react to the fractures, gaps, contradictions, repressions, and exclusions that are the inherent creations of the state of power and to never succumb to them through a constant self-reflection that is, in effect, a constant movement, a constantly changing self-definition—then a way out is back into the community. But as already discussed, there, within the community, one does not lose one's individuality (as he mourns, as she raises the flag, as she hugs a Muslim) and therefore also is not exempted from yet another burden of being in power, namely the burden of individual accountability.

Unlike responsibility, which might mean being politically educated and even active, if only to a minimal extent, accountability is that which the individual carries with him exactly because he is part of a community. Unlike acknowledgment, which can be demanded of anyone regardless of power or economic status, accountability is the burden of the member of a powerful community. A member in a powerful community cannot escape that accountability, precisely because he is what he is—in terms of his financially, politically, educationally, and culturally powerful status—only because he is a member of the community that at some point created the injustice. Realizing your personal accountability is traumatic because it requires a major change in your outlook on life as much as a change in your personal life. And the community, although a refuge from the implications of the trauma in the many other senses discussed earlier, becomes the jail of the powerful individual, who, as part of the community that is necessary for his refuge, is now being implicated because of the community's history.

The realization of personal accountability is so horrible because it relates not only to representations but also to the actual, material, corporeal flesh and blood. At first, the lack of bodily matter—the empty ambulances and hospital corridors, the volumes of dust that might contain corporeal remains—meant dealing, once again, with representations. As Thomas de Zengotita puts it, "So, if we were spared a gaping wound in the flesh and blood of personal life, we inevitably moved on after September 11. We were carried off by endlessly proliferating representations of the event. . . . Conditioned thus relentlessly to move from representation to representation, we got past the things itself as well; or rather, the thing itself was transformed into a sea of signs."[10]

However strong the case for this kind of exclusion of the material body from culture and its transformation into representation, the material body refuses to disappear, as Judith Butler argues.[11] In the case of 9/11, its material absence was a constant reminder of the presence of materiality. The corporeal body also left traces in the form of material dust of bones or pieces of flesh never exposed to the apparatuses of representation. The actual flesh and blood was kept out of sight. Its presence, as the presence of a dead casualty of war, would disturb the flow of the narrative of the community, a narrative relying on representations, which create, following Benedict Anderson, the imagined togetherness and sameness of all members of the community.[12] Representation, then, is in the service of creating an imagined community that will provide an easily digested set of morals applicable to representations rather than to flesh and blood. The ethics of representation (should Jules Naudet photograph the two people on fire to show the world the results of the wickedness of the terrorists, or would that be invading their privacy?) replaces the ethics of policymaking, since the results of the latter are prevented from the community, as they do not become representations due to the ruling ethics of representation. The community provides the representation as a gateway away from the horrors of responsibility and then accountability.

Unfortunately, the smell of burned flesh, the touch of warm blood, disrupts the smooth flow of the functioning of community. As long as the trauma is the realization of personal accountability for the suffering of corporeal bodies, and the cure is "the community," trauma will never go away. It's only when personal accountability is internalized, "community" is diversified and its inner fractures acknowledged, and a new sense of subjectivity, independent of Otherness and of the need to replace the material with representation, arises that trauma (or the causes thereof, perhaps) will disappear.

NOTES

I would like to thank Donald Mengay for his thoughtful reading of and extremely valuable help with this essay.

1. These words were written by the chief curator of the exhibit, Brain Wallis.

2. Sylvia Molloy, President's Column, *MLA Newsletter* 33, no. 4 (winter 2001): 3.

3. Karen W. Arenson, *New York Times*, Feb. 12, 2002, A11.

4. Susan Buck-Morss, "A Global Public Sphere?" *Radical Philosophy* 111 (Jan./Feb. 2002): 3.

5. Hilary Russ, "The Silence of the Lambasters," *City Limits*, March 2002, 30–31.

6. Caryn James, "Critic's Notebook: Experiencing the Cataclysm from the Inside," *New York Times*, Mar. 6, 2002, E1.

7. Laura Mulvey, "Visual Pleasure and Narrative Cinema," *Screen* 16 (fall 1975): 8–18.

8. Homi K. Bhabha, "The white stuff," *Artforum* 36, no. 9 (May 1998): 21.

9. Molloy, 3.

10. Thomas de Zengotita, "The Numbing of the American Mind: Culture as Anesthetic," *Harper's*, April 2002, 33–40.

11. For a lengthy example, see Judith Butler, *Bodies That Matter: On the Discursive Limits of "Sex"* (New York and London: Routledge, 1993).

12. Benedict Anderson, *Imagined Communities: Reflections on the Origins and Spread of Nationalism* (London and New York: Verso, 1983).

The Limits of Empathy and the Global Politics of Belonging

Jill Bennett

As part of a heated exchange of letters following the September 11 attacks, the *London Review of Books* published a letter from a man in Minneapolis who was indignant at foreigners who presumed to pass judgment on the United States rather than simply offering unqualified sympathy. "Imagine how you [the English] might feel if thousands of Londoners were blown to bits, and then intellectuals in America or France wrote about how England should have seen it coming."[1] Disregarding the fact that hundreds of U.K. citizens were killed in the attacks on the World Trade Center, and thousands more knew people who were killed or injured, the writer, by this statement, presumes himself to be part of a privileged "victim class" that implicitly excludes Europeans. In Benedict Anderson's terms, he invokes an "imagined community," based on nation, uniting people who neither know each other nor share the same experience.[2] Thus, as an American, he is able to identify with those directly affected by the attacks, without himself being a primary victim ("People I know in New York were affected . . . but luckily not killed or injured.").

Having watched the tragedy unfold from London, before traveling to New York a few days after the attacks, it seemed to me that in some quarters, at least, the impact was felt as profoundly in London as in parts of the United States. If this was, indeed, a global tragedy and an attack on trade, the devastating impact in the financial heart of London—where many had lost friends and colleagues—brought this home. While many commentators would argue that citizens of the United States suffered a kind of "collective trauma," it is also the case that the personal trauma of loss—not directly experienced by most Americans—affected bereaved families in many nations. The economic fallout of the tragedy also had a devastating impact worldwide. The term "national trauma," frequently used by the U.S. media in relation to September 11, is, then, something of a misnomer, insofar as it dramatically understates the reach of the tragedy.

But if "national trauma" is understood simply as a term coined to reflect the manifest depth of feeling across the nation, do such semantic quibbles matter? As the United States attempts to come to terms with the sudden realization of deep enmity and, together with its key allies, works to build allegiances, we could argue that it is precisely the time to investigate assumptions about national identity and shared identifications. A part of this process should entail interrogation of the imagined political boundaries of victim communities and of their exclusionary effects.

When trauma is coextensive with nation, where do the limits of empathy lie? Is the construction of "national trauma" an impediment to recognizing traumatic experience beyond the boundaries of nation and national identity? And if attributes of identity such as nationality, city of residence, and so on are understood to qualify one as, in some sense, a victim or traumatized subject, how might we acknowledge the range and specifics of experience within this grouping? Does the blurring of traumatic experience and empathy obscure not only the nature of trauma but that of empathetic experience? (If the correspondent from Minneapolis was demonstrably less "traumatized" than some British people, may he nevertheless have experienced a deeper and more enduring empathy for U.S. victims than did most people overseas?)

The limits of empathy were emphatically brought home to me when I returned to Australia, some two months after September 11. The conservative government—which prior to the attacks had looked certain to be voted out of office—had just been returned in a landslide victory. This turnaround was conventionally attributed to high levels of popular support for the "War against Terror" (we might call this a form of transnational identification) and for the government's continuing refusal to admit Afghan and other asylum seekers. The resurgence of patriotism in the United States was, it seemed, echoed in a rekindling of Australian national pride: a development that paralleled—and at times, fueled—the vehement rejection of refugees.

With the commencement of the Bush-led "War against Terror," the United States and Australia appeared to share a common enemy with refugees fleeing the Taliban regime. Yet in Australia, Afghan asylum seekers were frequently confused with the emergent enemy; reports circulated that the boats arriving were actually harboring terrorists. After September 11, a very clear image of the victim of terror—exemplified by the employee of the World Trade Center—had solidified. Neither the refugees, trapped for eight days in the hold of the container ship *Tampa*, nor those rescued off the Christmas Islands by the Australian navy after the Indonesian boat that had brought them began to sink were understood as victims, either in the sense of victims of circumstance (they had allegedly "chosen" to come, sunk their own boat, placed their children's lives in jeopardy) or victims of terror. In the public imagination, the horror of the World Trade Center attack was definitive and its victims were paradigmatic: self-evidently, unsuspecting, innocent people who had had no immediate hand in their own fate. Asylum seekers, who have, by definition, a case to prove, not only fell short of this paradigm but failed to gain public sympathy in the new climate of globalized fear, where anyone without established credentials, and anyone of Afghan, Middle Eastern, or Islamic origin, became a potential threat.

Is it fair to say, then, that transnational identification was, in this instance, founded on a (racist) preference for a notional American victim, that is, on the privileging of a particular cultural identity? Under such conditions, could the empathy generated for the victims of the World Trade Center attacks incorporate any kind of understanding of the traumatic experiences involved?

Kaja Silverman's distinction between idiopathic and heteropathic identification goes some way to illuminating the nature of empathic relationships in this instance.[3] Whereas heteropathic identification implies an identification with an alien body or experience, idiopathic identification is essentially self-referential, grounded on shared identity. In the latter mode, which appears to apply in this case, one evaluates the trauma of the other simply by asking, "I wonder what I would be like if this happened to me"; thus, unfamiliar experience is not encountered on its own terms but assimilated to the self.

Idiopathic identification with the victims of the World Trade Center attacks is, then, dependent on maintaining a sense of the victims as sufficiently "like us" to enable us to imagine ourselves in their place. Yet, in this regard, boundaries are slippery. There is no single image, identity, or lifestyle associated with the victims, despite the fact that the World Trade Center conjures up the figure of the corporate trader. Far from typifying the World Trade Center victim as a racially and economically privileged ideal, both national and international media coverage of the attacks reminded us of the fact that World Trade Center employees were a racially and ethnically diverse group, emanating from all strata of society. Such an image of a multicultural community within a traditionally Anglo-Irish society no doubt has particular resonance within Australia. But on what basis, then, were "alien" identifications repudiated and cultural affinities reinscribed?

And why did the suffering of one particular group engender empathy at the cost of another?

Silverman suggests that a capacity to locate oneself within the body of another is fundamental to the ability to witness—literally, to *see*—the pain of another. She describes a "specular panic" that arises when a subject is forced to witness the presence of a body that can "make no claim to what, in our culture, passes for 'ideality.'"[4] In her own experience, this panic occurs when she is faced with the specter of the homeless. The bodies in front of her eyes as she walks to work are too far from her to engender empathy; although they share with her a public space, the terms on which they inhabit this space render them alien.

Images of Afghan refugees in Australia after September 11 (behind the fences of detention centers—rioting, self-mutilating, and hunger-striking —or adrift on the ocean) reinforced a similar sense of cultural distance and radical difference. Indeed, one could argue that "dis-identification" was fostered through the mediation of these images; in particular, the way in which they were willfully misinterpreted was both symptomatic of, and productive of, a form of "specular panic."

The key image of the Australian federal government's reelection campaign of October/November 2001, notoriously fought and won on the refugee issue, was a navy photograph that the government opportunistically claimed showed children thrown into the ocean by their refugee parents as a tactic to oblige Australians to rescue them. For the prime minister, this "evidence" was enough to suggest that these were not "the sort of people" we wanted in Australia. In the months following the election, it emerged that there was no evidence to support this interpretation and that government ministers had rushed, with indecent haste, to capitalize on assumptions that they knew to be unsubstantiated.

This image had, however, served its purpose in characterizing the refugees as un-Australian, in a moment of patriotic regrouping and identification with the United States and its "War against Terror." Refugees were not simply "other" by virtue of race but because of their non-Western lifestyles and values: their lack of loyalty to a homeland, their decision to board a refugee ship for an uncertain future and expose their children to danger, to throw children overboard, to riot, to hunger-strike and sew their lips together.

By contrast, the values embodied by the victims, families, and rescuers associated with the World Trade Center could be readily endorsed. These people belonged to our world, as their association with the World

Trade Center demonstrated. Traders, janitors, waiters, and port authority workers—the victims were collectively made human for us by virtue of their identification as employees of the World Trade Center. These were not the desperate, dispossessed that constitute the refugee class. In the moment of transnational identification, it was the displaced refugee that posed the greatest threat to our sense of belonging. The very fact that many asylum seekers do not have papers counts against them, for it bespeaks the terrible condition of unbelonging. If one could imagine what it might be like to work in the World Trade Center—and hence fantasize about being the innocent victim of a terrorist attack—the refugee could not be located on this same axis of identification, linking us to the victims of the attacks; the refugee is, indeed, more easily aligned with those who oppose the values of belonging (to nation, place of employment, and so on). Both refugee and terrorist are, in effect, ruinous of such values. Thus, in spite of the fact that many refugees were fleeing the very regimes that supported the terrorists who attacked the World Trade Center, they could not be viewed as anything other than a threat.

The poignancy of the homemade missing person posters around Lower Manhattan after the attacks was perhaps the tangible evidence that most marked the World Trade Center victims as belonging or "placed." Speaking directly of the raw pain and desperation of those left behind, the posters told us that, in each case, this was someone's father, mother, husband. These were not images of people *in extremis*, in desperate situations, but of people defined through their belonging (to their family, company, or firehouse), images counterweighted precisely by those circulated in the Australian media of the anonymous refugee children apparently cast adrift in the ocean, images that became emblematic of unbelonging, of weak ties to family and nation. In this context, the eminently reasonable decision to suppress any images of bodies retrieved from the World Trade Center also served to reinforce a certain set of values around the management of suffering. We focused instead—and, apparently, exclusively—on the images of the managers, the firefighters, the rescuers, the mayor: those whose job it was to shield us from the unbearable evidence of death, to reestablish order in the wake of terror.

Furthermore, we mourned the loss of the World Trade Center itself. Among the memorials in the parks of Lower Manhattan were those RIP notices to the anthropomorphized "twins." It is no accident that the destruction of the World Trade Center captured more imagination and sympathy than the attack on the Pentagon. The edifice itself was a vehicle for identification—a symbol not just of trade but of Western capitalism's capacity to confer identity upon its diverse members. We, the other beneficiaries of capitalism—the employed subjects of First World nations, looking on from various points on the globe—knew through its destruction that we had ourselves been attacked; our sense of self was threatened.

Responses to September 11 showed that empathy grounded on an emotional response, on prior affinity or shared cultural values, or on what we might classify as an idiopathic identification may be both genuine and even potentially useful in a crisis. But it is benign only as long as the underlying principles of identification—and, conversely, of dis-identification—are hidden. Empathy directed toward a select kind of victim—that is, empathy that does not attend to the particulars of experience—serves inevitably to reaffirm cultural hierarchies. Such idiopathic identification is particularly problematic in the context of what is, paradigmatically, a global tragedy.

How, then, might critical forms of representation address affective responses to September 11 and attend to the global politics of trauma? Much of the early debate around the tragedy evinced a resistance to self-examination, principally in the political realm, where negative analysis of the U.S. government's foreign policy was perceived to undermine empathy for victims. Within the United States, articulating and validating the feelings of those affected by the events was a priority—and expressive forms of art and literature will no doubt continue to describe subjective responses. The greater challenge may be, however, to find a way to critically examine the nature of empathy—not simply in what might be perceived as an inflammatory or anti-American vein but in a manner that locates highly charged affective responses within a broader community framework. If, indeed, "the world changed" on September 11, we need to explore how representations might enable us to understand the impact of change at the global, local, and interpersonal levels—and the ways in which these levels interrelate.

The axiom that the world has changed may be a starting point for thinking about the simultaneous impact of trauma, first, within a designated space (such as New York City) and, second, in terms of interpersonal and international connections—connections that follow the trajectories of the various kinds of identifications and dis-identifications facilitated by mediations of the tragedy. Thinking through the impact of September 11, we might come to consider how the spaces of New York City are inhabited in the wake of devastation and loss—how local space or "home" has changed. But a related question becomes, What is it like to inhabit the space of the refugee, to live out the designation of unbelonging? In other words, where and in what ways (beyond our lived space) is this global change experienced?

NOTES

1. Todd Ojala, *London Review of Books* 23, no. 21 (Nov. 1, 2001).

2. Benedict Anderson, *Imagined Communities: Reflections on the Origins and Spread of Nationalism* (London: Verso, 1983).

3. Kaja Silverman, *The Threshold of the Visible World* (New York: Routledge, 1996).

4. Silverman, *Threshold of the Visible World,* 26.

first writing since

Suheir Hammad

1. there have been no words.
   i have not written one word.
   no poetry in the ashes south of canal street.
   no prose in the refrigerated trucks driving debris and dna.
   not one word.

   today is a week, and seven is of heavens, gods, science.
   evident out my kitchen window is an abstract reality.
   sky where once was steel.
   smoke where once was flesh.

   fire in the city air and i feared for my sister's life in a way never
   before. and then, and now, i fear for the rest of us.

   first, please god, let it be a mistake, the pilot's heart failed, the
       plane's engine died.
   then please god, let it be a nightmare, wake me now.
   please god, after the second plane, please, don't let it be anyone
   who looks like my brothers.

   i do not know how bad a life has to break in order to kill.
   i have never been so hungry that i willed hunger
   i have never been so angry as to want to control a gun over a pen.
   not really.
   even as a woman, as a palestinian, as a broken human being.
   never this broken.

   more than ever, i believe there is no difference.
   the most privileged nation, most americans do not know the difference
   between indians, afghanis, syrians, muslims, sikhs, hindus.
   more than ever, there is no difference.

2. thank you korea for kimchi and bibim bob, and corn tea and the
   genteel smiles of the wait staff at wonjo—smiles never revealing
   the heat of the food or how tired they must be working long midtown
   shifts. thank you korea, for the belly craving that brought me into
   the city late the night before and diverted my daily train ride into
   the world trade center.

   there are plenty of thank yous in ny right now. thank you for my
   lazy procrastinating late ass. thank you to the germs that had me
   call in sick. thank you, my attitude, you had me fired the week
   before. thank you for the train that never came, the rude nyer who
   stole my cab going downtown. thank you for the sense my
        mama gave me
   to run. thank you for my legs, my eyes, my life.

3. the dead are called lost and their families hold up shaky
   printouts in front of us through screens smoked up.

   we are looking for iris, mother of three. please call with any
   information. we are searching for priti, last seen on the 103rd
   floor. she was talking to her husband on the phone and the line
   went. please help us find george, also known as adel. his family is
   waiting for him with his favorite meal. i am looking for my son, who
   was delivering coffee. i am looking for my sister girl, she started
   her job on monday.

   i am looking for peace. i am looking for mercy. i am looking for
   evidence of compassion. any evidence of life. i am looking for
   life.

4. ricardo on the radio said in his accent thick as yuca, "i will
   feel so much better when the first bombs drop over there. and my
   friends feel the same way."

   on my block, a woman was crying in a car parked and stranded in hurt.
   i offered comfort, extended a hand she did not see before she said,
   "we're gonna burn them so bad, i swear, so bad." my hand went to my
   head and my head went to the numbers within it of the dead iraqi
   children, the dead in nicaragua. the dead in rwanda who had to vie
   with fake sport wrestling for america's attention.

   yet when people sent emails saying, this was bound to happen, let's
   not forget u.s. transgressions, for half a second i felt resentful.

hold up with that, cause i live here, these are my friends and fam,
and it could have been me in those buildings, and we're not bad
people, do not support america's bullying. can i just have a half
second to feel bad?

if i can find through this exhaust people who were left behind to
mourn and to resist mass murder, i might be alright.

thank you to the woman who saw me brinking my cool and
      blinking back
tears. she opened her arms before she asked "do you want a hug?" a
big white woman, and her embrace was the kind only people with the
warmth of flesh can offer. i wasn't about to say no to any comfort.
"my brother's in the navy," i said. "and we're arabs." "wow, you
got double trouble." word.

5. one more person ask me if i knew the hijackers.
    one more motherfucker ask me what navy my brother is in.
    one more person assume no arabs or muslims were killed.
    one more person assume they know me, or that i represent a people.
    or that a people represent an evil. or that evil is as simple as a
    flag and words on a page.

    we did not vilify all white men when mcveigh bombed oklahoma.
    america did not give out his family's addresses or where he went to
    church. or blame the bible or pat robertson.

    and when the networks air footage of palestinians dancing in the
    street, there is no apology that hungry children are bribed with
    sweets that turn their teeth brown. that correspondents edit images.
    that archives are there to facilitate lazy and inaccurate
    journalism.

    and when we talk about holy books and hooded men and death,
        why do we
    never mention the kkk?

    if there are any people on earth who understand how new york is
    feeling right now, they are in the west bank and the gaza strip.

6. today it is ten days. last night bush waged war on a man once
    openly funded by the
    cia. i do not know who is responsible. read too many books, know

too many people to believe what i am told. i don't give a fuck about
bin laden. his vision of the world does not include me or those i
love. and petitions have been going around for years trying to get
the u.s. sponsored taliban out of power. shit is complicated, and i
don't know what to think.

but i know for sure who will pay.

in the world, it will be women, mostly colored and poor. women will
have to bury children, and support themselves through grief. "either
you are with us, or with the terrorists"—meaning keep your people
under control and your resistance censored. meaning we got the loot
and the nukes.

in america, it will be those amongst us who refuse blanket attacks on
the shivering. those of us who work toward social justice, in
support of civil liberties, in opposition to hateful foreign
policies.

i have never felt less american and more new Yorker—particularly
brooklyn, than these past days. the stars and stripes on all these
cars and apartment windows represent the dead as citizens first—not
family members, not lovers.

i feel like my skin is real thin, and that my eyes are only going to
get darker. the future holds little light.

my baby brother is a man now, and on alert, and praying five times a
day that the orders he will take in a few days time are righteous and
will not weigh his soul down from the afterlife he deserves.

both my brothers—my heart stops when i try to pray—not a beat to
disturb my fear. one a rock god, the other a sergeant, and both
palestinian, practicing muslim, gentle men. both born in brooklyn
and their faces are of the archetypal arab man, all eyelashes and
nose and beautiful color and stubborn hair.

what will their lives be like now?

over there is over here.

7. all day, across the river, the smell of burning rubber and limbs
    floats through. the sirens have stopped now. the advertisers are
    back on the air. the rescue workers are traumatized. the skyline is

brought back to human size. no longer taunting the gods with its height.

i have not cried at all while writing this. i cried when i saw those buildings collapse on themselves like a broken heart. i have never owned pain that needs to spread like that. and i cry daily that my brothers return to our mother safe and whole.

there is no poetry in this. there are causes and effects. there are symbols and ideologies. mad conspiracy here, and information we will never know. there is death here, and there are promises of more.

there is life here. anyone reading this is breathing, maybe hurting, but breathing for sure. and if there is any light to come, it will shine from the eyes of those who look for peace and justice after the rubble and rhetoric are cleared and the phoenix has risen.

affirm life.
affirm life.
we got to carry each other now.
you are either with life, or against it.
affirm life.

5. Echoing

"There Is No Poetry in This":
Writing, Trauma, and Home
Michael Rothberg

What do we gain by naming the events of September 11, 2001, "traumatic"? Whether one approaches the events with a scholarly or a vernacular understanding, the events clearly were and are traumatic—most obviously for survivors of the attacks and the families of the victims but also potentially for eyewitnesses and even witnesses at a remove. My question, however, concerns the intellectual, ethical, and political consequences of the framework with which we approach September 11, not the adequacy of the adjective "traumatic" as a description for the events. While I am confident that the insights of trauma theory and psychoanalysis can provide essential therapeutic resources for individuals stricken with loss, in this essay I want to shift the focus away from the question of individuals' efforts to come to terms with trauma and to turn instead to questions about whether and how trauma theory can provide intellectual resources for more large-scale historical and political tasks.

I begin by addressing how the contemporary theory of trauma associated with Cathy Caruth can help us to understand trauma as a bridge between disparate historical experiences. I also address some of the limits of this theory, particularly its lack of categories for considering the global circulation of traumatic memory and its tendency to exclude from consideration the histories that precede potentially traumatic events. In the second half of the essay, I draw on Dominick LaCapra's reflections on trauma, absence, and loss and Suheir Hammad's poem "first writing since" in order to complicate the notion of "trauma at home" and to put forward tentative suggestions about ethical and political means for coming to terms with the violence of contemporary history.

I

Among the most important tasks that have appeared on the intellectual agenda since September 11 is the need to theorize the link between different experiences of suffering. The attacks on New York and Washington did not only leave unimaginable piles of rubble and ash in their wakes; they have awakened some people in the United States—at least momentarily—to a vista of global suffering. They have put Americans in touch with parts of the world, such as Afghanistan, that had previously occupied the most restricted possible zone of public consciousness for the majority of citizens. For some, the attacks have also resonated with more intimate sufferings in ways that suggest how traumas can feed off of each other. Such a recognition of a shared universe of suffering, momentary and incomplete as it has been for many, does not lead necessarily to any particular political agenda (or indeed to any political agenda at all). Yet the recognition that "we" are not alone in the world may be the first step to any productive engagement with histories of political and personal violence. Because of the way that it defines trauma, contemporary trauma studies appears to be well equipped to provide understanding of the volatile dynamics of intersecting experiences of suffering.

In the wake of the events of September 11, trauma theory can provide necessary attention both to how the experience of trauma isolates the victim and to how it can create the grounds for new forms of community. In her influential introduction to *Trauma: Explorations in Memory*, Cathy Caruth claims that "[i]n a catastrophic age . . . trauma itself may provide the very link between cultures: not as a simple understanding of the pasts of others but rather, within the traumas of contemporary history, as our ability to listen through the departures we have all taken from ourselves" (11). The possibility of understanding trauma as a cross-cultural link derives not simply from the kind of recognition of universal suffering that I alluded to above. Rather, Caruth suggests that this possibility is inherent to the structure of trauma:

> the pathology [of posttraumatic stress disorder] cannot be defined either by the event itself—which may or may not be catastrophic, and may not traumatize everyone equally—nor can it be defined in terms of a *distortion* of the event, achieving its haunting power as a result of distorting personal significances attached to it. The pathology consists, rather, solely in the *structure of its experience* or reception: the event is not assimilated or experienced fully at the time, but only belatedly, in its repeated *possession* of the one who experiences it. (4)

Caruth's version of trauma theory offers several relevant insights for an analysis of the events of September 11 and their aftermath. Most important here is the way that the belatedness of traumatic histories makes possible the "link between cultures." In its contemporary understanding trauma refers not simply to a wounding event but primarily to the *structure of its experience* or reception." The event is experienced belatedly (i.e., becomes traumatic) when the psychic apparatus is incapable of integrating it, when it "cannot be placed within the schemes of prior knowledge" (Caruth 153). The experience of trauma is thus an experience of accident or surprise. Such a perspective is indeed illuminating for the reception of the World Trade Center attacks. It is not simply the scale of violence that qualifies September 11 as traumatic but the way that the events surprised us, took us unawares, and broke with our previous horizon of expectations, thus disallowing our defenses against anxiety, our *Angstbereitschaft*. The novelist Don DeLillo captured this aspect of the events powerfully in a moving essay reflecting on the events: "First the planes struck the towers. After a time it became possible for us to absorb this, barely. But when the towers fell. When the rolling smoke began moving downward, floor to floor. This was so vast and terrible that it was outside imagining even as it happened. We could not catch up to it" (39). DeLillo's stuttering syntax emphasizes the fitful and belated understanding that constitutes the temporality of trauma. This temporality is not simply an effect of a traumatic event; it is part of the reception that defines an event as traumatic. The shift in the understanding of trauma from events, which are always singular, to a mode of reception, which can be shared because it is composed of structural features, opens up a possibility for linking together otherwise disparate histories. The understanding of trauma as adhering to a certain kind of belated experience rather than to a certain kind of event helps reveal how and why traumas become interlaced with each other, both within the individual psyche and in the social world.

Caruth usefully elucidates what it is about the phenomenon of trauma that opens it to the possibilities of shared experience, but it is important to supplement her approach in addressing events such as those of September 11. First, we need to develop criteria for evaluating the types of sharing that emerge in the belated space of traumatic reception. Like that of many working in trauma studies, Caruth's notion of reception is modeled on the psychoanalytic encounter between analyst and analysand: "the history of trauma . . . can only take place through the listening of another"; trauma's address is "a speaking and listening *from the site of trauma*" (11). Without wishing to discount the significance of the face-to-face encounter that is the model for this exploration of trauma, I would suggest that, in order to respond to the ethical and political implications of trauma's layerings and linkages, we need supplementary categories that attend to their circulation

in the public sphere.¹ It is important to consider what happens to speaking
and listening when those acts move away from intimate encounters through
the intervention of the media. For instance, when the implications of
trauma become social—and even national and global, as in the case here—
questions about commodification and ideological instrumentalization necessarily emerge. While the importance of confronting trauma cannot be
reduced to questions of political economy, and political economy cannot
be reduced to a one-sided condemnation of all forms of public circulation,
we cannot avoid asking about the structures and interests at stake when
certain traumatic experiences circulate globally and others remain more
closely tied to local or private contexts.² It ought not to be understood
as minimizing the suffering of survivors and families of victims of the
September 11 attacks to point out that, however "unique" those attacks
were, the hyper-visibility of "American" suffering reflects disproportionate
U.S. political, economic, and media power at least as much as it reflects the
specific terrors of the events. The "structure of experience" that is trauma
suggests possibilities for forging links between cultures, but whether those
links are actually forged will depend on worldly phenomena such as access
to media and ideological predisposition.

Trauma theory's account of the conditions of reception of trauma needs
to be further developed in order to provide insight into such worldly
phenomena. In addition, it needs to turn its attention to the structural
features that produce wounding events in the first place (whether traumatic
or not). Even if trauma cannot be linked to any particular kind of event
(certainly an important insight), trauma theory ought to have something
to say about the kinds of events that tend to produce traumatic effects—
especially if one traumatic history can provide the grounds for future acts of
violence (think of the histories of Afghanistan, Rwanda, Israel, Palestine, or
the Balkans). The ecumenical nature of Caruth's project is important—her
edited volume contains contributions on the Holocaust, AIDS, sexual abuse,
and natural disaster, among other traumatic experiences—but one wonders
if that strength does not threaten to become a weakness when trauma is
thoroughly caught up in geopolitics, as in the case of September 11 (and as
in the case of most of those other examples). Most disturbing would be the
possibility that a focus on trauma solely as a structure of reception might—
in this particular context, one that Caruth's book obviously could not have
addressed—actually end up unwittingly reinforcing the repressive liberal-
conservative consensus in the United States that attempting to explain
the events amounts to explaining them away or excusing them. In an
essay that helpfully distinguishes between explanation and exoneration,

Judith Butler has responded to this consensus: "[t]he cry that 'there is no excuse for September 11th' has become a means by which to stifle any serious public discussion of how U.S. foreign policy has helped to create a world in which such acts of terror are possible" (para. 1).[3] My claim is not that trauma theorists share this consensus (I'm quite sure that most do not) but rather that without theoretical supplementation the emphasis on the "accidental" nature of trauma may inadvertently contribute to the narrative framework in which there is no "relevant prehistory to the events of September 11th" (Butler 5). Even if our initial response to the events was the surprise described by DeLillo, we need ultimately to "catch up" to the events, to move forward and backward from them in order to work through their traumatic impact and to address the social and political contexts that help to foster (without necessarily leading to) acts of extreme violence.[4] Such contexts are not entirely outside the purview of trauma theory, nor, I should add, are they only explainable in terms of the problems of U.S. foreign policy. Nevertheless, any attempt at explanation must go beyond the local events of September 11 and their reception and must include discussion, among other aspects of the historical background, of how the United States has been complicit in preparing the grounds for terrorism, both at home and in the rest of the world.

2

This volume asks us not only to reflect on the usefulness of contemporary trauma theory for thinking through the recent violence but also to ponder the meaning of "trauma at home." The phrase "trauma at home" registers the sense of surprise, which has been voiced frequently in the media and by ordinary citizens, that violence could find its way to the shores of the United States. While this surprise at American vulnerability has been one of the dominant responses to the events, some other voices across the political spectrum have suggested that the "coming home" of trauma was inevitable—either because of "their" barbarism, because of "our" policies, or simply because one's fortunate isolation cannot last forever. What all of these types of responses have in common, despite their political differences, is a relatively stable sense of what home is or was, a sense that there once were clear differences between home and away, inside and outside, peace and violence, innocence and experience, but that those distinctions have been lost. Such responses (and I recognize that I am simplifying actual responses to make a point about "types") share a similar narrative structure, one that Dominick LaCapra has identified as typical in traumatic and posttraumatic contexts: they all blur the distinction between absence and loss. While the losses of September 11 are legion and essential to identify, we need to be careful about confusing their particularity with a preexisting or more general absence of "full unity, community, or consensus" (LaCapra 60) in the United States. We should therefore be suspicious of assertions that such "lost" (but actually absent) unity needs to be reasserted to compensate for the threat posed to the "homeland" by "terrorism." As LaCapra puts it, "one cannot lose what one never had" (50). This formulation speaks both to the purported unity and innocence of the world's only remaining superpower and to the condition of many people on the margins of the local and global political order, both inside and outside the United States, for whom the absence of peace, security, and even home is a structural condition (although emphatically not an unchangeable one). If, as LaCapra suggests, the blurring or conflation of absence and loss (or, I would add, of different kinds of absence or loss) "may itself bear striking witness to the impact of trauma and the posttraumatic, which create a state of disorientation, agitation, or even confusion and may induce a gripping response whose power and force of attraction can be compelling" (46), then it may be that the act of distinguishing between various absences and losses is a critical ethical and political task—a task that bears witness to the past and registers the problems of the present but also looks to a possible future.

While various kinds of theory are crucial to marking such distinctions, works of literature and art may also constitute and enable ethical and political interventions. In the anxious weeks immediately following September 11, I received what I believe constitutes one such intervention: Suheir Hammad's poem "first writing since." Hammad's poem arrived in my virtual mailbox via the e-mail listserv Professors for Peace, which was started in the wake of September 11. At the time, I was receiving dozens of messages from this group each day, and while many provided valuable and vital alternative sources of information and analysis they also began to produce in me a sense of being overwhelmed and sometimes numbed by a political rhetoric rapidly becoming familiar. Amid that excess of information and rhetoric, "first writing since," written by a young Palestinian American poet from Brooklyn, stood out as a response that succeeded in being both a multilayered work of mourning and an ethico-political call for justice. Hammad's poem, which is both emotionally powerful and analytically astute, clearly struck a chord with many people. Within a few months, references to the poem and often its full text could be found on more than 150 Web sites, including MSNBC.com and Middle East Report (www.merip.org), as well as various venues dedicated to poetry and peace;

it also circulated across the globe via e-mail, and Hammad read it on college campuses (including my own) and even on HBO.

"First writing since" consists of seven sections, each of which is made up of two or more stanzas of proselike poetry.[5] Written in lowercase with minimal punctuation, the poem reads like a series of diary entries that track the impact of the World Trade Center attack on the speaker, her family, and the anonymous people she meets (or imagines) in the streets of the city. The poem begins by locating itself in a tradition that questions art's ability to respond adequately to historical trauma: "there have been no words. i have not written one word. no poetry in the ashes south of canal street. no prose in the refrigerated trucks driving debris and dna. not one word" (1). The paradoxical temporality of this opening ("i have not written one word") emphasizes both the gap between language and bodily remains (ashes, DNA) and the attempt to saturate language with materiality—an attempt that is necessary precisely because "there is no poetry in this" (7).[6] The poet's temporary wordlessness attests to the stunned belatedness of traumatic shock—a latency period that quickly gives way to a flow of discourse. The tone of this outpouring is varied and ranges from stricken to searching to accusatory and even to comic—as in section 2, in which we find a chorus of "thank yous" by those who narrowly avoided being at the site of the tragedy: "thank you for my lazy procrastinating ass. . . . thank you, my attitude, you had me fired the week before." This comic and slightly blasphemous litany attests to the poem's commitment to working on multiple levels and mobilizing conflicting affective responses.

Crucial to the poem, as the "thank yous" also demonstrate, is its choral structure. While mostly spoken in an autobiographical first person, the poem attempts to document something of the collective dimension of the trauma and of the heterogeneity of the city. Hammad alludes to the most visible emblems of collective mourning that emerged spontaneously after the attacks, the posters and flyers featuring the names and images of the missing (which were reminiscent of the images carried by the Mothers of the Disappeared throughout Latin America):

the dead are called lost and their families hold up shaky printouts in front of us through screens smoked up.

we are looking for iris, mother of three. please call with any information. we are searching for priti, last seen on the 103rd floor. she was talking to her husband on the phone and the line went. please help us find george. also known as adel. his family is waiting for him with his favorite meal. i am looking for my son, who was delivering coffee. (3)

These lines, which follow immediately after the comic section 2, shift the tone dramatically and catch the reader by surprise, thus providing a distanced mimetic analogy for the shock of the events themselves. The victims are semianonymous and yet rendered in their particularity, identified in relation to family, personal taste, and work. However, they are not offered up for our unmediated consumption; we are at several steps remove from them, witnessing only through smoky screens and via shaky printouts. While Hammad refuses to let her readers confuse themselves with the position of the victims, she does bring us closer to their loss by temporarily inhabiting the voices of the relatives. This negotiation between proximity and distance is itself an ethical act and produces in the reader what LaCapra names "empathic unsettlement": "a kind of virtual experience through which one puts oneself in the other's position while recognizing the difference of that position and not taking the other's place" (78).

While Hammad elicits empathic unsettlement in relation to the victims of the World Trade Center attack, she employs other forms of unsettlement to address the wider context of the events and the contemporary political scene. Just as she refuses to speak in the voice of the victims, Hammad also does not attempt to provide direct access to the perspective of the perpetrators: "i do not know how bad a life has to break in order to kill. i have never been so hungry that i willed hunger i have never been so angry as to want to control a gun over a pen. not really. even as a woman, as a palestinian, as a broken human being. never this broken" (1). There is no attempt at exoneration here, although the poem also does not allow us to distance ourselves from the conditions that may lead to violence (without excusing it): the brokenness attendant upon various forms of sexual, national, and class-based oppression. In the place of exoneration or even simplistic attempts at explanation, Hammad stages skepticism: "today it is ten days. last night bush waged war on a man once openly funded by the cia. i do not know who is responsible. read too many books, known too many people to believe what i am told. i don't give a fuck about bin laden. his vision of the world does not include me or those i love. . . . shit is complicated, and i don't know what to think" (6). Knowledge of the world—even, or especially, unsettled knowledge based on doubt—emerges as the counterpoint to terror: the pen, not the gun.

"First writing since" is unsettling: it unsettles us through empathic address by families of victims, and it unsettles us by refusing to provide easy explanations or exoneration for the violence of September 11, by refusing to take sides in the "us or them" logic of the dominant political class. Furthermore, it seeks to trouble our settled assumptions about what

constitutes home by confronting us with what it means not to have *one*—
that is to say, to have both more than one and less than one: to be
simultaneously at home and in exile. The poet describes receiving comfort
from a woman on the street: "'my brother's in the navy,' i said. 'and we're
arabs.' 'wow, you got double trouble'" (4). Writing about what it's like
to occupy this double position as insider and outsider, Hammad shifts
into a more confrontational mode: "one more person ask me if I knew
the hijackers. one more motherfucker ask me what navy my brother is
in. one more person assume no arabs or muslims were killed. one more
person assume they know me, or that I represent a people. or that a people
represent an evil. or that evil is as simple as a flag and words on a page"
(5). Using repetition and a fragmented, metonymic syntax, this passage
discloses the racist syllogisms that underpin restrictive notions of "home"
and "foreignness." The poem both stakes a claim to speaking from American
space and challenges the hegemonic construction of Americanness by
reasserting the local: "i have never felt less american and more new yorker,
particularly brooklyn, than these past days" (6). Hammad's articulation of
a complex poetic vantage point as Arab and American, as New Yorker and
Palestinian, poses difficult and timely questions about the links between
disparate geographies and histories and about the too often taken for
granted opposition between trauma and home.

Hammad moves at once above and below the national radar, taking apart
assumptions of a prelapsarian American unity in order to assert bonds
of local and transnational solidarity. Making the kind of link between
cultures that Caruth sees as the potential of responses to trauma, the
poet proposes that "if there are any people on earth who understand
how new york is feeling right now, they are in the west bank and gaza
strip" (5). Hammad's claim is political, of course. Her claim coexists with a
series of others that have sought, for local political reasons, to create links
between September 11 and political contestations worldwide (including,
naturally, the counterclaim that was heard often that it is Israelis who truly
understand the events in New York). Surely there are more than enough
people worldwide who can justly claim to live in a traumatized home or
to be deprived of a home altogether. It cannot be wrong if more of these
people listen and speak to each other across their traumatic experiences.
And yet, once again, we are confronted with the limits of a framework
established solely around the category of trauma. For not all claims to
"understanding" the other's suffering are equivalent. In the months since
September 11, nation-states around the globe have used the suffering in New
York to solidify hard-line positions; in the United States there has been a

crackdown on civil liberties and threats to forms of dissent. Claims to traumatic experience, to vulnerability, to violence do not tell us everything we need to know about matters of justice and responsibility. Trauma theory helps make us attentive to suffering and thus, in principle, to justice and responsibility, but it needs to be supplemented by a positive vision of social and political transformation: "you are either with life, or against it. affirm life" (Hammad 7).

NOTES

1. In *Traumatic Realism: The Demands of Holocaust Representation,* I develop a framework for responding to representations and memories of traumatic histories. In the context of a consideration of the impact of the Nazi genocide, I argue that traumatic histories make three types of demands on our response: they demand documentation, they demand reflection on the limits of representation, and they demand engagement with the public sphere and commodity culture. While the events of September 11 bear no resemblance to those of the Holocaust, I am suggesting in this essay that what we can learn from coming to terms with events such as the Shoah can be illuminating for our current concerns. Caruth's account of trauma plays a very important role in my formulations, but in *Traumatic Realism,* as here, I imply that that account needs to be supplemented with social theoretical and Marxist categories if we want a more complete understanding of historical trauma.

2. I have found Andreas Huyssen's essay "Present Pasts: Media, Politics, Amnesia" helpful in conceptualizing a nonreductive approach to the global circulation of traumatic (and other) memories.

3. *Theory and Event,* the on-line journal by Project Muse from which Butler's article is taken, does not include page numbers but rather numbers each paragraph; therefore, all references will refer parenthetically to paragraph numbers.

4. The notion of working through alluded to here finds its most convincing expression in the work of Dominick LaCapra. See the subsequent discussion.

5. I am grateful to Suheir Hammad for her kind permission to quote from her poem. Parenthetical references will refer to the seven sections of the poem. The poem's seven sections seem to correspond to the poem's moment of enunciation: "today is a week, and seven is of heavens, gods, science" (1). Given limitations of space I will not be able to address all of the most important features of Hammad's poem. A more complete discussion would need to include consideration of the poem's feminist sensibility as well as its debt to African American cultural forms such as hip-hop.

6. Perhaps the most famous instance of this kind of "thinking against itself" in

relation to the aesthetics of trauma comes in Theodor Adorno's dictum that "to write poetry after Auschwitz is barbaric." On Adorno, see my *Traumatic Realism*, chap. 1. For a useful anthology of poetry that bears witness to various traumatic histories, see Carolyn Forché.

Works Cited

Butler, Judith. "Explanation and Exoneration, or What We Can Hear." *Theory and Event* 5, no. 4 (2002).

Caruth, Cathy. "Trauma and Experience: Introduction." In *Trauma: Explorations in Memory*, ed. Cathy Caruth. Baltimore: Johns Hopkins University Press, 1995.

DeLillo, Don. "In the Ruins of the Future." *Harper's*, December 2001, 33–40.

Forché, Carolyn, ed. *Against Forgetting: Twentieth Century Poetry of Witness*. New York: W. W. Norton, 1993.

Huyssen, Andreas. "Present Pasts: Media, Politics, Amnesia." *Public Culture* 12, no. 1 (2001): 21–38.

LaCapra, Dominick. "Trauma, Absence, Loss." In *Writing History, Writing Trauma*. Baltimore: Johns Hopkins University Press, 2001.

Rothberg, Michael. *Traumatic Realism: The Demands of Holocaust Representation*. Minneapolis: University of Minnesota Press, 2000.

Fallout of Various Kinds

Elizabeth Baer

This is not 'Nam. This is bowling. There are rules. – Walter, in the Coen brothers' film The Big Lebowski

Dear Mom,
A book that connects White Plains to Poland to Vietnam seems to be the perfect book for you! I hope it helps you think about the connections between your interest in the Holocaust and your experience with Vietnam (a connection I'd like to see you write about). Happy Vergangenheitsbewältigung. Love, Hes

When I was eight months pregnant with our first child, my husband was sent unexpectedly to Vietnam. We had both protested the war as college students but graduated in that worst of years for avoiding the draft, 1968, after they had eliminated the deferments for graduate school and fatherhood and before the lottery was initiated. Coming from a small town in Massachusetts, my husband was informed of his impending draft notice before our commencement; our wedding took place soon thereafter. Like many people in dire situations, we had counted on at least avoiding the most horrifying fate: going to Vietnam. Clint qualified for Officer Candidate School—which delayed things for awhile. He signed up for an extra year of service in order to choose his post. Surely, we thought, this war has to end soon.

Hester, our daughter who wrote the above inscription in Wayne Karlin's book *Rumors and Stones: A Journey*, was born three weeks after my husband landed "in country."[1] In Faulknerian fashion (I had read all nineteen of Faulkner's novels and written my senior thesis on him just before graduating from college), Hester and I endured the next seven months together. Almost daily I had the same recurring nightmare: a long, olive-green army car drove into the driveway of my parents' home, where I was living with my new baby. This, of course, meant that my husband had been killed: the army always sent a person to give you the bad news. (In fact, the couple from whom we had bought used baby furniture fled to Canada after the husband had spent a year in Brooklyn delivering such devastating news to families and then, in the government's infinite wisdom, had been assigned a year's duty in Vietnam himself.)

I survived the terrifying absence by not reading a book for the entire eight months that my husband was gone. This was not an intentional abstinence. Rather, I could not abide having my intellect alive. I closed it down for the duration. Before Clint and I actually met in the flesh at the age of seventeen, we had had a two-hour argument on the telephone about *Moby Dick*. Books were and still are at the center of our love for each other. I simply could not afford to read while he was gone: to do so was to experience too painfully the void in our lives.

Since our joyous reunion in May 1971, I have returned with avid desire to "the pleasure of the text" and exult in sharing that love with my students. But it took my daughter, with whom I was writing a book at the time she wrote the above dedication to me, to point out a pattern in my scholarly work: much of it focused on the topic of women and war. I am taking seriously her urging that I write about these connections. It is the events of September 11 that have been the catalyst to doing so.

At this very moment, particles of an atomic energy or hydrogen bomb lurk somewhere in your body. Every day you absorb more and more of these bits of atomic dust when you drink water and eat food.[2]

As my daughter was conceived in the waning days of Vietnam, so I was conceived shortly after VE day. The "sunny" 1950s were my childhood: Bishop Fulton Sheen, Pinky Lee, and the Mickey Mouse Club on television and daily mass and the lives of the saints at my parochial school. Spunky Nancy Drew, who drove a blue roadster and could take or leave Ned, was the literary character whose exploits I most enjoyed following. My father went off to work at his life insurance office daily, dressed nattily in a carefully chosen tie and his gray felt hat. My pretty mother taught her four daughters domestic skills, gardened magnificently, and entertained my father's business associates elegantly.

But the schizophrenia that was the 1950s was just barely under wraps. I vividly recall early exposures to the Holocaust. A *Life* magazine article about lampshades concocted by the Nazis from human skin is perhaps my earliest memory; I sat in the wing chair in the living room as I looked at the

photograph of prominent Nazis sitting in their living room. A television
program about a Jewish man being hidden from the Nazis in the basement
of his non-Jewish wife's family home is another early memory. The plot
of the program turned on the crisis that resulted when she, living above
ground, became pregnant. Naive about the "facts of life" (as we called an
understanding of sexuality in the 1950s), I could not grasp why this was a
crisis. I asked my mother during the next commercial, and she dutifully
explained those facts before the program resumed. I recall, too, the coverage
in *Life* of the Eichmann trial. I clipped the stories and saved them in a file,
perhaps an early indication of my future as an academic and a Holocaust
scholar. By then, my parents had moved to a newly constructed home in
the suburbs and my father had seen to it that a study room was created for
my sister and me, equipped with tables made of doors and a filing cabinet.
Many a happy Saturday was spent doing extra credit assignments for my
favorite eighth grade nun, Sister Emma, in that room.

Fallout is dangerous to man because of its radioactivity.
I sensed but could not articulate a tension, a paradox between the smiling
life in the American suburbs of the 1950s and the genocide of the previous
decade, which killed eleven million human beings. My father, a naval officer
during World War II, never spoke of his experiences, like most men who
were veterans. Certainly the nuns never invoked the Holocaust in our
history lessons; instead, these lessons focused on moments when Catholic
hegemony had been threatened in the past. The Crusaders were heroes;
Martin Luther, a villain; Mary Queen of Scots, a martyr. (Although a part
of me resents the misplaced orthodoxy of these lessons, I believe that the
passion with which history was taught, with no facade of objectivity, kindled
my love of learning.) Peter Novick, in his book *The Holocaust in American
Life,* suggests that one reason we were not taught about the Holocaust in
the 1950s is that we did not wish to sully Germany, our ally in the cold
war.[3]

If one cause of the schizophrenia of the 1950s was the rush toward comfort
and modernism as an escape from the grim realities about human nature
revealed by the Holocaust, another was the stark contrast between the
smiling suburbs and the threats of the atomic age. It was a commonplace at
St. Stephen's School to be given holy cards of St. Joseph on his feast day (or
whoever the saint du jour was) and then to have an air-raid drill. A shrill
siren would suddenly erupt, and we would be swept under our beige metal
and wooden desks or into the hallway to cower under our crossed arms and
the stern warnings of the Dominican sisters.

Radioactivity is the ability of certain atoms or elements to spew forth rays.
The threat of nuclear war was palpable. The fears it generated expressed
themselves in many ways in my childhood: for example, my father went
bowling every Tuesday evening with his league; I could never fall asleep
until he returned home and my sense of security was restored. "Cold" was
not an apt adjective for this war as far as I was concerned. The Iron Curtain,
the violence of Khrushchev banging his shoe against the lectern, the Cuban
missile crisis, the Berlin Wall—all were real and profoundly troubling to me,
despite my seemingly safe white middle-class existence, with its Ginny dolls
and platter parties and babysitting income. It was perhaps inevitable that I
would join the ranks of antiwar protesters in the 1960s—going to college
just outside Manhattan afforded me the opportunity to join demonstrations
and to read *The Village Voice* and to participate in much of hippie culture.

How deeply I had been marked by this childhood of fallout shelters and
cold war crises I did not fully recognize until I went to Moscow in 1993.
Standing on Red Square, being barked at to stay in the pathway marked off
for those in line to see Lenin's embalmed body, I recognized the soldiers'
red uniforms as those from the *Life* magazine of my childhood, and even in
this post–Berlin Wall world, I was paralyzed. All the fears of my childhood
resurfaced. That happened again on September 11.

The rays emitted by radioactive elements are truly death rays. They can kill
living things. They can penetrate your flesh and cause chemical changes.
I remained adamantly opposed to all wars throughout my husband's three
years in the army. Desperately unhappy, we at one point seriously contemplated deserting and fleeing to Canada. But the penalty was high: we could
not foresee the amnesty that was granted to draft dodgers and deserters
after the war and hence believed that such a decision would mean that we
were forever barred from returning to the United States. Raising a family
without access to their grandparents seemed too high a price to pay. Clint's
experiences in Vietnam were profoundly disillusioning: if he had gone to
the war with some shreds of patriotism, these were quickly stripped away.
His letters were full only of plans for our life after he returned home. Like
my father, he has rarely spoken of his experiences as a soldier since that
return in 1971.

Like Paul D in Toni Morrison's *Beloved*, I folded away the pain of our
separation, the absence of my husband at the birth of our first child. It
resided in something like the rusted tin that Paul D has in his chest where
his heart should be, until I was tricked into taking that pain out and coming
to terms with it. I was tricked by a film, which I saw when it was released

in 1978—*The Deer Hunter*. One of the first films to deal with the Vietnam War, the movie is set largely on the home front and not "in country," which is why it affected me so deeply—it told the story of the war I had endured rather than that of my husband. Shortly after this experience, I had another that revealed to me the importance of teaching undergraduates about history. General Westmoreland was invited to speak at Dartmouth College, where I was teaching, as part of a course being offered on Vietnam. He was, of course, one of the most loathed of the military by those of us who protested the war, and I went with much skepticism to hear his talk in a large auditorium filled with students. My skepticism was rewarded: he layered the truth and lies so skillfully that he provoked a standing ovation. I recalled his constant mantra on the radio through the war years—"Just one more week and we can win this war"—but the students in the audience had been too young then, and when he reiterated that gross falsehood on this evening, they believed him.

It was on my first trip to Europe in 1987, at the age of forty-one, that questions began to surface about the still adamant antiwar stance I held. Until then, I had had the luxury of thinking about war entirely from an American perspective. In England to evaluate study abroad locations as part of my responsibility as the dean of faculty at a small liberal arts college, I met a most impressive Oxford undergraduate named Clement. Of all the places he could have taken Clint and me as newly arrived tourists, he took us to the moldering graveyard of Bladon Church in Woodstock, where Winston Churchill is buried. The reverence with which Clement approached this spot—so sacred to him—shook me to the core. He knew so much about his country's history and was so earnest about England, unlike the American college students I taught, who knew little about their own history and, instead, affected cynicism. A few days later, in London, we visited St. Clement Dane's Church on the Strand. Here is an excerpt from the entry in my travel journal at that time:

> A church designed by Christopher Wren, it was seriously damaged during wwii and rebuilt in memory of the members of the Royal Air Force. Usually I shirk from things having to do with war and stick to a strict antiwar attitude. But during this first day, in London, my understanding of wwii has thickened and shifted in a rather startling way. . . . As I walked around St. Clement Dane's, looking at the roll books along the walls of the men who were killed during wwii, I suddenly felt with conviction that these men *were* heroes (where I

might have sneered before). But now I understood what they were fighting for. . . . I was very, very moved by this church.

Three years later, I experienced another epiphany while abroad. This time it occurred in Germany, at Dachau. A three-hour visit to the first concentration camp, established by the Nazis in 1933 right after Hitler came to power, made me realize I had been taught virtually nothing about the Holocaust in my formal education. How could this have happened? And could it happen again? These were the stabbing questions with which I began to wrestle upon leaving the camp. Now World War II took on a whole new dimension as I returned home and began to study the Holocaust obsessively. Gradually, all the important questions about war, evil, and human nature coalesced for me in the study of the Shoah. After extensive reading and a month-long Jewish Labor Committee study tour to Poland and Israel, I began to teach courses on the Holocaust and then to do scholarly work on it.

> *Local fallout can deliver enormous radiation doses. In a hydrogen bomb war, it's likely that the belligerents will depend on local fallout to wipe out populations of very large regions.*

On September 11, I was just driving to an 8:00 A.M. (Central Standard Time) English department meeting when I heard a somewhat stunned announcer on NPR say that it appeared a plane had hit the World Trade Center. By the time I was parking my car ten minutes later, the radio announced a second plane had hit the other World Trade Center tower. Terrorism came to my mind immediately. By the time my meeting ended at 10:00 A.M., the Pentagon had been hit and the plane in Pennsylvania had gone down. Clearly something was terribly wrong. Unlike most of my colleagues, who decided to cancel classes, I convened my first-year seminar of sixteen students, who had been on campus less than ten days. Entitled "Images of the Holocaust," the course was designed to raise ethical issues about the representation of the Holocaust in film, fiction, memoir, and visual art. The previous day, I had talked about the founding of Israel in the aftermath of World War II and the resulting tensions in the Middle East, which were being manifest in early September in a controversial conference in South Africa. When my class met at 1:30 P.M. on September 11, it appeared that the American involvement in Israel was a factor in the terrorist attacks, and my students asked me to explain about Palestine and Israel again. Yesterday's lesson had a sudden new relevance.

As we lived out the fall semester together, my students just seemed sad on many days. Granted, the topic of our class may well have contributed to that. But I thought so often of how their world changed dramatically on Labor Day weekend when they left home for orientation and how it then again changed irrevocably on September 11. My first semester in college in the fall of 1964 was idyllic by comparison. And I, too, was sad for much of the fall term.

I recorded the following entry in my journal on September 19:

> Still struggling to come to grips with the terrorist attacks on NYC and DC last week, September 11. What will it mean for the future? War? For air travel? For the economy? For daily living? Over 5,000 [as it was reported at the time] people missing and unaccounted for. So many sad stories, so many eerie parallels to the Holocaust in terms of the consequences of hatred, racism, and religious fanaticism. I've watched more TV in the past week than in a whole month or more—and we've had no sunshine for days, adding to the gloom and doom. In the midst of the beginning of a new school year, a sense of endings: end of the warmth and light of summer, end of the ethos of invulnerability in America.[4]

If you could get into a basement shelter of moderately good design and have enough food and water to hold out for a week or two, you might be able to avoid the effects of local fallout.

Additionally, I was struggling with a very difficult decision: I was scheduled to take twenty-four American students to Germany and the Czech Republic for the month of January 2002 to study the Holocaust. Our itinerary included sites of early Nazi history, the Haus der Kunst, and the White Rose Memorial in Munich; four concentration camps; the Jewish Quarter in Prague and the memorial at Lidice; and the Wannsee Center, the new Jewish Museum, the Topographie of Terror, and many other sites in Berlin. I had never taken students abroad before and my co-teacher and I had worked for a year to set up this course. Again, many colleagues were canceling their study abroad courses, choosing the safety of a Minnesota classroom instead. I wavered between listening to all my cold war childhood fears, which counseled cancellation, and listening to the encouragement of my International Education Office, which urged me to go forward. Each day I listened to NPR, read the *New York Times*, scanned Web sites, and tried to read the tea leaves: would it be too big a risk to go? As October lengthened into November and no further attacks occurred, I began to take heart. In the end, despite the sneaker bomber, we boarded a plane on January 3. I took courage from the belief that there had never been a more important time to teach the Holocaust than now, and to do so on the soil of the perpetrators was to engender for my students some of the understanding I had gained only in an international context.

While in Prague, we had the chance to hear Mozart's *Requiem* in a magnificent art nouveau building in the center of the city. That bittersweet music is a favorite of mine, and I took my seat with eager anticipation. Almost as soon as the first notes were played, however, tears sprang unexpectedly to my eyes. This music of mourning for so many dead was, at the same time, healing. A few months earlier, I had attended a Bob Dylan concert in Minneapolis, a celebration of the Minnesota native's sixtieth birthday. It was a very different venue than Prague: a huge ice hockey rink cum rock concert hall with a crowd of thousands. I first saw Bob Dylan play at the Newport Folk Festival before he "went electric," and there was something reassuring about connections with the past when he sang "Masters of War" in Minneapolis that night, a clear reference to the bombing of Afghanistan. There was also something healing about being in a place with so many people; academics like me tend to spend a lot of time alone, and after the terrorist attack, solitude was not always my friend.

Don't count too heavily, however, on such shelters saving you or your family. Pestilence would spread. Fires would be uncontrolled. There is no need to labor the point: An atomic attack is no pretty business.

The uneasy sense during my childhood that danger lurked close by; the loss of my husband for almost a year, during which time an event we should have shared took place without him; a decade of devotion to studying the Holocaust; and September 11—the device of autobiography allows me to draw connections and parallels that objective scholarship would not. Fallout of various kinds. Literal, figurative, atomic, psychological. *Trauma at home: this is the essence of it.* Those fallout shelters: because even being in one's home was not safe. So a home within a home, a secret home, a subtext had to be constructed. The most intimate of physical acts, giving birth, raided by a war ten thousand miles away; I sent her umbilical cord to him; a small piece of his daughter, whom he would not know for eight months. A small shelter in my chest carried the pain for eight years.

The pogrom of November 1938, called *Kristallnacht* by the Nazis: the sanctity of how many Jewish homes defiled. Feathers flying from bedding ripped apart.[5] Again, secret annexes and shelters are built. Unimaginable to so many that the Nazis would actually expropriate their furniture, their dishes and paintings, their bank accounts, their careers, would separate their families. The final expropriation: hair and gold fillings in the teeth.

A survivor shares with my students a document he found in his parents'
home when he returned after the war: shoved to the back of a drawer was
the careful list the Nazis had made of all his parents' belongings as they took
control. *Trauma at home.* Women standing on the street in New York City
with photos of their missing husband or son or daughter. Such a low-tech
approach to finding the missing after such high-tech terrorism, reminiscent
of the searches conducted for loved ones in displaced persons camps in the
aftermath of the Holocaust.

Trauma at home. Yes, this is new to us Americans in that such an attack
on our soil (assuming one excludes attacks of the Civil War) is new. But as
I think back over my own life, as I make connections among the threats
I have experienced and studied, trauma at home is not so new after all.
Perhaps, in fact, this is just where most women have experienced war over
the centuries. And this is where the fallout—of various kinds—lands.

The fragile hope for peace when the Berlin Wall came down was shortly
thereafter shattered as the Gulf War took place. I was appalled by the yellow
ribbon fervor that engulfed my small campus, as I have been appalled by
the "axis of evil" rhetoric of the current administration. While the study of
the Holocaust has forced me to confront the capacity for evil in all human
beings, I have also learned the dangers of singling out any group as the
Other. Such a tactic so easily escalates into violence, which results in the
fallout of retaliation, and so the cycle continues.

> *Therefore strontium 90, like calcium, will seek out bones and teeth; iodine
> makes a beeline for the thyroid gland, and cesium 137 and carbon 14
> distribute themselves throughout the body and lodge in the reproductive
> organs to do damage there.*

Taken as a metaphor, the biological prediction in this last quotation seems
prescient: that fallout of various kinds will "lodge in the reproductive
organs," where it will reproduce itself as well as spawn damaged offspring.
I realize as I write this that one of the reasons I have studied the Holocaust
is to penetrate the schizophrenia of the 1950s, to bring to the surface for
recognition and contemplation what the nuns called "original sin." "We
ain't gonna study war no more" went one anthem of the 1960s. Perhaps not.
But it is incumbent on us to study—and teach—how these wars come about
and how they can be avoided. The combination of factors that launched
the war against the Jews—Germany's defeat in World War I and resulting
economic difficulties, the need for a scapegoat, centuries of anti-Semitism,
a misplaced belief in eugenics (the purported ability of humans to create

a superrace), a charismatic leader—are lessons we need to learn. And we need to learn them not for what they teach us about another country in another time but for what they teach us about ourselves, now, and the arrogance, the racial hatred, the social injustice, the genocide of which we are all capable.

NOTES

1. Wayne Karlin, *Rumors and Stones: A Journey* (Willimantic CT: Curbstone Press, 1996). Karlin is a Vietnam veteran who has published four novels as well as two anthologies of writing about the Vietnam War. *Rumors and Stones* recounts his 1993 journey back to the Polish village from which his mother came; while there, he learned the plight of his other Jewish forebears: they had been shot by invading Nazis in 1941.

2. This and all subsequent epigraphs in the text are taken from a fifteen-page brochure entitled "The Fallout Question" by Earl Ubell (New York: Koster-Dana Corporation, 1960). Though I found this particular pamphlet in an antique store, it is the rhetoric of my nuclear childhood, which I read often in similar brochures distributed in school.

3. Peter Novick, *The Holocaust in American Life* (Boston: Houghton Mifflin, 1999), especially pages 85–123. Novick comments: "Between the end of the war and the 1960's, as anyone who has lived through those years can testify, the Holocaust made scarcely any appearance in American public discourse" (103). Novick persuasively details the displacement of Nazism as the "apotheosis of evil" by the term "totalitarianism," referring to Communism (86).

4. I have been a scholar of the Holocaust long enough to know that to compare the Holocaust to other events is a risky endeavor, and I want to be clear that in this journal entry I am not suggesting an equivalence between the Holocaust and the events of September 11 but rather searching in human nature for the causes of both events.

5. Holocaust historian Marion Kaplan explains that Jewish women's memoirs of the so-called *Kristallnacht* often focus not on broken glass but rather on feathers spread throughout the home, feathers from bedding that has been ripped apart by marauding Nazis: "This image of feathers flying, of a domestic scene gravely disturbed, represents women's primary experience of the pogrom." See Kaplan, "Keeping Calm and Weathering the Storm: Jewish Women's Responses to Daily Life in Nazi Germany, 1933–1939," in *Women in the Holocaust*, ed. Dalia Ofer and Lenore Weitzman (New Haven: Yale University Press, 1998), 46.

9/11/01 = 1/27/01:
The Changed Posttraumatic Self

Irene Kacandes

To speak to you, the dead of September, I must not claim false intimacy or summon an overheated heart glazed just in time for a camera. I must be steady and I must be clear, knowing all the time that I have nothing to say—no words stronger than the steel that pressed you into itself; no scripture older or more elegant than the ancient atoms you have become.

And I have nothing to give either—except this gesture, this thread thrown between your humanity and mine. – Toni Morrison, "The Dead of September 11"

For me, much of how I experienced September 11 was determined by events that had taken place months earlier. On January 27, 2001, two of my closest friends, Susanne and Half Zantop, were brutally murdered at midday in their own home in the rural town of Etna, New Hampshire. The cryptic title of this essay proposes a private equation that doesn't make much sense to illustrate an aspect of trauma that on the surface of it may not make much sense either: radically different traumas can be experienced as similar by those who have already been traumatized. The death by stabbing of two individuals by two other individuals has essentially little in common with terrorist attacks using hijacked passenger jets as bombs, collapsing buildings, and the death of thousands. Indeed, putting these events together could be considered obscene. And yet, that's just what my psyche did—put the events together. The experience of my friends' murder did more than just resonate when I learned of the September 11 attacks in the United States. As I watched the television news and first saw the images of my beloved native New York from where I was teaching in Berlin, Germany, I was transported back to the steel-cold New Hampshire winter that mirrored the hearts of family and friends as we grieved for Susanne and Half. I immediately had the uncanny sense that I "knew" what was transpiring in the United States, that I knew the actors and their victims. It was dreadful knowledge that made my body shake uncontrollably. Perversely perhaps, it was also knowledge that I believe allowed me to process the terrorist attacks more quickly than most others around me.

In light of Toni Morrison's passionate warning—which I take as a warning about how to address the survivors as well as the deceased—it would be unforgivably solipsistic to share some features of how I experienced my friends' murder and how I reacted to the news of September 11, were it not for my conviction that other people might recognize aspects of their own experience in this account. These others may include the previously traumatized, who, regardless of the directness of their connection to the places, the events, or the actual victims of the September attacks, sensed similar uncanny knowledge about what was happening. But my hope is that individuals with very different histories of closeness to tragedy may also find some information here that can be of use. What I can't emphasize enough is that I am not at all interested in suggesting, much less adjudicating, who has been traumatized in the medical sense by the events of September 11. (I certainly have not been.) Nor would I want this essay to contribute in any way to establishing some kind of hierarchy among those who suffer in its wake.[1] As a recent study published in the *New England Journal of Medicine* shows by looking at Manhattanites alone, sufferers whose distress warranted psychiatric treatment are an unpredictably heterogeneous group with highly divergent connections to the events and the victims of the World Trade Center attack (Galea et al. 2002; see also Goode 2002, a15). It is relevant to my essay that huge numbers of people witnessed this calamity; most have grieved, many have become depressed, and a not insignificant number have developed the symptoms of posttraumatic stress disorder (PTSD). My aim here can only be to offer clarification about a few features of the phenomenon of trauma in the hope that this analysis might allow some readers to become more compassionate toward themselves and others by better understanding what they might otherwise have considered inappropriate responses. My method eclectically relies on professional trauma literature, my own personal experience, and anecdotal evidence. This might seem inexcusable in other contexts, but in relation to September 11 I can't think of any other way to try to follow Toni Morrison in "throwing a thread."

SOME PRELIMINARIES

Words like "atrocity," "calamity," "catastrophe," and "disaster" have been around for a long time. The word "trauma" has, too. Its use to describe psychic wounding, however, is only a century old. And in those hundred or so years, medical, psychoanalytic, and psychotherapeutic professionals and lay people have used the term in myriad ways, most confusingly to refer both to the forces or mechanisms that cause a psychic disorder and to the resulting psychic state. In 1980, the American medical establishment designated as a disease a certain set of symptoms resulting from trauma in the first sense, complex PTSD, trauma in the second sense. One of the most intriguing developments leading up to this technical definition was the recognition that victims of exceedingly different types of violations (for example, rape versus captivity; single versus prolonged exposure to a stressor) can exhibit astonishingly similar symptoms. In *Trauma and Recovery*, psychiatrist Judith Herman traces the sometimes parallel paths of work with hysterical women, combat veterans, and victims of domestic and sexual abuse that eventually led up to the institutional recognition of PTSD ([1992] 1997, esp. 7–32).

While this designation and inclusion in the diagnostic manual represented quite a breakthrough at the time, numerous revisions of our understanding of the disease and its etiology have been necessary. One such revision concerned the characterization of the events that can trigger PTSD as uncommon, as "outside the range of usual human experience" (APA 1980, 236; also quoted in Herman [1992] 1997, 33). Herman's own work with incest and sexual abuse victims contributed to wider recognition that some forms of sexual and domestic violence were anything but outside the range of human experience; they were and are horribly constituent of it for far too many women and children. Regrettably, war, totalitarian control, and now terrorism seem to be part of life's fabric for more people in the world as well. Herman (and others) clarified that: "Traumatic events are extraordinary, not because they occur rarely, but rather because they overwhelm the ordinary human adaptations to life" (33).

In a related but distinct aspect of trauma, casual and professional students of trauma have observed that persons do not react to the same stressors in the same way; what causes trauma for one person might not for another (Wigren 1994, 417; Caruth 1995, 4). We know little about why one psyche will experience a set of circumstances as life-threatening while another submitted to the very same events will not, and we know hardly more about why previously traumatized individuals and victims of racism, poverty, and sexism are more susceptible to traumatization than the general population (Root 1996; Galea et al. 2002). There is one other dimension of the medical definition that seems particularly relevant to this volume's consideration of September 11: witnessing or even hearing of the violation or death of another can be stressors that lead to depression or PTSD (APA 1994, 424, Criterion A1).

Cathy Caruth, following Freud's original observations, describes trauma as "unclaimed" or "missed" experience (1996). Philosopher Susan Brison argues for modifying that characterization: "at least in the case of a single traumatic event, the event is experienced at the time and remembered from that time, although the full emotional impact of the trauma takes time to absorb and work through" (1999, 210). Regardless of which account one gives of the initial intake of traumatic events by the brain, Brison, Caruth, Herman, and numerous practicing psychotherapists like Jodie Wigren emphasize the critical act of creating narratives about what has happened in order to "absorb and work through" the trauma. Dori Laub (Felman and Laub 1992) and Wigren (1994) emphasize the importance of sympathetic witnesses in enabling the creation of such narratives. Following Herman and Martha Minow (1993), I have suggested that such witnessing can contribute to restoration of the social order, a point to which I will return at the end of this essay (Kacandes 2001, esp. 89–140).

In fundamental ways trauma is connected to incomprehensibility. Sometimes, as Brison (1999) suggests, one can "say" what happened but cannot register its (full) impact. And sometimes one can "see" the external consequences of a trauma (such as losing a leg) but cannot put into words what happened.[2] Being able to move on from this threat to the self involves in part accepting the fact that what seemed impossible did actually happen by telling a narrative about it and feeling the appropriate affect for such an occurrence. Most important to my analysis here is this: contact with uninvited disaster, the working through, and the acceptance of the presence of the impossible in one's life will *change one*. Brison's recent book, *Aftermath: Violence and the Remaking of a Self* (2001), takes this change as its main subject. I believe this is also what Holocaust survivor Rabbi Baruch G. was trying to get at when he characterized his own suffering after liberation as greater than that during his internment in concentration camps: "I suffered probably more from the loneliness and the isolation, *more* than during the Holocaust period. And I thought about it the other day and I suppose it has to do with the fact that after life around you seems to be normal, but *you* are abnormal" (edited testimony, near beginning). Exposure to certain kinds of events may transform one's view of the world, and, consequently, one simply cannot be in the world in the same way as prior to exposure. In Baruch G.'s framework, the forced changed self and world-view create a gap between the self and most others.

About the rape and attempted murder perpetrated on her, Brison writes: "I would rather not have gone down that road. It has been hard for me, as a philosopher, to learn the lesson that knowledge isn't always desirable, that the truth doesn't always set you free. Sometimes, it fills you with incapacitating terror and, then, uncontrollable rage. But I suppose you should embrace it anyway, for the reason Nietzsche exhorts you to love your enemies: if it doesn't kill you, it makes you stronger" (2001, 21). Although my experiences and Baruch G.'s and Brison's are incommensurate in many respects, I, too, would rather not have gone down that road. I would rather not have lost my friends to murder. I would rather not have experienced the numbness, the paralyzing fear, the panic, the hysterical grief, the amnesia, the loss of interest in my job, my family, and my friends. And yet, I came out of those experiences with views of the nature of the world and my own mortality that seem truer, if less comforting, than the views I had before. When I first saw the images of the planes crashing into the World Trade Center, I was not incredulous. Rather, what I saw were strangers killing strangers out of hate, out of an unwillingness and cultivated inability to see the humanity of the other. What I saw were two adolescent boys stabbing my friends to death.

LOSING SUSANNE AND HALF

On Saturday, January 27, 2001, my husband and I were spending a quiet evening in my apartment in Lebanon, New Hampshire, when the telephone rang. I was immediately concerned since I never receive phone calls on Saturday night unless my husband and I have been unable to get together for the weekend and he is calling me. Since Philippe was with me, I feared it would be a family member telling me that something had happened to my father, who has not been in good health. But no, it was my colleague, Bruce Duncan. He said that another departmental colleague and our chairwoman, Susanne Zantop, and her husband, Half, also a professor at Dartmouth, had been murdered. They'd been found in their home by a friend, he reported. The dean of the faculty had appointed Steven Scher, another colleague, interim chair. I wasn't able to take in what Bruce was saying about Susanne and Half; in that moment only the dean's act registered with and frightened me. The single thing I do remember saying is that Bruce should call me back the moment he found out that there'd been a mistake. No, he didn't think there'd been a mistake, but he promised to call me if he found out anything. He asked if I was alone, and I said that Philippe was with me. The next half-hour is a black hole. I did tell Philippe what I'd been told, but I don't remember how. We just sat there in stunned silence. It had to be a mistake. The phone rang again; it was Ulrike Rainer, another departmental colleague, asking if I was alone. No, I said, and begged her to tell me the news was false. I think it was she who told me which of our friends had discovered the bodies of Susanne and Half. I remember thanking her for checking on me. More stunned silence. The phone rang again; it was Gerd Gemünden, another departmental colleague, to whom I am very close and who also was particularly close to the Zantops. He told me he and his wife were at the house of our friend Roxana Verona, who had found Susanne and Half that night. Two other very close friends, Marianne Hirsch and Leo Spitzer, were there. Did we want to come over? Yes, I said, right away. I remember insisting to my husband that I drive. But mainly I remember how frigid it was in the car and how dark it seemed going up and down the long hill that separates my town from Hanover.

When I first wrote out these words, some six months after the events they recount, I broke off at this point. I experienced strong internal resistance to going back into that car to travel the road that took me to the place where I found out that what had seemed completely impossible had in fact happened. And yet, after breaking myself off, as in interrupting the narrative here, the next feeling was deep sadness about the difference between the "before" and the "after." Let me explain, because this is key to the idea that trauma changes the individual. Before the night of January 27, 2001, it seemed completely impossible—not just improbable but actually impossible—that two individuals could be killed in their home in our beautiful, peaceful, safe, rural area. Transplanted New Yorker that I am, I was the only person I knew who consistently locked her car, office, and apartment. Of course, there had been murders before in our area. But for one thing, they had occurred prior to my arrival in New Hampshire, and, for another, almost all murders here are crimes of passion between people who know each other, which brings me to Susanne and Half. It is easy to transform people into saints after they have died. But Susanne and Half's marriage had always been admired by everyone who knew them well. It was beyond the limits of imagination that they had hurt each other. And because they were such kind, generous people, it seemed completely impossible to me that anyone who knew could kill them. The only thing I could grasp onto that first night in the car was the idea of a robbery. But a robbery where people get killed? Here? It couldn't happen.

But it did. My friends were murdered by two young male strangers who wanted money to start a new life for themselves in Australia. We couldn't possibly have imagined such a thing then. And while it certainly doesn't make any sense to me more than a year later and after the perpetrators' admissions of guilt, I do now *know* that a terrible, vicious death can be inflicted on people I love. No, not just "can" happen—it's not just possible—it has happened. Right here. Right in my own backyard—or, rather, in their study. Susanne and Half were killed in their beautiful window- and book-lined study. Midday. Together. Much of this we found out later. For now I have to return myself to that horrid night because a few other things transpired that began to effect the changes in me.

Roxana answered the door. There was something about that act of the hostess answering the door. I guess in relation to what she'd just been through, the idea that she could walk to the door, open it, and hug us was reassuring. We'd enjoyed so many delicious dinners in her home. But then, to walk into the living room and see five of my closest friends without two of my closest friends was horrifying. That vision alone functioned as the dreaded confirmation that this awful thing I'd heard on the phone was true. When I looked into their faces I saw what I was on the verge of feeling but hadn't yet let myself feel. It was only then that I began to cry. I was crying for Susanne's and Half's being killed, for myself, for the sadness I felt as the news began to sink in, but I was also crying for my friends, these people in the room, who were feeling the same painful incredulity and grief. I can't remember whether the police were already there or if they arrived after we did. But at some point they questioned Roxana privately. In the meantime, Philippe and I learned more of what was known at the time.

I'm not going to repeat those details here—not because I am trying to save myself pain but rather because it seems too much like the furnishing of a crime story. And one of the hurtful lessons we learned in the wake of Susanne's and Half's murders was about the pull of crimes stories in our society, how the gory details fascinate. The murder story trumped interest in who our friends were over and over again. Each time this happened, it inflicted pain. What I do want to mention is that the first time I wrote out this narrative I broke myself off at this point, too, after listing what we had learned that night. In this case, writing out the details reminded me of the agony that started that night and continued for several weeks of trying to figure out what had happened. There was a desperation in our detective work that still upsets me to recall today. On the one hand, each detail that came out forced us into a reconstruction of the Zantops' last moments of life. Even that first night when we knew so little, it was clear that they must have experienced fear and pain. And they did not deserve to die a horrid death! On the other hand, the details exercised a magical power over us, because we each seemed to share a fantasy that, when we figured out what had happened, we would get them back. This fantasy was, of course, just that, a fantasy. And the spell it exercised over us was actually malevolent, not benevolent or even benign, because thinking through possible scenarios felt not only like living through their deaths with them, and thus losing them over and over, but also like losing the other people we put into those scenarios—and therefore losing ourselves as well. Let me explain.

That very first night, for example, after the police had questioned Roxana, they asked us as a group if we could think of anyone who would want to kill the Zantops. No, we immediately replied. The detectives asked if they could have killed each other. Well, there you have it again: we were beyond the limits of plausibility, and yet we were forced to go there. No, we cried, no couple was more loving. No, we insisted, they couldn't possibly have killed each other. No, we protested, no murder-suicide. No, we puzzled, no illness-suicide. If Half had died of a heart attack, Susanne wouldn't have killed herself out of grief. She would have thought of their daughters. No, neither had a lover. No! No! No! The very act of thinking through such possibilities was like losing a part of them, because thinking of those scenarios didn't fit with the Susanne and Half we knew. Merely posing the question somehow tore at our sense of them. The facts of their deaths (and specifically the police investigation) made us have to keep asking ourselves similar questions. For me, to think about each person I knew who knew them and to consider whether that person could have killed them were themselves transformative acts—destructive transformative acts. I connected them at the time with Jesus' stern pronouncement in the New Testament that to have looked at a woman with lust in your eye is to have committed adultery. This judgment had always puzzled me. But last year, as I thought about the possibility of each person I knew being the perpetrator of this terrible crime, the act of having the thought changed those people *and me*. I felt dirty, even evil. I need to dwell on this point, because I have come to think of this phenomenon as one type of "collateral damage" in relation to the main trauma of losing Susanne and Half. Although similar phenomena are described in memoirs and in the technical trauma literature, I am unaware of any term to name them. Another term I've coined for myself is "concomitant loss." While the details of my experience remain just that, I believe that such concomitant losses may be numerous for trauma victims and that they may constitute a significant factor in the larger issue of the changed posttraumatic self that is my topic here. One more thing about January 27, 2001, might better convey what I mean.

Just as we were departing from Roxana's house, Dick Birnie, a longtime collaborator and friend of Half and the chair of the Geology Department of which Half was a member, arrived with his wife. I didn't know Dick well, but I did know him a bit. My first reaction upon seeing him was a sharp pang of sadness for him and others who were already or shortly thereafter would be grieving: Half's friends and colleagues. The main reason

I need to mention seeing Dick, however, is that he arrived with a clue: he'd overheard an altercation between Half and a student the day before. I've already tried to explain the psychological need to do detective work, to grasp at anything that could help explain how this completely inexplicable thing had happened. But in recounting this specific detail here, I want to draw attention to the way that a group of dedicated professors could so quickly consider the possibility that a student had committed this heinous crime. Given that the two victims and the vast majority of their associates worked on a college campus, this might not seem remarkable. But it pains me to remember everything associated with this aspect of the investigation. The instant Dick mentioned what he'd seen, I myself began to think of times I'd been threatened by students. None of these threats were to harm me personally; they more often involved insinuations that students would be hurt by their parents or would hurt themselves if they didn't get a certain grade. My thoughts were racing; Dick's recital made me create the scenario of sour students killing their teachers. I must quickly add, especially for those who are not familiar with the Zantop case, that the young men who were eventually apprehended and charged with the crime were not Dartmouth undergraduates—though they did pose as students conducting an environmental survey from a particular private local secondary school to gain access into the house. However, the point about collateral damage and concomitant loss I want to make here is that the perpetrators did even more harm than they thought they did—as if the murders weren't enough. Who knows how many teachers have walked into their classes in the wake of the Zantop murders and asked themselves how many of these students could kill? I did. Of course, the spate of student gunmen in numerous public schools in the 1990s probably caused and still causes many teachers to pose this question. For me, to have asked that question is also to have forever changed the student-teacher relationship. I have lost a trust I cherished.

In addition to the initial shock, the emotions engendered by losing Susanne and Half included a roller coaster of numbness and intense grief that alternated with persistent refusals to accept that my friends were dead. There were almost paralyzing bouts of fear, especially before the suspects had been identified and apprehended. (Some of us slept with baseball bats next to our beds; some repositioned guns they owned or acquired one. I, who love the dark, slept with the light on for three months.) I despaired bordering on panic when confronted with my amnesia of people and facts I had once known. There was also the insecurity generated by never knowing what might trigger a bout of sobbing, whose length and intensity I could not control. In the first months I was selfishly afraid to come in contact with the Zantops' friends who did not live locally or had not been present during those first weeks; I found bumping into their (different) stages of grieving almost unbearably painful. Professional situations became fraught because my Dartmouth affiliation alone provoked questions about what had happened; I couldn't respond in any neutral, factual way, and I didn't want to explain that I was very close to the Zantops to people who didn't know that I was. So this situation too only produced hurt. I felt confused by my anger at friends who didn't get in touch and my inability to return the calls of those who did. I think I felt the closest to insanity when I would look into the faces of people I loved and be overpowered by a sense that they were going to die soon; sometimes I would break down weeping, sometimes I managed to hold myself together until the conviction faded a bit. Very little related to my teaching, research, or normal leisure activities could rouse my interest. This apathy began to dissipate in early September, as I settled in Berlin to prepare for running a study abroad program. Before I return to my starting point of September 11, however, I need to describe that person in Berlin and how she was different from the woman spending a quiet evening at home with her husband on January 27.

THE CHANGED SELF

The first change I consciously registered in myself was the attitude that I need to be ready to die at any moment. Given that, especially initially, we had no idea why the Zantops had been killed, that the killers were on the loose, and that my own profile as well as that of most of my friends were very similar to theirs, it makes a certain amount of sense that we thought we could be the next target. But the attitude I developed and still have has more to do with the swiftness of their deaths. One moment they were there making lunch, and the next moment they were not. The particular manner of their deaths also preoccupied me. Will I be numb with fear or will I be able to pray in my last minutes? Will I fight or will I be still? If I get sick, will I become depressed or will I accept my physical state? This could sound morbid, but I don't experience it that way. I experience my running through of various scenarios as realistic and helpful preparation for the inevitable—not an inevitably violent or tragic death but simply an inevitable last moment of my life. Frequently at first but still today, I ask myself about the present moment: is it a good one? Such thoughts have led me to be vigilant about attending to relationships; if in the next instant my life will be over, I want to leave as much felicity behind as possible. Similarly, I try to take any unpleasant situation I might be in and to discover some beautiful or positive aspect of it, because, again, if it's going to be my last moment in this world, I don't want to have spent it in frustration or anger. This attitude fits well, I suppose, with my transformed sense of the future.

I became (and remain) incapable of thinking that I know anything about the future. Losing Susanne and Half the way we did made it so incontestable to me that one simply cannot know what is going to happen next. On the most mundane level, I recall having essentially every hour of that last weekend in January 2001 scheduled with activities from Friday morning to late Monday night. I distinctly remember running through the list in my head on Thursday evening: teaching, tennis, grocery shopping, dinner with Philippe, house hunting, quiet evening at home, church, a birthday brunch, a Super Bowl party, a mammogram, lunch with a younger faculty member, a television show. I was determined to keep everything low-stress, but it didn't occur to me for one second that things wouldn't unfold approximately as planned. Well, that Saturday night phone call cancelled not only all plans but the idea of planning itself. Admittedly, I am finally back to making lists of things to do, but each list carries an invisible, insistent proviso—"if I'm around."

When the reality sunk in that Susanne and Half truly were dead, I realized how much my sense of the longer-term future had vanished. There are the specific ways in which whatever sense I had had of the shape of the rest of my life was wrapped up with them personally because of the deep friendship I had with each of them and the close professional association I had with Susanne. But there was also the way the act of murder, my cognizance of evil as a local force, led to a transformation of my sense that I will live out my life and the world will go on after me. I no longer remember at what stage the thought crystallized, but at some point I realized that this "new" feeling was actually not new but a reemergence of my conviction as a child of the cold war that nuclear war could make my world disappear at any moment. Somehow there had been a luminous, hopeful phase in between.

I was also aware since childhood that murders are not a rare occurrence in the United States. But I myself had never lost a loved one to murder before—only to illness. Murder became real to me in a way that it simply hadn't been before losing Susanne and Half. Losing a loved one to murder entails a very different kind of grieving process. While I still cannot fathom for myself what state a human mind must get itself into to thrust a knife into another human being, I have played this scene in my head over and over again. And I now *know*—in a way that doesn't just have to do with my brain—that humans kill humans by any number of means. Though I had been researching and teaching the Holocaust for more than a decade, the quality of murder committed literally millions of times over in that genocide and others became real to me in a way that it simply had not been, and I believe could not have been, prior to the Zantops' murder. The fact that the perpetrators of the Zantops' murder were so young, grew up in a town so very similar to so many towns around here, and look like so many young adult males one sees every day impressed on me this knowledge that humans, not monsters, kill. I don't want to be misunderstood on this point. Violence is evil. But what I believe I learned, the way this experience changed me, was by forcing myself to understand that murderous violence is human; it is potentially in every one of us and therefore also everywhere.

<h2 style="text-align:center">9/11/01 = 1/27/01</h2>

It was this knowledge of evil that led me to "recognize" the planes flying into buildings as humans killing other humans. While I could no better get into the heads of the hijacker-terrorists than into those of the Zantops' murderers, I felt that the essence of the two crimes was the same even if the scale was so profoundly different. That's why the images from New York and Washington instantly transported me from autumn in Berlin to winter in New Hampshire. That's how 9/11/01 came quickly to equal 1/27/01. For this reason, I found myself alienated in the next days from most others around me who couldn't believe what had happened. I read in the bewilderment of my local German friends and even more so in the shocked question—why do they hate us?—that was repeatedly broadcast from the United States to all corners of the world not only political naiveté but, more especially, ignorance and disbelief about evil. I couldn't share in this ignorance and disbelief, though I did share in the overwhelming sadness; for me, "it" had happened again. What had seemed completely impossible on January 27, 2001, but had become part of my everyday reality had taken new victims— not only those individuals who had died but also those perhaps countless individuals who would no longer be allowed to believe in a benevolent world. An image came to me of Holocaust survivor Edith P., who at the end of her videotaped testimony about her own experiences (given in February 1980) grieves for Cambodia. She speaks of her feelings of impotence and guilt, lamenting that the world has not learned the lesson of the Holocaust. She testifies to how terribly that ignorance pains her.

<h2 style="text-align:center">HEALING?</h2>

To the question of individual healing, Susan Brison has given the most articulate and honest answer I know: "People ask me if I'm recovered now, and I reply that it depends on what that means. If they mean 'am I back to where I was before the attack?' I have to say, no, and I never will be. . . .

But if recovery means being able to incorporate this awful knowledge into my life and carry on, then, yes, I'm recovered" (2001, 21). Brison makes clear that the knowledge acquired during the traumatic encounter changes the individual and that there is simply no retrieving the pretraumatized self. One can go on, however, and Brison affirms that "Sometimes I even manage to enjoy myself" (21). Taking Brison's point one step further, I have posited that this "awful knowledge" possessed by the posttraumatic self can profoundly influence how one reacts to new traumatic events, near or remote, individual or collective. And I have suggested that this knowledge may retraumatize one (as it did some of those New Yorkers surveyed by Galea et al. [2002, see esp. table 2]) or it may help one register the reality of a new calamity faster, as I believe it helped me on September 11.

To my mind, no answer is as satisfactory as Brison's when one considers the question of healing from *collective* trauma. Judith Herman admonishes that "remembering and telling the truth about terrible events are prerequisites both for the restoration of the social order and for the healing of individual victims" ([1992] 1997, 1). I take hers as the best action plan available, vague though it might be. Holocaust survivors and researchers have talked and written eloquently about the need to tell.[3] That telling does not necessarily give much relief to the survivor, and, as Edith P. observed, it doesn't appear to prevent the reoccurrence of genocide. Yet, who knows what hateful person who might have become a perpetrator did not do so because of something she or he learned from a witness to atrocity? Edith P. herself gives testimony in the hope that it might make some difference. Telling about suffering seems better than denying it.[4]

As I've already recounted, some of us who were close friends of the Zantops began to get together even before we could really "speak." Susanne and Half had loved so many people that one of their (intended?) legacies was the sense of commitment we felt to one another. In the course of the next days, weeks, and, for some of us, months, the Zantops' close friends, the college community, family members, and colleagues from other places gathered in various configurations and forums to share their grief and fear, to comfort one another, and to commemorate Susanne and Half. To give just one example, some of their numerous local friends marked the one-year anniversary of their deaths by publishing two pages of anecdotes about them in our local paper (see "Susanne and Half Zantop" 2002). As for me, even though my grieving did require professional attention, I believe that my recovery was aided enormously by these various forms of "telling." With the help of a supportive family, group of friends, priest, and psychotherapist, I did not try to rein in my grief. For perhaps the first time in my life I was able to turn down the volume a notch on my own self-criticism and just accept what was happening to me, accept the emotions that seemed to be running my life. I have already mentioned that, through Susanne's and Half's deaths, violence became real to me in a way and to a degree that it never had been before. I've long considered myself a pacifist—maybe that's the burden of being named Irene, which means "peace" in Greek—but since January 27, 2001, I have come to feel even more strongly that any act of violence is wrong. Forcing myself to do things can be a sort of violence. And so, a large part of my personal healing has involved registering any thought or act that feels like self-coercion and then desisting from it. This is in part why I have not told this story until now. Previous attempts have felt too unbearable to complete. Even this attempt, I observe, displays signs of trauma, such as phobia of the events (I note my lengthy preliminaries) and the inability to tell of the events concisely (I note that my essay is considerably longer than others in the volume).

Though I have only been in Washington DC once and New York a handful of times since the September 11 attacks, it seems to me that many venues have been created for people to commemorate their loved ones, to share their grief, and to express their sorrow. I myself have found the *New York Times*' "Portraits of Grief" section moving and helpful. I have not heard anything about how close relatives of the victims have experienced this particular mode of memorialization—surely inadequate for their needs—but I am struck by the role this one thing can play for the community at large. As legal scholar Martha Minow suggests in an analysis of contemporary (pre-9/11) North American society, to decide "whose suffering we care about" is also to "define ourselves and our communities" (1993, 1445). These portraits have helped make each individual vivid to those of us who might otherwise feel only a general sadness about anonymous fellow citizens. The portraits' form, particularly their brevity, disallows a "claim of false intimacy" and yet contributes to Morrison's early gesture of throwing a thread between the victims' humanity and ours. Who else's suffering we decide to care about in our post-9/11 world is still an open question.

NOTES

1. Similarly, it is anathema to me to think that some people might interpret the gesture of this essay as claiming some special right to grieve for Susanne and Half Zantop. I loved them very much, and they showered me with affection. But that's not the point. The very process of mourning for them myself has shown me that one cannot predict who will grieve, how, and to what extent.

2. See, for example, Wigren's patients Hugh and Kathi (1994, 418–21); on the problematic of "seeing and trauma," consult Herr 1978, 20; and Caruth 1996, 28–29.

3. The literature on this subject is voluminous. Primo Levi's memoir, *Survival in Auschwitz* ([1958] 1961), and Lawrence L. Langer's *Holocaust Testimonies: The Ruins of Memory* (1991) are good places to start.

4. In my own scholarly work I have argued for testifying to traumas described in and enacted through literary writing. Even though literary witnessing can change no historical fact, it can contribute to social healing by implicitly expressing the judgment that those things depicted were wrong and that we currently endorse a value system that considers such actions crimes (Kacandes 2001, 113, 139).

Works Cited

American Psychiatric Association (APA). 1980. *Diagnostic and Statistical Manual of Mental Disorders*. 3d ed. Washington DC: American Psychiatric Association.

———. 1994. *Diagnostic and Statistical Manual of Mental Disorders*. 4th ed. Washington DC: American Psychiatric Association.

Baruch G., Rabbi. Edited Testimony. A-50. Fortunoff Video Archive for Holocaust Testimonies. Yale University Library, New Haven CT.

Brison, Susan. 1999. "The Uses of Narrative in the Aftermath of Violence." In *On Feminist Ethics and Politics*, ed. Claudia Card, 200–225. Lawrence: University of Kansas Press.

———. 2001. *Aftermath: Violence and the Remaking of a Self.* Princeton NJ: Princeton University Press.

Caruth, Cathy, ed. 1995. *Trauma: Explorations in Memory*. Baltimore: Johns Hopkins University Press. Originally published as "Psychoanalysis, Culture and Trauma" *American Imago* 48, nos. 1 and 4 (1991).

———. 1996. *Unclaimed Experience: Trauma, Narrative, and History*. Baltimore: Johns Hopkins University Press.

Edith P. Edited Testimony. A-539. Fortunoff Video Archive for Holocaust Testimonies. Yale University Library, New Haven CT.

Felman, Shoshana, and Dori Laub. 1992. *Testimony: Crises of Witnessing in Literature, Psychoanalysis, and History*. New York: Routledge.

Galea, Sandro, et al. 2002. "Psychological Sequelae of the September 11 Terrorist Attacks in New York City." *New England Journal of Medicine* 346, no. 13 (March 28): 982–87.

Goode, Erica. 2002. "Thousands in Manhattan Needed Therapy after Attack, Study Finds." *New York Times*, March 28, A15.

Herman, Judith Lewis. [1992] 1997. *Trauma and Recovery*. New York: BasicBooks.

Herr, Michael. 1978. *Dispatches*. New York: Avon.

Kacandes, Irene. 2001. *Talk Fiction: Literature and the Talk Explosion*. Lincoln: University of Nebraska Press.

Langer, Lawrence L. 1991. *Holocaust Testimonies: The Ruins of Memory*. New Haven: Yale University Press.

Levi, Primo. [1958] 1961. *Survival in Auschwitz*. Trans. Stuart Wolf. New York: Macmillan.

Minow, Martha. 1993. "Surviving Victim Talk." *UCLA Law Review* 40:1411–45.

Morrison, Toni. 2001. "The Dead of September 11." *Vanity Fair*. Special Supplement, November, 49.

"Portraits of Grief." *New York Times*. http://www.nytimes.com/portraits.

Root, Maria P. 1996. "Women of Color and Traumatic Stress in 'Domestic Captivity': Gender and Race as Disempowering Statuses." In *Ethnocultural Aspects of Posttraumatic Stress Disorder: Issues, Research, and Clinical Applications*, ed. Anthony J. Marsella et al., 363–87. Washington DC: American Psychological Association.

"Susanne and Half Zantop: In Memoriam: The Imprints of Two Lost Friends and Colleagues." 2002. *Valley News,* Jan. 27, C1, 10.

Wigren, Jodie. 1994. "Narrative Completion in the Treatment of Trauma." *Psychotherapy* 31, no. 3: 415–23.

6. Working Through

Rubble as Archive, or 9/11 as Dust, Debris, and Bodily Vanishing

Patricia Yaeger

At the close of World War II American B29 bombers dropped 1,665 tons of napalm bombs on Tokyo, "leaving almost nothing standing over 16 square miles." Although the death toll exceeded that of Nagasaki, this event disappeared with astonishing speed from American and Japanese memories, and yet the scale of death and destruction was enormous. Ikuyo Misu wept as she remembered her escape: "Ever since then, there have been parts of Tokyo I can't bear to visit. . . . The next day, the bodies were splayed on the ground everywhere you looked, just like mannequins, but blackened. You couldn't tell male from female" (French 4).

The inability to distinguish, to tell body from body or flesh from rubble, has also marked American responses to 9/11. Governor Pataki refused to clean the shoes he wore on his first trip to ground zero. "They were caked with the gray glue-like substance that sticks to everyone who wades through the debris," Christy Ferer, the wife of one of the World Trade Center victims, explains. "This, to me, is like the ashes of the dead" (A21). How do we think about "gray glue-substance" and "the ashes of the dead" simultaneously? What range of stories are people generating about the matter that clings to the governor's feet?

The materials of the World Trade Center have been coercively discarded: the remaining two-million-ton pile of debris forced us to encounter a formally built environment as its components—as lost labor, lost structure. But to think of the bodies of the dead mingling with this debris, to think of the results of the 9/11 explosions as detritus, gives one pause. In the documentary *9/11* by Jules and Gedeon Naudet, one of the firefighters exclaims, "You have two 110 story office buildings. You don't find a desk, you don't find a chair, you don't find a computer; the biggest piece of a telephone I found was a keypad, and it was this big. The building collapsed to dust. How are we supposed to find anybody in this stuff—there's nothing left of the building." How do we respond to trauma when the only thing left is "stuff"?

In *Testimony* Dori Laub says that the experience of trauma "leaves no hiding place intact." The experience of survival demands that we condense our sensibilities; it forces survivors and their listeners to think about "a great many existential questions that we manage to avoid in our daily living, often through preoccupation with the trivial" (72). But post-9/11 Americans have encountered a world sheathed in the trivial, in what has been variously labeled as "rubble," "dust," "debris," "ruins," "detritus," "wreckage," "dirt," "powder," "waste," or "cartage." How do we contemplate a trauma cradled in all this "stuff"? What rites of passage does debris undergo in the many stories that bear witness to trauma?

In *Rubbish Theory* Michael Thompson defines rubbish as the zero degree of value. As the nadir of usefulness, as any economy's lowest point, rubbish acquires an aura of invisibility that recreates trash as the neutral backdrop or transfer point between two other categories of value: "the transient" (consumer goods as they change status, skidding from object of desire to kipple: things marching toward decay on a path of decreasing value) and "the durable" (objects like works of art, whose value endures or escalates). Within this triumvirate—rubbish, transient objects, and durable goods—meanings can shift abruptly. As Thompson explains, "the rubbish to durable transition is an all-or-nothing transfer. An object cannot gradually slide across from one category to the other as is the case with the transient to rubbish transfer" (26). This transition breaches boundaries separating "the worthless" from "the valuable." The polluting qualities of rubbish completely disappear, and the object collects aesthetic or sacred value.

This transition from rubbish to transcendence describes a first-order response to the phantasmatic piles of debris haunting ground zero: namely, the impulse to convert this detritus into something hallowed and new. When profiteers pilfered and then sold the Twin Towers' remains to grief-stricken relatives, officials called in a ceremonial unit of the police department to repackage this material as ceremonial debris. Blessed on site by a chaplain, the powdered remains of the World Trade Center were shoveled into fifty-five-pound drums and taken to One Police Plaza by police escort. Flanked by honor guards and covered with American flags, these drums became a ritual source of ash to be spooned into polished cherry mahogany urns and bestowed upon victims' families at a memorial service a month after the attack. The preparations for moving this debris from flag-covered drum to urn were highly ritualized. The urns could only be handled with gloved hands—each urn placed in a blue velvet bag inside a dark box. But in the *New York Times*' description of this ritualized process, we find, once again, an uneasiness, an awkwardness or nervousness, with this strange sense of residue: "An officer scoops a large spoonful of soil into a plastic bag. The soil, brown with a slightly grayish cast, is unhealthy in appearance. It crunches slightly when the spoon is placed in it, and is thick enough that the spoon stands on its own" (Waldman B11). This is dirt that bites back, that does not lend itself to the cleanliness of ceremony.

This resistance to transformation—a refusal to find within detritus either a hoard of the transcendent or the sacred qualities of the durable—suggests a second-order response to the World Trade Center's remains: the deeply felt nausea associated with rubbish. In "Down the Drain: Shit and the Politics of Disturbance" Gay Hawkins describes the sanitary social body that has become a Western ideal. "Encounters with the 'ugly face of what ends' unsettle boundaries. . . . The hint of shit [or death and debris] in a public space doesn't just call the self into question but technologies of governance, faith in the infrastructure. The belief that systems for waste removal will efficiently protect us" from injurious knowledge about where refuse really goes is one method for shoring up our need to maintain a category of objects "without value" and to keep those objects concealed (33). But since, in the cacophony of 9/11, the bodies that allow us to mourn have vanished, or merged with polluted air, or simply turned into construction debris, the media has been compelled to elaborate stories out of leftovers, to foreground the World Trade Center as dusty remains.

I am particularly haunted by a picture in the *New York Times* that shows a worker standing in big yellow boots, his face covered with a red plastic face mask, his body swathed in an industrial jumpsuit, a platoon of shovels behind him as he stands like a moonwalker, confronting an eerie landscape covered with debris. This is Fresh Kills landfill on Staten Island, the site where much of the detritus from the World Trade Center has gone to be sorted and recycled or thrown away: a strange place to store the dead. "It gets cold up here. When the wind shifts, it smells like what it is, a half-century's worth of trash" (Barry and Waldman A1).

Food or bathroom breaks require decontamination for workers looking for "bits and pieces" of people's bodies or lives "among thousands of tons of dull-gray pieces of debris that have been carted from the World Trade Center disaster site." After a backhoe lays out debris piles—half as long as a football field—to be raked, thirty investigators move in one another's direction, "raking and poking the grayish matter as they walk along." Usually they find nothing, and the sanitation workers take over. The desire to keep things separate, "to coordinate the piles of debris in exact relation to downtown streets," remains impossible. "I defy anyone to tell me where everything came from," an inspector intones. Workers watching the conveyor belt for too long get motion sickness; fighting vertigo, these workers are repaid with a few body parts, a credit card, photo I.D.s. Across the water, they can see "the luminous towers still rising from Lower Manhattan. 'It is a beautiful sight,' Lt. Bovino said. 'You can almost forget you're in a landfill'" (Barry and Waldman A1, B11).

Lieutenant Bovino's forgetting suggests a third response to the detritus left by 9/11, namely, a mode of shape-shifting debris that alters under the pressure of divergent emotions. Again we bear witness to an oscillation in the value of rubble as it fluctuates from sheer matter to the stuff of mourning to debris as polluting agent or antimatter, but this time the detritus itself quakes with the power of the uncanny. In October 2001 the executive director of Cross-Cultural Solutions, Steven Rosenthal, was serving meals for workers at ground zero when he told a *New York Times* reporter that, for him, the procession of family members mourning their dead had become the most powerful image to define the disaster since the horror of the explosions themselves. "It is easy to work down there and just see it as a big pile of steel and a construction problem and forget that it is a grave for thousands of people," he said. But while some families are eager to visit "the pile" to give their grief a habitus, others "cannot contemplate setting foot anywhere near what they regard as a mass grave or a killing field" (Murphy B10). "To me it is unbearable to imagine a loved one under all that debris," said Lynne Cillo-Capaido, whose twin sister worked on the ninety-seventh floor of One World Trade Center and has not been found. But when another victim's sibling, Frank Saiya, applied for a death certificate for his brother Edward (who "made it to the roof of Two World Trade Center but was swept away when the building collapsed"), Saiya told reporters that he found surprising comfort in the twenty pounds of rubble that a friend managed to pick up for him. "He became part of that building when it came down," said Saiya, who lives in Topeka, Kansas. "I choose to believe that there may be one speck of Ed in that rubble" (Murphy B10).

If the zero degree of rubble permits a sense of variable remains—of detritus that becomes, for its different viewers, neutral, intolerable, or a source of comfort—a fourth way of defining the World Trade Center wreckage emerges in Saiya's affection for the one speck of his brother that may remain: a sense of detritus as a space that gathers corporeality, of rubble as a site where bodily trauma passes through. The stories that both cameramen and firefighters tell in the documentary *9/11* capture this sense of dust or debris as both source and origin of bodily fragility—as dead matter that can also kill. In the rain of debris that followed the collapse of the second tower, the French cameraman who captured the firefighters' worry and bravery inside the towers fell to the ground (I felt "someone jumping on top of me and then the dust"), his camera focused randomly on a piece of paper and then on debris in the air, an aftermath of small, drifting, floating, blowing particles. Another firefighter described the impact of the second collapse: "You heard the ground rumble and debris was just chasing you," while someone else remembered the mingling of rubble and body parts: "That whole day I searched through rubble. The roof of the Marriott, we were on the roof of the Marriott. There were parts all over the place—legs, feet." The cameraman remembers his ordeal in the lobby: "First it was debris falling and then it was people falling. It was not something you could get used to and the sound was so loud." After the first tower collapsed, "this white powder [was] everywhere." Detritus is frightening and animated. Is it rubble or body part? World Trade Center debris gains both the animation of blood and the killing power of a weapon.

Oddly, even the shrines consecrated to 9/11's victims have acquired the weird corporeality we associate with bodily remains. A local museum decided to provide a permanent home for makeshift memorials at risk to weather or decay, and "the exhibition's artifacts have posed a daunting set of conservatorial issues never before encountered. . . . Disintegrating shrine constituents include dried flowers, cracking pain, yellowing missing posters, mold-incubating plush toys and unstable adhesives" (Collins A21). On every side we encounter the terrors of disintegration; this disaster has left few objects and fewer bodies, but what is left trembles with instability.

In this genealogy of the World Trade Center as ruins, a fifth way of narrating this residue emerges. David Halperin has insisted that "nothing that retains value qualifies as waste" (6). But the dilemma of this disaster has been to keep the fact of waste and its re-creation as value constantly in mind. The detritus of 9/11 evokes, for most Americans, deep reservoirs of personal and cultural sadness. The residue left from each explosion stirs up the fact of bodily vanishing. It also suggests the lost work, the fallen labor that went into the making of such massive buildings. "Rather than old clothes and tattered furniture, acres of misshapen girders and beams from the wreckage of the World Trade Center lie piled up on Staten Island to be cut for scrap and sold" (Glanz A19). Misshapen beams evoke the connection of metal remains to lost work or production. Detritus and work go hand in hand. We find junkyards, recycling centers, and scrap heaps across continents because what we make produces an excess or leftover that becomes—in a time of global profligacy—more poignant and coercive when we throw it away.

"Stacked as neatly as possible in a separate place, hundreds of vehicles that were smashed in the buildings' collapse—passenger cars, police cruisers, ambulances and fire trucks slumping next to what is left of their hook-and-ladders—will almost certainly end up in the maw of a scrap-yard shredder themselves. . . . Slightly lower on the hill, the great beams and columns of the trade center lie in stacks as much as thirty feet high. The steel is bent and torn in ways that veteran scrapmen find shocking. 'You don't see this—ever,'" says the manager of a scrap metal firm that will cut beams for recycling. The beams are molded like licorice twists, the wreckage personified: "as this destroyed metal waits for an appointment with a shredder or smelter or perhaps another landfill, it is thoughts about those who died that will endure" (Glanz A19).

If the residue of the World Trade Center has been variously narrated as the sacred, as nausea, as the uncanny, as corporeality, as a remnant of the lost work of production, then each speck of debris also suggests this narrative function: each part-object or crumpled portfolio offers an archive for exploring an era already vanished, opens a frightening portal into the past. "To the extent that wreckage advertises itself as a residue or trace of the past, its materiality also possesses a manifestly diachronic component. We understand junk here not simply as the material property of its setting . . . but also as a portal that opens up to alternate temporalities in which may be glimpsed otherwise forgotten historical processes" (Harris and Neill 69). In the rhetoric grappling with what should or should not be included in 9/11's memorials, the promise is that the World Trade Center's rubble will open another dimension in the crease of the real. In search of these portals, every architecture critic seems to champion a different building part for monumentalization. Before the crumpled facade was fully disassembled, Herbert Muschamp declaimed: "Clearly the walls have become a landmark, whether or not we choose to preserve them. Even if the decision is made to remove them, they can no longer be treated as junk. . . . And it does seem weird that a city now thought to be so deeply protective of its history should look the other way as a big chunk of history disappears" (37).

Numerous memorials use the remains of disaster to make a diachronic opening in the present to summon the power of the dead. In America the most powerful of these may be the Civil Rights Museum in Memphis—built on the site where, on a visit supporting the local sanitation workers' strike, Martin Luther King was assassinated. The museum offers a historical overview of the civil rights movement spanning every epoch of American history. But the last room of the museum moves every viewer into lowly, sad space: into the minimalist 1960s décor that adorns the room King slept in before his death. We peer at the balcony where he was shot, squint to see the bloodstains that docents claim are still there. This motel-room-under-glass suggests an odd conflation of debris and death. The exhibit just before the motel room tenders a full-scale replica of the sanitation workers' strike. A huge orange garbage truck towers over the workers who surround it, a line of men wearing placards that say, "I AM A MAN." Next to these protestors, plaster casts of National Guardsmen protect city turf, menacing black men with their rifles. And spewing out of the big truck, covering the ground, we see refuse: the uncollected, undisposed-of garbage of Memphis: excessive, potentially smelly, offensive.

This cacophonous focus on an orange truck that refuses a city's leftovers creates a strange scene of chaos and fear. What we see is too orange; there are too many strewn-about objects; this rubbish is an ominous, powerful sign of work stoppage, of the power, even in the midst of squalor, for every man of color to say to the world and to his white employers: "I AM A MAN." As you walk from this trash-strewn scene to the window facing Dr. King's room, on a table so close you could touch it if the glass were not there, is more refuse, the leftovers from a meal Dr. King just consumed, a tray covered with plates, saucers, half-eaten toast, crumbs, crumpled napkins: a meal in disarray.

The juxtaposition is unexpectedly powerful. The huge truck, the line of men, the rifles: each gives a momentary sense of the scale, the menace that King and other protestors were facing. But the imagined odor, the stench of the leftover, the mess and chaos of the lives of sanitation workers not paid a decent wage, re-creates the anger one needs to breath while confronting the pain of shared history. How does one cope with devaluation and with the body's vanishing? This odd concatenation of trauma and trash, death and debris continues in the aftermath of 9/11. Should we preserve the World Trade Center's great walls with their monumental unshapeliness? If we do this, will we also find space to remember the everyday world of detritus that these lost buildings, so filled with lost people, became?

WORKS CITED

Barry, Dan, and Amy Waldman. "At Landfill, Sifting Mountains of Debris for Slivers of Solace." *New York Times*, Oct. 21, 2001, A1, B11.

Collins, Glenn. "Impromptu Shrines Expressed a City's Grief." *New York Times*, Mar. 8, 2002, A21.

Ferer, Christy. "Unforgotten Soldiers." *New York Times*, Oct. 25, 2001, A21.

French, Howard. "100,000 People Perished, but Who Remembers?" *New York Times,* Mar. 14, 2002, A4.

Glanz, James. "Mounds of Twisted Steel Silently Evoke the Dead." *New York Times,* Oct. 1, 2001, A19.

Halperin, David. "Out of Australia." *UTS Review: Waste* 7 (2001): 3–8.

Harris, Jonathan Gil, and Anna Neill. "Hollywood's Pacific Junk: The Wreckage of Colonial History in *Six Days and Seven Nights* and *Rapa Nui.*" *UTS Review: Waste* 7 (2001): 68–85.

Hawkins, Gay. "Down the Drain: Shit and the Politics of Disturbance." *UTS Review: Waste* 7 (2001): 32–42.

Laub, Dori, and Shoshana Felman. *Testimony: Crises of Witnessing in Literature, Psychoanalysis, and History.* New York: Routledge, 1992.

Murphy, Dean. "Slowly, Families Accept the Ruins as Burial Ground." *New York Times,* Sept. 29, 2001, B1, 10.

Muschamp, Herbert. "The Commemorative Beauty of Tragic Wreckage." *New York Times,* Nov. 11, 2001, 37.

Naudet, Jules and Gedeon. *9/11.* New York: CBS, 2002. Documentary.

Thompson, Michael. *Rubbish Theory: The Creation and Destruction of Value.* Oxford: Oxford University Press, 1979.

Waldman, Amy. "With Solemn Detail, Dust of Ground Zero Is Put in Urns." *New York Times,* Oct. 15, 2001, B11.

A Not So Temporary Occupation
inside Ground Zero

Donna Bassin

September 11 led me away from the text and the relatively protected space of the consulting room to the site of ground zero, where

> the unmentionable odor of death
> offends the September night.
> –W. H. Auden, "September 1, 1939"

All of us have been forced to attend to the multitude of losses directly created by the attack on the World Trade Center and/or to prior losses that have been merely reawoken and exposed by this trauma.

July 2001—A Personal Middle East

My family and I traveled to Egypt to commemorate my fiftieth birthday. Before my grandfather died, I had promised I would try to find the gravesite of Victorine, my Egyptian-born great aunt, buried without family in Cairo shortly after my birth. The Jewish cemetery was filled with trash, the marble gravestones stolen to decorate storefronts in Cairo. Without identifying markers, Victorine would remain missing, one of thousands of anonymous Jews in the cemetery.

I felt robbed. Yet days later I became the robber. Given the opportunity to buy an ancient relic, I took it, trying to deny the reality of loss, and transported it illegally out of the country. An evil eye for an evil eye.

As tourists, we came to see the ancient sites of the pharaohs' power and the commanding mosques of the Moslem faith. Everywhere we went we were approached with open palms for *baksheesh*. We dug into our pockets with annoyance and exasperation, paying the penalty of being Americans abroad. Eventually the painful discrepancy between our resources and those asking for money was impossible to ward off. *Baksheesh* means "share the wealth" and is, as we came to understand, a legitimate request from those whose wealth resides mostly in their homeland's history and beauty.

Large portions of Islamic communities around the world have been depleted by repressive political regimes, military violence, acts of torture and sexual assault, forced relocation, the loss of loved ones, and the ongoing deprivations from a lack of the basic essentials such as food and shelter.

SEPTEMBER 11, 8:56 A.M.

The first plane hit the World Trade Center. A few weeks later Osama bin Laden stated in a frightening videotaped message to the United States: "America has been filled with horror from north to south and east to west, and thanks are to God. What America is tasting now is only a copy of what we have tasted. Our Islamic nation has been tasting the same for more than eighty years of humiliation and disgrace. Its sons killed, and their blood spilled, its sanctities desecrated." Bin Laden, "the face of evil and the enemy incarnate," and the Al Qaeda network forced us to share and directly witness in our nation the anguish, deprivation, trauma, and terror others have suffered for generations. Vengeful attacks legitimized in the name of "sons killed" bypass the difficult task of working through loss. When terror, revenge, and/or robbery (my own) are used in the name of traumatic loss, the dead are perversely used rather than mourned.

SHORTLY AFTER SEPTEMBER 11

New Yorkers were in a state of anxious uncertainty; conversations were sparse, words failed to comfort. A patient of mine feared that the city was having a collective nervous breakdown. Long walls of missing person posters populated the city. We waited for news of survivors. Many heard echoes of their own past and present grief in the acts of public mourning. Many of my own patients who had not lost family or close friends in the September 11 attacks expressed, with shame, their envy of the families who had, because those victims, they felt, had legitimate reasons to grieve and an external environment in ruins that mirrored the inner world of a mourner. These patients struggled with what they experienced as more invisible and "objectionable" losses, such as the loss of security and the illusion of immortality.

Bereaved families tried to protect their dead from the anonymity of being a statistic, turning these posters into memorials. Those who viewed them could not retreat into an abstraction as they were confronted with the names and images of the beloved missing and dead.

Grief fueled other activities of mourning as well. Volunteers did what they could at ground zero or by giving blood, making donations, offering prayers. Mourning is really not about getting rid of the dead or the past, as an overly concrete reading of Freud might suggest. Rather, and in part, it seems to be an attempt to manage intense grief and to activate the constantly recycling process of deconstructing the lost other(s) in their idealized singularity and reconstructing them internally in all their complexity, individuality, and separateness. Ritual activities and ceremonies can support this loving task of memorializing, a lifelong process of reinscribing memory.

SEPTEMBER 25

The mayor's language describing the activity at ground zero began to shift. No longer hopeful, his tone registered deep notes of despair. All expectations of rescue and even confidence in the recovery of bodies dimmed. New York City's Department of Mental Health called me to join a small problem-solving group whose task included the facilitation of bereavement for the victims' families. We all faced many challenges. How could family members mourn without a body? What could the city do to facilitate the families' painful acceptance of the reality that their loved ones were dead? Would the process of mourning become more difficult, even traumatic, if they were confronted with ground zero?

RESEARCH AT GROUND ZERO

My experience *inside* ground zero was visceral. The word "inside" is important in my attempt at description, because even a temporary occupation within ground zero is different from the experience of viewing the site from without, as an object, as something other. I traveled to ground zero with the first group of families who were ready to acknowledge that their loved ones were dead, not missing, and were willing to accept a death certificate. We traveled down the Hudson River by water ferry from the Family Crisis Center at Pier 94 to the western bank of the World Trade Center district. We rode mostly in silence. On board were the mayor, clergy, the Red Cross, mental health counselors, community police, and fifty family members of those who were killed. All of us were briefed about what we would see, but language could not capture what we experienced. Family members were given face masks, tissues, flowers, and a stuffed animal. While the face masks and tissues were for the living, the flowers and stuffed animals were for the dead. Did any of us believe that these objects could stand up to a life lost or could assuage the anger we imagined the dead must feel? When it was time for us to return to the ferry, it was difficult for some to leave. One mother told me how painful it was to be at ground zero. If her son had to die there, she explained, she could at least stand there and be with him. One woman wanted to leave a blanket for her daughter. This mother knew her daughter was dead, but there was still a wish to comfort and protect her.

Being inside this violated and dismembered space of ground zero evoked terror and anguish. I lost all sense of scale, of embodiment, all sense of myself as a human being with resources. It felt like life in a nightmare that is real. The rubble screams the collapse of individuality, security, and mastery that is impossible to represent. Words don't suffice, because the experience taps into helplessness known before words can be uttered to represent and contain experience. It is all gray at ground zero. Life becomes not a range of color but only its absence.

I had a nightmare that evening: My life was in danger. I was in a holocaust of sorts. I was trying to fill a backpack up with supplies, and the container kept breaking open. I looked around the room and saw only blank faces.

What is useful in the mind's attempts to return to the images of trauma? Is there something reassuring about recognizing a reality outside one's own subjectivity, even when that reality is profoundly traumatic? There is a need to replay and reconstruct our understanding of what hate can do. We need to try to discover something that may always remain undiscoverable or unidentifiable, but, nevertheless, the attempt to make some comprehensible narrative continues even in sleep. I began to confront my anxiety of losing my grip as a designated driver on this ride and my dismay at the lack of useful psychoanalytic texts. Despite the frequency in which mourning appears in our literature, those texts felt rather thin.

By the Middle of October

For most of the families of the New York victims of September 11, there were no corporal remains to be found and properly buried. How then could the bereaved bury their beloved dead with the kind of burial their traditions supported? After the crash of TWA flight 800, families filled empty coffins with the belongings, letters, and mementos of their loved ones. Some included debris from the crash. In New York, a decision was made to provide each bereaved family with a wooden urn containing cremated remains of the rubble: "dust" from ground zero. The urns would be presented after a memorial service at the site.

October 25

Under the direction of the Port Authority of New York and New Jersey, some of the rubble left from the September 11 attack is being tagged for future archival use. Although these material remains are mute, their shape and silence testify to the impact of what happened. They will always remember, but how will future generations read them? Will they become symbols of what hate can do?

Perhaps much of the individual and collective activity of finding literal and metaphoric remains of September 11 can be partially understood as an attempt to co-construct a comprehendible narrative from bits and pieces. We sensed growing concern and heard overheated discussions regarding the nature of a memorial at the site. What wishes and fears underlie the process of making the all too present event a part of our past? Did we want to bury our dead so we could attend to the living? So we could remove ourselves from our terror of death? So we could attempt to keep alive the task of remembering as much as we tried to forget?

At the end of *Maus*, Art Spiegelman calls his father a murderer after discovering that his father destroyed his mother's wartime memoirs without ever reading them. I imagine that Spiegelman experienced his father's relentless preoccupation with his tormenters and his grief not only as a way to avoid the work of mourning but also as a way to obliterate the memories he and his wife held from the war. Despite the son's own experience of being a victim, he becomes the perpetrator when he calls his father a murderer. Neither father nor son can, seemingly for the purpose of individual survival, allow mourning to reconstruct the lost other in all her complexity.

A "New Normal" Halloween

Where is Halloween this year? In my town in New Jersey there was a noticeable change in home displays. American flags and "United We Stand" posters replaced the usual displays of skeletons, grim reapers, and severed plastic limbs rising from the earth. The ubiquitous witches and ghosts costumes were gone, and many children dressed up as police officers and firefighters, the heroic defenders against death. The twenty-eighth annual Greenwich Village Halloween parade muted its usual mocking of death out of respect of the enormity of so much unexpected death in the city. In Mexico and increasingly in communities with large Mexican populations, the first two days of November are set aside as a fiesta, "Los Dias de Los Muertos" or "The Days of the Dead," to mourn and remember the dead. The fiesta helps to make death familiar and a part of everyday life. The symbols of death are playfully managed to facilitate comfort with how life is always becoming death.

By the End of November

Ground zero has become a construction site and, increasingly, a site of souvenir stands. Widows of the firefighters have organized the "9/11 Widows' and Victims' Families Association" to protest the disregard for what might be the final burial ground of their loved ones. They want a mourning site that is comforting, accessible, and dignified, one that can stand in for their loved ones' physical presence. The site of the attack has taken on heightened significance because so few bodies were found. These families are rightfully aware that, without an attempt to keep memory alive, history will bulldoze over landscapes that are charged and imbued with symbolic power.

But what is the story that needs to be inscribed? In a *New York Times* article, Edward Linenthal suggested that "the purpose of memorials is not just to mourn the dead but to actively reshape the moral conscience of people who come through."[1]

Early in December

The Israeli-Palestinian conflict has escalated. How complicated will mourning become when we have to legitimate the suffering of others as well as our own? When will we learn to hold onto the multiplicity of our positions—as victims, bystanders, and victimizers? Will we also learn new ways to protect ourselves while still afraid?

December 29—The Platforms

Platforms have been erected at ground zero, and over five thousand people per day get tickets to stand for thirty minutes to view the gaping hole. All of us have collected and replayed a range of images of September 11. The desire to take in and surround ourselves with images—to see, to get closer to, to be part of—has been a constant presence since the attack. Televised vigils substituted a sense of presence for those who were not there. What is this insistent hunger to see the evidence of loss—images of flaming buildings, ash-covered people fleeing for their lives, the blasted ruins, the faces of grief? *Memento mori*—"remember the death."

Do we collect images, remains, and mementos to try to undo the discovery of absence, to prove that we have something—some remains, a shrine, love, hope, a belief in justice, heroes, a collective identity? Many objected to the seemingly ghoulish need to see ground zero. Death, like sex in the nineteenth century, is taboo. On the other hand, perhaps they missed the painful urge in this spectatorship to undo the aloneness of death. There is something useful in being connected, even virtually, with the community of mourners. What exactly does the site offer? Is it the body of the traumatized group or a symbol of the destroyed mother who would have comforted us if she could?

Under the direction of architect Laura Kurgan, a folding map of the area from Duane Street to Bowling Green has been created and distributed. Kurgan, I read, was inspired by an artists' group that produced a map of war-torn Sarajevo in 1996. The documentation of the physical impact of September 11 will hopefully remind us to remember despite the rebuilding that will occur.

FEBRUARY 2002

The British psychoanalyst Hannah Siegel has declared that psychoanalysts who believe in the therapeutic power of speech must not be silent.

What can we say? In *Civilization and Its Discontents,* Freud located the origins of suffering in the mighty forces of nature, in the weakness of our own bodies, and in our inadequacies in managing relationships in family, state, and society.[2] Freud recognized how limited we are in dealing with mighty nature and the frailty of our bodies and cautioned against feeling a paralyzing despair about our inadequacies in managing human affairs. Instead, he suggested we use our awareness to direct our activity.

How will we choose to remember instead of repeat our past?

How do we keep from encapsulating September 11 into mere history and inert monuments that detach us from the atrocities, making our experience of them remote and abstract? Despite our best efforts, the Holocaust has largely become "history." As history sheds its skin on the past, mass destruction in Rwanda, Bosnia, and Afghanistan is repeated rather than remembered. Mourning as a way to work through our political history has not occurred. The number of civilians killed in Afghanistan as a result of U.S. air attacks has received little attention. I want to organize and install walls of missing person posters for each Afghani killed and include their families' portrait of grief in the *New York Times* in order to retrieve them from the abstraction of collateral damage.

MARCH 11, 2002

On the six-month anniversary of the attack, eighty-eight searchlights at Battery Park City pooled into two pillars of light, evoking a reminder of what once was and serving as an ephemeral double for the Twin Towers. In his paper "The Uncanny," Freud speaks of the phenomenon of the double,

which serves the wish for immortality.[3] The immortal soul doubles for the transience of the body. Together, our memory of the Twin Towers and its double, the Twin Towers of Light, stands as avowal and disavowal of all that has been associated with it: our financial potency, our phallic mastery, our defiance of mother earth's gravity, and our invulnerability. Designed to be temporary, the Twin Towers of Light echo the impermanence of memory itself. These light beams across the night sky create two cuts into the dark and call to mind Maya Lin's description of her Vietnam Veterans Memorial: "I thought about what death is, what a loss is. . . . [It is] a sharp pain that lessens with time, but can never quite heals over. A scar. Take a knife and cut open the earth."[4]

Maya Lin's memorial uniquely bypassed religion and patriotism in coming to terms with the past and the dead. Providing a minimalist but embracing structure, this memorial space has provided a possibility for a working through of loss that transcends specific political content and propaganda and resists a homogenized understanding of the motives and consequences of war. Veterans and antiwar activists can find something of their own experience there. Remembrance in this space of mourning pushes for an ongoing questioning of any singular understanding.

MOURNING AND MEMORIALS

Mourning requires a confrontation with the emptiness occasioned by loss. It requires a body and a place. It is ongoing and requires a constant effort to recycle the remains of the past into the present. Memory displaced to the

Candles, flowers, mass cards, and
stuffed animals at Union Square.
I left my pinhole camera on the
ground here, and this is what it saw.
Many shared the need for a permanent record.
I guess many of us just couldn't believe "our
own eyes." We go over the same image again
and again in an attempt to understand.

external world leaves us only with ghosts or monuments of stone. Freud
emphasized the conservative aspects of mourning—rescuing lost parts of
the ego from the wreckage inflicted by the reality of loss. But mourning
offers generative possibilities as well if the past is not simply ossified and
displaced into history but used in the service of transformation.

We are still working through our private and collective grief. Perhaps
the search for a memorial for the September 11 attacks is itself part of the
quest that mourning demands—that is, for the discovery of what has been
lost and the integration of that loss to form a new identity. Is it possible
that community rituals of mourning can retain the singularity of each
meaningful life needlessly lost and yet can support a moral conscience that
aggressively demands collective responsibility?

Notes

1. Dinitia Smith, "Competing Plans Hope to Shape a Trade Center Memorial,"
New York Times, Oct. 25, 2001.

2. Sigmund Freud, *Civilization and Its Discontents* (1930), in *Standard Edition
of the Complete Psychological Works of Sigmund Freud,* vol. 21 (London: Hogarth
Press, 1955).

3. Sigmund Freud, "The Uncanny" (1919), in *Standard Edition of the Complete
Psychological Works of Sigmund Freud,* vol. 17 (London: Hogarth Press, 1955).

4. Maya Lin, quoted in Robert Campbell, "An Emotive Place Apart," *A.I.A.
Journal,* May 1983, 151.

September 11, 2001—An Event
without a Voice

Dori Laub

September 11 was an encounter with something that makes no sense, an event that fits in nowhere. It was an experience of collective massive psychic trauma. Nearly six months after the event that shook our world and our assumptions about our lives, there is no coherent narrative about September 11. This, too, is in the nature of massive collective trauma. We are still involved with the ongoing struggle between an imperative need to know what it is that has happened to us all—not only to those who were in the buildings into which the planes crashed and to their families and friends but to all of us in America, no matter how distant from the scene of the attacks—and an equally powerful urge to not know, a defensive wish to deny the nature of the tear in the fabric of our shared lives.

The events of September 11 left world leaders and scholars seeking a context for such extreme, catastrophic violence. In an address to a Joint Session of Congress on September 20, 2001, President George Bush said of the terrorists, "They are the heirs of all the murderous ideologies of the twentieth century. They fall in the path of Fascism, Nazism, and totalitarianism." This statement was much more highlighted in the Israeli and European press than it was here. It was an obvious connection for those who experienced the Nazi terror firsthand. The drawing of parallels between September 11 and the terrorism of Nazism and Fascism recalls the comments of Michael Naumann, the German minister of culture, in his address at the Stockholm International Forum on the Holocaust on January 20, 2000, when he described the Holocaust as a form of terrorism whose target was life itself: "Hitler's Germany deliberately set out to abolish the sanctity of life. The extermination of the Jewish belief that the protection of life is the highest human principle was the ideological terrorist epicenter of the Holocaust."[1] I believe Naumann offers us an insight into what we in America experienced on the beautifully clear autumn day of Tuesday, September 11. It was a blow against our commonly held beliefs about the value of life. Later in his speech, Naumann said that, since the final defeat of Hitler's Germany in May 1945, one hundred acts of genocide have been documented in the world, every one of them an attack on the sanctity of life itself.

Following the events of September 11, we witnessed an instantaneous sense of paralysis, a helpless confusion experienced mostly in the United States but also in many parts of the Western world. Normality abruptly ceased. Life as we have known it stopped. It seems gone, perhaps for good. Having seen the United States experience a massive deadly terrorist attack against which it had proven unable to protect itself, Western society nearly lost its balance.

On Being a Psychoanalyst

I want to switch now to the mode of an analyst, or therapist, because that's what I know best. I am also a Holocaust survivor. My life's work is listening to those who are seeking psychic healing. Many if not most of my patients have endured massive trauma. Our work together involves a kind of witnessing that I have written about extensively. On September 11, we were all, doctor and patient alike, witness to, and victims of, a kind of terror that was, until that morning, unknown to us as Americans.

On that Tuesday I was in my office seeing patients. My day began early. My second patient was late because she had been listening to the radio when she heard about the first plane crashing into the World Trade Center, and the only thing she could talk about was what was happening in New York City. Patient after patient kept talking about it all day long, and so it continued for the whole week. Those patients who did not mention it were the ones who were the most fragile, totally detached from life. Even psychotic patients who were not as damaged came back, joining the community of anguish and fear; they became part of the event. Yet somehow, as the days passed, I felt that the September 11 experience lacked form. It was amorphous. Yes, there was a culprit found by the name of bin Laden. But there seemed to be no clear direction emerging. Even the president was nowhere to be found on the first day, except for a five-minute address on the radio.

As someone who experienced the chaos of World War II in Europe directly, I found myself wanting a Winston Churchill to come and address the nation, but there wasn't one. In America, it was very unclear what happened during the first day. Yet the foreign press gave a clear account of the events of the day. That week, the Israeli press published precise profiles of all nineteen hijackers; it took much longer for the American press to do so. There was no dearth of media coverage here, but it either had a pervasive emotional flavor of flooding or took the direction of a defensive battle cry, a patriotic rally, or that of an obsessional, endless, but superficial repetition of the scanty news that was known. European nations, indeed, came out very early with political statements of support. Arab leaders, on the other hand, were silent, except for one man who took a stand from the very beginning: King Abdullah of Jordan unequivocally condemned the attacks. (This is the grandson of the first King Abdullah, who was murdered in Jerusalem in 1950 when he secretly entered into negotiations for a peace treaty with Israel.) The present terrorists are but a continuation of the Muslim Brotherhood of Egypt, who were involved in the murder of President Anwar Sadat, a murder carried out by a group of extremists, a member of which, Ayman Al-Zawahiri, was the second in command to Osama bin Laden. History is continuous. Trauma survivors' responses to September 11 bear witness to this.

One female patient, the daughter of a bipolar father who grew up in a very chaotic family, stopped sleeping after September 11 because her sense of not being safe had been further confirmed. Holocaust survivors living in New York City began to reexperience their terrors and their nightmares; some even needed to be hospitalized. It all goes on, they felt; it never stops, and no place is safe. Four months after the attack, the *Harvard Mental Health Letter* (January 2002) reported that "The number of new prescriptions for sleeping pills rose by a reported 28% and the number of new prescriptions for antidepressants by 17% in the New York area." On March 5, 2002, CBS News reported that "The greatest danger from a traumatic incident is now, the period from six months to a year, and psychologists say the second wave of trauma may be even tougher to treat than the first." Therapists in New York reported a new wave of symptoms among New Yorkers—anxiety, depression, and other posttraumatic stress disorder–related symptoms. The effects of a trauma experienced some five or six months earlier were being felt again. This phase of symptomatology seems to be more pronounced than that immediately following the attack. Recently, a New Haven, Connecticut, hospital reported its first case of a September 11–related psychosis—a woman who was experiencing a bottomless terror and suspects that terrorists are everywhere around her. Homeless people in the streets of New Haven were more scared about what might happen, but they also experienced a sense of familiarity with the lack of safety they had known all their lives. I had worked with them as their psychiatrist for six years. September 11 was a communal experience that not only confirmed their worst fears but also, ironically, brought them relief. Now, perhaps, the society that has shunned them has caught up with them and has begun to know what they have intimately known all along. There is no such thing as the safety of a home—it can vanish in a moment. Now, perhaps, they might feel a bit less isolated from the rest.

A child survivor of the Holocaust told me that she remembers her sense of despair and fury when her father, who was always so in charge of life, couldn't find an answer to the questions she asked when her family was among the crowds of Polish Jews fleeing the advancing German armies in 1939. Once more, now, there is no authority who knows, can protect, and can give direction. Statements of compassion, participation in the mourning and the loss, and sharing in the new uncertainty of life are simply not enough. They do not lessen the pain and the overwhelming terror. There is an overpowering need for a promise of safety, for reassurance and clarity of purpose. To say that the Al Qaeda network has a new chief of operations, a Palestinian whose whereabouts is not known but who is said to know all the sleeper cells in the United States and other countries, is at best disquieting. To speak of a dark lurking danger that can come from anywhere only intensifies the dread. Perhaps, though, all of this brings us closer to the truth of what has actually come to pass—that something unimaginable and incomprehensible has happened. Civilian airplanes carrying innocent civilian passengers to their destination were turned into deadly missiles that brought the Twin Towers down, caused everything to crumble and to implode, leaving only rubble—a huge pile of ruins and debris. Thousands of people simply vanished. Are they really dead? I found myself thinking of Paul Celan's poem "Death Fugue," about the rising smoke over the crematoria, the graves in the sky. "We shovel a grave in the air there you won't lie too cramped."[2]

Perhaps, after all, there is a resemblance between the attacks of September 11 and something equally unimaginable that happened in the Holocaust. I want to emphatically stress that there can be no equating them. The scale is too disproportionate. The landscape around the destruction of the Twin Towers continues to be humane, filled with people attempting to comfort and to restore. This is completely different from the landscape of the Holocaust, in which the surrounding world was dumbfounded by the extraordinary impact of death or stood back and let it happen. During the Holocaust, and for many years after it was over, nobody was willing to hear and to know what truly was happening, in spite of overwhelming evidence. It took decades for a dialogue of testimony to emerge. Yet there is this similarity: the absence of narrative. No one can really tell the story of the Twin Towers disaster, and no one is really ready to hear it.

Trauma and Speechlessness

This generalized amorphousness, bewilderment, and, most of all, numbness seems to me a hallmark of collective massive trauma, a sense of shock so profound that it leads to both cognitive and emotional paralysis. It leads, too, to the loss of voice, and in this it feels akin to the speechlessness that Walter Benjamin wrote about in his essay "The Storyteller," as he witnessed the state of soldiers returning from World War I. He describes the incommunicability of trauma, the demise of both storytelling and listening.

> With the [First] World War, a process became apparent which has not halted since then. Was it not noticeable at the end of the war that men returned from the battlefield grown silent—not richer, but poorer in communicable experience: What ten years later was poured out in the flood of war books was anything but experience that goes from mouth to mouth. And there was nothing remarkable about that. For never has experience been contradicted more thoroughly than strategic experience by tactical warfare, economic experience by inflation, bodily experience by mechanical warfare, moral experience by those in power. A generation that had gone to school on a horse-drawn streetcar now stood under the open sky in a countryside in which nothing remained unchanged but the clouds, and beneath these clouds, in a field of force of destructive torrents and explosions, was the tiny, fragile human body.[3]

During the week after the attacks of September 11 in New York and at the Pentagon, although I listened for hours to patients talking of their inner horror, of their unsettledness, of a sense of things having changed perhaps forever, of innocence and safety irretrievably lost, I found that I myself couldn't focus. I could not formulate a clear account of what was happening either, much less write about it. Whenever I turned to my Dictaphone and tried to speak into it, I had to put it away. It was a struggle. Then I spoke with a colleague in New Jersey, a daughter of two Holocaust survivors, who was treating casualties from the Twin Towers, and she helped me understand what we were both experiencing. "Yes, I know," she began, when I said I could not yet say anything coherent about what had happened. "I work with people and I help them, but I don't know what I'm doing and I cannot write about it, I cannot speak about it. When I speak to you now I begin to understand not knowing what I'm doing, but other than that, I cannot put it into thought." Coming back again to clarity from the cognitive paralysis in response to trauma is a long and cumbersome journey, even for those of us who have made such a journey once already.

As I have written elsewhere, what occurs in massive trauma is the loss of the internal "other." People are so affected by the violence that has broken into their lives that they can no longer maintain the dialogue with themselves that is ongoing in normal life. What they felt, what they saw, what they experienced, what they remembered—it suddenly becomes unavailable to them. It's all a haze, like walking in a dream. There's both an inability and a total refusal to keep one's gaze centered on the eye of the trauma. Strategies are employed to avoid it, individual and collective—patriotic gestures, sentimentality, pseudo-unity, fantasies of revenge, concepts of justice or of bringing those responsible to justice. All of these in their own right can be very valid, but at this particular juncture they are definitely being used to avoid the full absorption and recognition of the traumatic event, the primary step that would allow the resumption of that internal dialogue of knowing. With this internal dialogue comes the possibility of agency and of action—informed and effective response.

Let me discuss for a moment a patient I see who was shaped by another culture, a Japanese journalist born long after Hiroshima who works in New York. Her office is in midtown, and through her windows she could see the World Trade Center. She described the scene for me: "I could see the fire, smoke, it was so thick, but I was so busy. I had to prepare for the meeting taking place that day. People were coming in, flying in. I had no time to look. Only now it dawns on me what was really happening; the towers collapsed. Ben, that's my husband, could have been killed. I walked out to the street. When I looked up the street in Manhattan, I saw that brilliant sky, the sun shining; looking down I saw billowing clouds of smoke. People covered with ashes." We need to remember that she is Japanese, remembering stories of other ashes. "People were running. A few hours later, nobody was there. New York was a ghost town." Weeks later, she was very angry with me. For a moment her defensive armor of being matter-of-fact, task oriented, and tough had cracked. She experienced "the abyss"— intense terror, helplessness, and loss. I had witnessed and acknowledged her softness, attachment, and longings, the "weaknesses" she had worked all her life to overcome. Now she could no longer return to her former well-defended self. She revisited New York after having been absent for months, and the smell was still there, and she didn't want to go to ground zero. She refused to look at it, refused even to smell the trauma.

Breaking through Screen Memories

Instead of looking directly into trauma, one encounters screen perceptions and screen memories. Perhaps describing a memory of my own will help here. As a child, I was deported to Transnistria, the part of Ukraine occupied by the Romanian army, who were allies of the Germans. What I remembered for years was sitting with a little girl on the bank of the River Bug, the demarcation line between German and Romanian occupation areas. It was a beautiful summer day; there were green meadows and green hills and a blue river. It was like a summer camp. We were having a debate at age five, arguing whether you could or could not eat grass. I recounted this memory in my second week of analysis in 1969, and luckily enough my analyst was Swedish. He said, "I have to tell you something. The Swedish Red Cross liberated Thereisenstadt and took depositions from women inmates in the camp. Under oath, they declared that conditions in the camp were so good that they received each morning breakfast in bed brought by ss officers." There could not have been a more powerful interpretation of my denial. I stopped talking about young girls, green meadows, and blue rivers and started remembering other things, my own experience of trauma.

In the days following September 11, I myself felt impelled to break the grip of silence, to be released from the hypnotic fascination of the endlessly repeated television images, the continual repetition of already well-known bits of information, fragments that did not cohere. I did so by going ahead with a planned trip to Israel on September 16. Specifically, I went to help plan a video testimony project about Holocaust survivors who themselves had never broken the seal of their silence. All have been living in psychiatric hospitals for decades since the end of the war.

I had a meeting set up in Israel for September 16. My departure for Israel was scheduled for September 13. On September 11, I received an e-mail asking if I was going to be at the meeting, and I decided that yes, no matter what, I was going to make it to Israel for this meeting. The skies were closed—there was no flying. I couldn't get through to El Al in New York by phone. I could get El Al in Israel, but they would put me on hold, and after a half-hour or so of listening to music someone would pick up the phone and give me the flight information that was not available in New York. Once I started for the airport in New York but turned back, having heard that no planes were taking off. But then, on September 14, I decided to try again in spite of all the statements on TV and radio that the skies were closed. The trip to New York was eerie. Usually there is heavy traffic. That day there were no cars. For long stretches, the highway was completely empty. Then, for no apparent reason, there would suddenly be a slowdown.

Soon I realized this was the result of rubbernecking. On the other side of the road, oncoming traffic was at a halt. Several cars had been involved in accidents. They were overturned and smashed up, and everywhere there were ambulances, fire trucks, and wreckers waiting to clear the road of ruined cars. The drivers, it seemed, had simply lost control.

When I finally got to JFK, the parking lot was empty. Arriving at the departure building, I just walked in. Any terrorist could have gotten in. There were only a few people milling around. When I asked at the counter about El Al, I was told that, yes, there were two flights leaving that day. When I landed in Israel, it was, for me, a return to normalcy. That evening there was a party in my family, with fifty people coming from all over the country, a gathering for a six-year-old girl's birthday. The place was only about five kilometers from Kalkilia in the West Bank. Yet it felt safer, more normal, despite being so much closer to danger.

THE TOWER OF BABEL

The multitude of diverse voices, public and private, that we are hearing about September 11 testifies to the absence of a coherent narrative voice for the event itself. We are faced with versions of the event's meaning that continue and coexist, some driven by a wish to know, to bear witness, and some driven by an equally powerful need to not know, to deny and suppress the truth of witnessing. The latter meet with too little moral rebuttal. The Egyptian press, as well as newspapers in other Arab countries, claimed from the very beginning that the Israeli central intelligence agency, the Mossad, was behind the acts of terror against the United States on September 11. Proof of that was the claim that more than two thousand Israeli workers employed in the Twin Towers didn't come to work on that day, having been warned of what was going to happen. Other newspapers claimed that the number of Jewish workers who were absent on that very day numbered over four thousand. It is no secret that the Egyptian government controls the press and could have prevented such allegations, but obviously it chose not to. When an Egyptian scholar who attended a rabbinical meeting in Chicago in October 2001 was asked about these allegations, he promptly responded that the public relations services of the United States and of Israel had not been effective enough in counteracting such rumors. Not for a moment did he hesitate to wonder why he or other scholars who did not believe these allegations remained silent while they were published and republished in the Egyptian press. Some sources trace these allegations to a Muslim college in northern India, part of the Deobandi movement that has influenced public education in many Muslim countries—Saudi Arabia, Pakistan, and others. This school is thought to be the origin of this particular theory, which spread throughout the Muslim world. General Rashid Qureshi, the public relations chief for President Pervez Musharraf of Pakistan, stated the theory to *Newsweek* a few days after the attack.[4] And a poll cited by Andrew Sullivan in the *Sunday Times* stated that 48 percent of Pakistanis believed that Jews flew the planes into the World Trade Center.[5]

In a somewhat less extreme vein, Arab propaganda still blames the Palestinian-Israeli conflict for the terrorist attacks against the United States. Were it not for the Israeli subjugation and the endless Palestinian suffering, such terrorism, it is claimed, would not have happened. Notwithstanding bin Laden's declarations of hatred and threats of destruction toward the West, specifically toward the United States, which put the Palestinian question lower on his list of priorities, Arab governments repeated the anti-Jewish allegations while being rather silent about condemning the September 11 terrorist attack. Palestinian crowds were indeed celebrating the events of September 11 in the streets until Yasir Arafat forbade such public celebrations and confiscated the videotapes that documented them.

On our side of the Atlantic, voices have been less vociferous and extreme. On several campuses, students and faculty demonstrated a short time after the bombings, some pressing for peace negotiations with the Taliban and against any kind of military intervention. One academic who represents herself as an expert in terrorism went as far as to state in an open forum for faculty and students that "Terrorism is a communication of helplessness." Students in American universities held marches and demonstrations in that particular kind of tenor, at odds with the majority of the nation. What is striking is not the opinions that were expressed—after all, this is a society in which free speech is allowed and even encouraged—but that there was no powerful rebuttal of such opinions. It is as though the voices of those who experienced the terrorist attack more directly were muted and those most directly affected remained speechless in the face of such political expressions. Even though many opinions were voiced in different forums, there was little direct response either to the extremist claims of the Arab press or to the political agendas of certain academics who influenced vast bodies of students across the country.

What is most striking, in view of the multiplicity of voices that tell "the story of September 11," is that no unified voice has emerged to challenge, dispute, and contradict the radically divergent, often mutually exclusive, versions of reality that are being spouted from different corners of the earth. It is as though there is no truth and no sense of conviction, a collective uncertainty regarding the veracity of the truth and of one's own experience. Therefore, no source exists for an indignant rebuttal of the distortions and lies that are being repeatedly voiced. Something about our ability to feel and to know what happened on September 11 has been muted. Propaganda and distortions go unchallenged, and those affected, including those who witnessed the disaster and its aftermath, remain silent and cannot yet create an authoritative narrative that could put things straight.

This mutedness about the truth is not a new or unfamiliar phenomenon, particularly when it is related to events of massive violence and massive destruction. We need only to think about the genocides of the twentieth century and the silence, even denial, bordering on revisionism that regularly engulfed them. Let me refer to an article from the *New York Times* in October 2000 having to do with Rwanda. In 1999 the United Nations released a report of an inquiry into its failure to prevent or stop the genocide in Rwanda. It was harshly critical of the Americans and the French and of most officials of the UN, including Kofi Annan, who was then the head of the UN peacekeeping function. There was one man of whom the report was not critical. This was the commander of the UN forces in Rwanda, Lieutenant General Romeo Dalaire of Canada. After the massacre, the officer returned to Canada and continued to serve in the Canadian army as a general. Four years later, he decompensated—he became alcoholic and started suffering from a severe case of posttraumatic stress disorder, with flashbacks, insomnia, and hallucinations. In an interview, he described a scene that he kept seeing over and over again: "I'm in a valley at sunset, waist deep in bodies covered in blood. I'm holding up my arms trying to get out. Each time it comes back, the scene gets worse, and I can hear the rustle of bodies and I'm afraid to move for fear of hurting someone."[6] In January 1994, Dalaire had received information that the Hutu regime was planning an act of genocide. He learned that they were working out how to kill one thousand people in twenty minutes. The general notified the UN. No response. In the beginning of April, he had twenty-seven hundred soldiers. Six times he asked the UN to increase the number to five thousand and to give him a mandate to intervene. Six times he was refused. Instead of increasing the number of troops, 90 percent were withdrawn. Fewer than three hundred soldiers remained under his command, and he could not intervene. In the ensuing two months, eight hundred thousand people died. In October 2001 the UN Security Council and Kofi Annan received the Nobel Peace Prize. A few years after the slaughter but before the awarding of the Nobel Peace Prize, President Clinton, on a visit to Rwanda, apologized, saying that what happened had not been fully "appreciated."

The mutedness of trauma is perhaps most visible in the public domain.

It took nearly a half-century for a meaningful dialogue on the Holocaust to begin taking place in Germany, and Austria has not yet reached this phase. The same holds true for the Armenian genocide. That this very mutedness is a direct consequence of massive traumatic experience is again and again observed with traumatized individuals. It is quite common that victims of massive trauma do not know, do not remember, and do not believe what they really experienced and what was done to them. Recall my screen memories of the lovely days spent on the grassy banks of the River Bug with a charming girl, while in reality we were both Jewish children held prisoner by Nazis. Trauma survivors desperately seek confirmation that the events that shattered their lives were real, sometimes even through wanting corroboration from the perpetrator of the violence. It is a common phenomenon for women who have been victims of rape or incest to remember the events only decades after they happened. When such memories led to court action in the 1980s, a whole movement was created, the False Memory Foundation, supported and generously endowed by people who identified with the accused perpetrators and perhaps were concerned about being accused themselves. Experts were hired, studies were conducted, legal action was funded, and publications were sponsored to support the theories of the false memory movement. What is unfathomable about this is that no movement originated to protect the truth. No such foundation was created on behalf of the victims, and their advocates— including their therapists—were often sued for libel, convicted in courts, and ordered to pay millions of dollars in damages. To this day, no "True Memory Foundation" exists, and no resources comparable to those of the False Memory Foundation are available to those who protect the truth and give it expression. It's as if truth, when it comes to traumatic experience, has no voice and no advocate.

This holds true for a narrative of the extremely violent events of September 11. Its truth is still fragmented, piecemeal, and disorganized, a story in search of a voice. I do not want to foreclose the emergence of that truth by declaring that September 11 is about evil—because I don't know yet. What I do know is that it was about something unfathomable, at the root of which there may be evil for which no ways of explaining or understanding yet exist. September 11 stands alone in its starkness, in its deliberate, whimsical exercise of total power.

We can neither give up on creating a cohesive narrative nor succumb to our need to create a story that will quell our fears and give direction to our rage and grief.

On the one hand, both approaches may bring us temporary relief. On the other hand, we know that it takes time (sometimes decades), sustained effort, and, most of all, the courage to hear and to know for the truth of witnessing to come into being. But time alone is not enough. "Time has not apparently healed children's psychological wounds after the attack," Marla Diamond of CBS News reported on April 5, 2002. A six-month follow-up of 421 parents by the Children's Health Fund "found the same number of kids, 52%, still worried about their own safety." A health care specialist added, "Almost four out of ten children are having problems like being distracted or nervous or anxious." What do the children know that the rest of us may be too good at hiding?

Now that we have had our own experience of suicide bombers, it is harder for us to distance ourselves from the terror that Israelis are feeling and from the international threat that terrorist bombers pose for all of us. We have no choice. As journalist Thomas L. Friedman put it in the *New York Times* on March 31, 2002, "If America, the only reality check left, doesn't use every ounce of energy to halt this madness and call it by its real name, then it will spread. The Devil is dancing in the Middle East, and he's dancing our way."[7]

NOTES

1. The quote by Michael Naumann is taken from *http://www.holocaustforum.gov. se/conference/official-documents/speeces/naumann-eng.htm.*

2. Paul Celan, quoted in John Felstiner, *Paul Celan: Poet, Survivor, Jew* (New Haven CT: Yale University Press, 1995), 31.

3. Walter Benjamin, "The Storyteller: Reflections on the Works of Nikolai Leskov," in *Illuminations: Essays and Reflections,* trans. Harry Zohn, ed. Hannah Arendt (New York: Harcourt, Brace, and World, 1969), 84.

4. *Newsweek*, Apr. 1, 2002, 26.

5. *International Jerusalem Post*, Mar. 22, 2002, 16.

6. Lieutenant General Romeo Dalaire, quoted in Tina Rosenberg, "The Unbearable Memories of a U.N. Peacekeeper," *New York Times,* Oct. 8, 2000, editorial.

7. Thomas L. Friedman, "Suicidal Lies," *New York Times*, Mar. 31, 2002.

Remember Life with Life:
The New World Trade Center

James Young

In Jewish tradition, it takes a year of mourning before the gravestone is unveiled for a deceased loved one. In this time, a number of ritual stages allow us gradually to move from the work of mourning to that of memory. Having first worked through the sense of loss, finding meaning in it and internalizing the memory of our loved one, we then mark this grief and our loss externally with a stone. It is a decent interval, and I would counsel such an interval here.

Indeed, as stages of mourning turn into stages of memory, we see that this is a process, a continuum. Before settling on a final plan for the World Trade Center, as urgent a task as this may be, I think it might help first to articulate the stages of the memorial process itself—as a guide to where we've been, where we are, and where we would like to go. In so doing, we begin to define a conceptual foundation for this site, which takes into account all that was lost and all that must now be regenerated. Here we need to ask, What is to be remembered here and how? For whom are we remembering? And to what social, political, religious, and communal ends?

If memory begins with how we name it, then let's call this complex the "New World Trade Center" and thereby affirm its regeneration and its central place in America, the "new world." In this way, the terrorist attack will be regarded not as the beginning of a new era but as the end of an old one. We thus define our post-9/11 reality by rejuvenating construction and new designs, not by the attack and destruction it wrought. Conversely, we will come to regard the New World Trade Center as the ground zero of a renewal and the ultimate expression of a modernity so abhorred by the terrorists. Indeed, let us embrace the ideological roots of modernity: the affirmation of life itself, change, and rejuvenation, all things abhorred by the antimodern zealots of religious fundamentalism and absolutism.

Will this be a site commemorating the old World Trade Center and the thousands murdered there or one that merely replaces what was lost in the attack? By necessity, it will be both. This is why we need to design into this site the capacity both for remembrance and for reconstruction, the space both for memory of past destruction and for present life and its regeneration. This must be an integrative design, a complex that meshes memory with life, embeds memory in life, and balances our need for memory with the present needs of the living. Our commemorations must not be allowed to disable life or to take its place; rather, they must inspire life, regenerate it, and provide for it. We must animate and reinvigorate this site, not paralyze it, with memory. In this way, we might remember the victims by how they lived and not merely by how they died.

This is also why we must not turn this devastated site into a memorial only to the three thousand lives lost there. Such a memorial may preserve the sanctity of this space, as former New York City mayor Rudolph Giuliani has suggested, but it may also inadvertently sanctify the culture of death and its veneration that inspired the killers themselves. For whether we like it or not, memorials to death and destruction can also monumentalize and privilege such death and destruction. Our memorial to the destruction of the towers and the lives lost could even become the terrorists' victory monument to the deadly success of their attacks. Our soaring shrine to the victims and our sorrow could become the murderers' triumphal fist, thrust into the air.

And what of the ruins? All cultures preserve bits of relics and ruins as reminders of the past; nearly all cultures remember terrible destructions with the remnants of such destruction. But Americans have never made ruins their home or allowed ruins to define—and thereby shape—their future. The power of ruins is undeniable, and while it may be fitting to preserve a shard or piece of the towers' facade as a gesture to the moment of destruction, it would be a mistake to stop with such a gesture and allow it alone to stand for all those rich and varied lives that were lost. For by itself, such a remnant (no matter how aesthetically pleasing) would recall—and thereby reduce—all this rich life to the terrible moment of destruction, just as the terrorists themselves would have us remember their victims.

I know that for many it is similarly tempting to leave the void behind as a permanent symbol of the breach in our lives, the emptiness we feel in our hearts. I know that for many the physical void left behind is nearly unbearable, a constant reminder of life changed, of mass death nearby, a personal assault on our "home." And sometimes nothing seems to remember such loss better than the gaping void itself. I can sympathize with this need to remember loss by preserving loss. But this, too, would be an unmitigated capitulation to the bombers: it would be to remember the site exactly as the killers have forced it upon us. It is they, not we, who created this void in our city and in our lives: to preserve it would be to extend the deed itself for perpetuity. Instead, let us regard this present void as a necessary, yet transient stage in the memorial process. Let it lie fallow for now, akin to the Biblical injunction, so that it may ultimately regenerate and become a source for life itself.

Indeed, in our rejection of the absolutist tenets of the killers, let this site become an evolving memorial, one that not only will accommodate every new generation's reasons for coming to it but will be animated by every new generation. And let this memorial recall its own constantly evolving meanings and reasons for being over time. The site has, after all, already changed radically since the attack—and not by accident. Where the seven-story mountain of tangled and jutting ruins stood literally as remnant of the ferocity of the attack, its sheer physical devastation, terror, and mass death, the gigantic hole in the ground now stands literally for the immeasurable loss of life and buildings. For the thousands of visitors, tourists, families of victims, and neighbors who stand on the edge of this gaping hole, the void stands for both itself—a gaping wound in the cityscape—and for the void in these people's lives and hearts. The feverish pace of attempted rescue and cleanup that has led to this moment bespeaks the need of all to repair this terrible breach, the need to remember this loss by repairing it.

Let this be a place where all the stages of memory—recalling the terrible attack in all of its immediacy, recalling the void left in the aftermath, recalling the attempt to commemorate life with life—are remembered as parts of a living continuum and necessarily evolving memory.

In Israel, a forest of six million tress is being planted in the Judean hills between Jerusalem and Tel Aviv, in the words of B'nai B'rith, "as a living memorial to the six million Jews who perished in the Holocaust" (*Israel: A Traveler's Guide* [Washington DC, n.d.], 14). Begun in 1954, this planting clearly takes on several layers of practical and symbolic meaning in Israel: it remembers both the martyrs of Nazi genocide and a return to life itself as cultivated in the founding of the state. Rather than remembering the victims in the emblems of destruction left behind by the Nazis, thereby succumbing to the Nazi cult of death, these trees recall both the lives lost and the affirmation of life itself as the surest memorial antidote to murder. It was also with this traditional veneration of life in mind, as symbolized in Jewish tradition by the Etz Chaim (tree of life), that Yad Vashem has planted a tree to remember and to name every single Gentile who rescued a Jew during World War II.

As it turns out, I'm very happy to say, tree planting as a memorial act is not only a Jewish tradition. Two years after the "great Hanshin earthquake" of January 17, 1995, in Kobe, Japan, architect Tadao Ando proposed a very similar commemoration for the 6,000 victims of this catastrophe (plus another 300,000 who were left homeless). In an article entitled "Green Net Works," which appeared in the *Royal Institute of British Architects Journal* in 1997, Ando proposed planting 250,000 trees, including some 50,000 white blossom-yielding trees such as cucumbers or magnolias. "The white flowers," he wrote, "will serve as both a prayer for those who perished in the disaster and a reminder of what has happened to those who survived it. Trees and plants are living things, and caring for them is not easy. By cooperating to protect and nurture the living things as they grow, I believe that little by little the community will rejuvenate itself. . . . We must leave the children of the next generation irreplaceable assets. Like twirling a baton, we must foster life itself. . . . This is what I hope for." In fact, the architect's dream has been realized, as the emperor himself has recently gone to Kobe to plant the 300,000th tree, and planting continues to this day.

One of these is a commemoration of a mass murder, the other of a natural catastrophe. But in both cases, the dead are remembered by living forms, with the regeneration of life itself, so that the victims' lives—and not just the terrible moment of their deaths—are at the center of our memory now. At the same time, we make ourselves responsible for nurturing and sustaining such memory. We remind ourselves that, without the deliberate attempt to remember, memory itself is lost, that like life itself, memory needs to be cultivated and attended to.

I recall these "living memorials" not merely as explicit models for our own memorial downtown but also as possible conceptual foundations and backdrops for our memorial thinking. As is quite clear by the consensual outlines suggested by the Lower Manhattan Development Corporation, downtown will be rebuilt according to an integrated design of new office buildings, living spaces, and memorials to the victims of the 9/11 attacks. But underpinning any particular design must be both a conceptual and foundational setting for this sixteen-acre site of the former World Trade Center complex. In keeping with the regenerative and rejuvenating memorial models above, I would propose that we locate whatever else is built here—and I hope it will be a complex of high-rise office buildings, cultural centers and museums, new housing, and a memorial—amid a setting that includes memorial groves of some 2,850 white blossoming trees, each one planted and dedicated in the name of one of the victims of the World Trade Center attacks. Moreover, because these two attacks were coordinated as part of a larger attack on the nation, I propose that similar groves also be planted simultaneously on the other 9/11 attack sites as well, one tree for each of the victims who died at the World Trade Center, at the Pentagon, and in that field in Pennsylvania. In this way, the individual victims can be recalled both separately for the lives they lived and collectively for their mass murder, as both individual trees and as a canopied forest. At the same time, these three memorial groves in Lower Manhattan, Washington, and Pennsylvania will create a national memorial matrix, allowing us to remember them separately and together, as a way to commemorate the significance of the attacks and the significance of individual lives lost.

Thus, I can see why there will surely be an interim park, with names of victims, names of decimated fire companies, names of nations who lost citizens. There must surely be an interim memorial for the buildings themselves, my favorite being the "Towers of Light" conceived and proposed by artists Julian La Verdiere and Paul Myoda and architects John Bennet and Gustavo Bonevardi. A temporary memorial garden may last, as may the "Towers of Light," especially if, as seems likely, the Twin Towers themselves are not rebuilt in their former proportions. But it may not be up to us now to decide just how long these memorials will last but rather up to the generations who visit them, who will need to decide for themselves why they continue to recall what seems to be, so selfishly, our own special loss.

In this spirit, let's build into this site a world-view that allows for competing, even conflicting agendas—and make this, too, part of our process. Rather than fretting about the appearance of disunity (all memorial processes are exercises in disunity, even as they strive to unify memory), we should make our questions and the public debate itself part of our memory work. Memory is, after all, a process and is everlasting only when it remains a process and not a finished result. For just as memory is a negotiation between past and present, it is also an ongoing negotiation among all the groups of people whose lives were affected by this event and whose lives will be shaped by what is built there. How will the needs of competing constituencies, all with profoundly legitimate concerns, be balanced against each other? If, as part of a well-defined process, the debates are conducted openly and publicly, they will be as edifying as they are painful. Firefighters and their families, police officers and their families, office workers, traders, and bankers from around the world, city officials, developers, architects, artists, immediate neighbors, outlying neighbors, tourists—all may want something a little different in this site. And the hundreds of victims from eighty-four other nations, all with their own reasons for being there, will be remembered in their own national and cultural traditions. There must be room in both the process and the actual commemorative site for the memory of all these people and their families. Memory at ground zero is not zero-sum: it is an accumulation of all these disparate experiences and needs. Just as we accommodate ourselves to the competing needs of others every day of our lives in this city, just as we live together but separately, just as we come and go together but separately, we must build into both the process and this site the capacity to remember together but separately. Thus, city planners should hold coordinated competitions for new building designs and memorial designs, should decide what to build based on what the city's skyline needs, on what the city's economy needs, and on what our inner topographies of self need. These needs must be explicitly articulated and should constitute the very basis for these competitions.

Should the New World Trade Center complex be home to a permanent museum and memorial to the attack and the lives it took? Of course. Appoint a design committee of architects, curators, and cultural historians of memory to work in tandem with a commission of developers and city planners in their search for building designs. Make clear from the outset that this will be an integrative design. What form will the buildings, museum, and memorials take? In addition to memorial gardens, walls of the victims' names, and freestanding monuments, perhaps every building will designate a permanent place in its lobby for exhibitions or leave an empty floor reserved for showing the history of this site and its changing face over time. The office buildings themselves might also be marked architecturally with some sign of the attacks and the resulting void in our lives they are being asked to fill. Thus might a standing shard of one of the old towers recall the destruction, even as soaring new towers negate the killers' cult of death.

In the conceptual précis for this complex, we must be absolutely clear in our governing mandate: Let life remember life. Name your children after the victims, love life itself more fervently because of how they lived, not because they died so horribly. Defeat the culture of death with emblems of life, with trees teeming with birds, with gardens and flowers, where life is contemplated and death is rejected. Let the new complex breathe with more open space and allow the surrounding water—our greatest natural emblem of life—to permeate and animate this site. Instead of consecrating this site as a graveyard only, one forced upon us by the killers, let's dedicate the New World Trade Center complex to everything the terrorists abhor: our modernity, our tolerance, our diversity, our egalitarianism. If they hate our buildings, let's rebuild them here; if they hate our lives, let's live them here; if they hate our culture, let's celebrate it here; if they hate our prosperity, let's prosper here.

Were we now to reinvigorate this sixteen-acre site with both life and commerce, with cultural centers and office space, we might actually improve on an area of Manhattan that had already been wanting in cultural institutions and habitable environs. Bring the office workers back to the neighborhood and keep them here at night, with restaurants, theaters, centers for the arts and interreligious study, housing and studios for artists, writers, and students. Humanize the icons of our capitalist culture by building into them spaces for life, reflection, and memory. Let's build the New World Trade Center in precisely the modernist vernacular that the killers hate us for embracing. To do otherwise would be to grant the terrorists an absolute victory over New York.

Finally, by dint of its location at the tip of lower Manhattan, the New World Trade Center will necessarily become part of a national memorial matrix and landscape much larger than itself. It will be within sightlines of the Statue of Liberty, Ellis Island, the war memorials in Battery Park, and the Museum of Jewish Heritage—A Living Memorial to the Holocaust. But whereas these neighboring national shrines had previously been dwarfed, and literally overshadowed by the towering twin icons of American commerce, they will now find themselves highlighted, perhaps even rejuvenated, by the New World Trade Center. As a result, these national markers will themselves begin to assume a much greater prominence in the minds of New Yorkers, visitors, and memorial pilgrims—all trying to find their place in America's ever-changing landscape of memory.

Contributors

Elizabeth Baer serves as a professor of English at Gustavus Adolphus College, where she holds the Florence and Raymond Sponberg Chair of Ethics. She is also a visiting professor at the University of Minnesota. She is the coeditor, with Hester Baer, of the first English edition of *The Blessed Abyss: Inmate #6582 in Ravensbrück Concentration Camp for Women* (Wayne State University Press, 2001) and editor of *Shadows on My Heart: The Civil War Diary of Lucy Buck* (University of Georgia Press, 1997). Forthcoming from Wayne State University Press in 2003 is her anthology of essays, coedited with Myrna Goldenberg, entitled *Experience and Expression: Women, the Nazis, and the Holocaust*. She has received several awards and grants for her work on the Holocaust.

Donna Bassin, a clinical psychologist and psychoanalyst with a private practice in Manhattan, is a member of the International Psychoanalytic Association and a faculty member at the Institute for Psychoanalytic Training and Research. She is a professor of psychology at Pratt Institute and a fine art photographer. She has coedited *Representations of Motherhood* (Yale University Press, 1994), edited *Female Sexuality: Contemporary Engagements* (Jason Aronson Publishers, 1999), and authored papers and reviews in the *International Journal of Psychoanalysis, Journal of the American Psychoanalytic Association, Psychoanalytic Psychology, Gender and Psychoanalysis*, and *Studies in Gender and Sexuality*. She is currently working on a manuscript tentatively entitled "What Remains: Memorialization and the Working Through of Mourning."

Jill Bennett is a senior lecturer in art history and theory at the University of New South Wales, Sydney. She is currently writing a manuscript on trauma, conflict, and visual art and has recently edited, with Rosanne Kennedy, *World Memory: Personal Trajectories in Global Time* (Palgrave, 2002).

James Berger, associate professor of English at Hofstra University, is the author of *After the End: Representations of Post-apocalypse* (University of Minnesota Press,

1999). He is currently working on a manuscript entitled "Those Who Can't Speak: Language Impairment in Modern Literature and Culture" and has been awarded a National Endowment for the Humanities Fellowship for 2002–2003.

Peter Brooks is the Sterling Professor of Comparative Literature and French at Yale University. His most recent publications are *Troubling Confessions: Speaking Guilt in Law and Literature* (University of Chicago Press, 2001) and, as coeditor with Alex Woloch, *Whose Freud? The Place of Psychoanalysis in Contemporary Culture* (Yale University Press, 2000).

Ann Cvetkovich is an associate professor of English at the University of Texas at Austin. She is the author of *Mixed Feelings: Feminism, Mass Culture, and Victorian Sensationalism* (Rutgers University Press, 1992) and *An Archive of Feelings: Trauma, Sexuality, and Lesbian Public Cultures* (Duke University Press, 2003).

Judith Greenberg holds a Ph.D. in comparative literature from Yale University. She is completing a manuscript on echo and trauma and has written on the topic in *American Imago.* She has published on trauma and Virginia Woolf in *Woolf Studies Annual* and in *Virginia Woolf: Turning the Centuries,* edited by Ann Ardis and Bonnie Kime Scott (Pace University Press, 2000). She has also written on women and the Holocaust, including a chapter on women in the French Resistance in *Experience and Expression: Women and the Holocaust,* edited by Elizabeth Baer and Myrna Goldenberg (Wayne State University Press, 2003) and a chapter on Charlotte Delbo in *Teaching Representations of the Holocaust,* edited by Marianne Hirsch and Irene Kacandes (Modern Language Association).

Suheir Hammad is a Palestinian American poet and political activist. She has published a book of poems, *Born Palestinian, Born Black* (Writers and Readers, 1996), and a memoir, *Drops of This Story* (Writers and Readers, 1996).

Geoffrey Hartman, Sterling Professor Emeritus of English and Comparative Literature at Yale University, is the cofounder and project director of the Fortunoff Video Archive for Holocaust Testimonies. He also holds many national and international honorary positions. His latest books include *Scars of the Spirit: The Struggle against Inauthenticity* (Palgrave, 2002); *The Longest Shadow: In the Aftermath of the Holocaust* (Palgrave, 2002); *A Critic's Journey: Literary Reflections* (Yale University Press, 1999); and *The Fateful Question of Culture* (Columbia University Press, 1997).

Marianne Hirsch is the Ted and Helen Geisel Professor in the Humanities at Dartmouth College. Her publications include *The Mother/Daughter Plot: Narrative, Psychoanalysis, Feminism* (Indiana University Press, 1989) and *Family Frames: Photography, Narrative, and Postmemory* (Harvard University Press, 1997). She is the editor of *The Familial Gaze* (University Press of New England, 1998) and coeditor of *Conflicts in Feminism* (Routledge, 1991) and a special issue of *Signs*, "Gender and Cultural Memory" (2002). She is currently writing a manuscript with Leo Spitzer entitled "Ghosts of Home: Czernowitz and the Holocaust."

Irene Kacandes is an associate professor of German studies and comparative literature at Dartmouth College. Her areas of specialization include twentieth-century German cultural studies, Holocaust studies, narrative theory, gender studies, orality, and literacy. She is the author of *Talk Fiction: Literature and the Talk Explosion* (University of Nebraska Press, 2001) and coeditor of *A User's Guide to German Cultural Studies* (University of Michigan Press, 1997).

Claire Kahane is a recently retired professor of English from the University at Buffalo and currently is a visiting professor at the University of California. For many years a member of the Center for the Study of Psychoanalysis and Culture at Buffalo, she is now a research candidate in psychoanalytic training at the San Francisco Psychoanalytic Institute. She is the author of *Passions of the Voice: Hysteria, Narrative, and the Figure of the Speaking Woman* (Johns Hopkins University Press, 1995) and coeditor of *In Dora's Case* (Columbia University Press, [1985] 1990) and *The M/Other Tongue* (Cornell University Press, 1985). She has written widely in the area of feminist-psychoanalytic theory and criticism and is now working on a collection of essays on Holocaust trauma and literary representation.

E. Ann Kaplan is a professor of English and comparative literature at SUNY at Stony Brook, where she also is the founder and director of the Humanities Institute. A companion volume to her 1983 *Women and Film: Both Sides of the Camera* (Routledge), titled *Looking for the Other: Feminism, Film, and the Imperial Gaze* (Routledge), appeared in 1997, along with her coedited volume, *Generations: Academic Women in Dialogue* (University of Minnesota Press, 1997). Recent edited volumes include a revised expanded version of *Women in Film Noir* (University of California Press, 1998) and *Playing Dolly: Technocultural Formations, Fantasies and Fictions of Assisted Reproduction* (with Susan Squier) (Rutgers University Press, 1999). Her Oxford University Press anthology, *Feminism and Film*, appeared in 2000, and she is currently working on a new manuscript, "Performing Age: Trauma, Cinema, the Body."

Dori Laub, M.D., F.A.P.A., is a practicing psychoanalyst in New Haven, Connecticut, who works primarily with victims of massive psychic trauma and their children. He is the deputy director of trauma studies at the Yale Center for International and Area Studies. He is an associate clinical professor at Yale University School of Medicine and chairman of the Fortunoff Video Archive for Holocaust Testimonies at Yale. He has published on the topic of psychic trauma in a variety of psychoanalytic journals and has coauthored *Testimony: Crisis of Witnessing in Literature, Psychoanalysis, and History* (Routledge, 1992) with Shoshana Felman.

Orly Lubin is the chair of the Department of Poetics and Comparative Literature and head adviser of the National Committee of Jewish Women and Gender Studies at Tel Aviv University. She is also the assistant editor of the journal *Poetics Today*. She has written on feminist theories, theories of reading and spectatorship, women's autobiographies, and the moral discourse of testimonies of post-Holocaust catastrophes.

Nancy K. Miller is a Distinguished Professor of English and Comparative Literature at the Graduate Center, CUNY. Her most recent books include *Bequest and Betrayal: Memoirs of a Parent's Death* (Oxford University Press, 1996) and *But Enough about Me: Why We Read Other People's Lives* (Columbia University Press, 2002). She is coeditor, with Jason Tougaw, of *Extremities: Trauma, Testimony, and Community* (University of Illinois Press, 2002).

Toni Morrison is the Robert F. Goheen Professor in the Council of the Humanities at Princeton University. Her seven major novels—*The Bluest Eye, Sula, Song of Solomon, Tar Baby, Beloved, Jazz,* and *Paradise*—have received extensive critical acclaim. She received the National Book Critics Award in 1978 for *Song of Solomon* and the 1988 Pulitzer Prize for *Beloved*. She has received honorary degrees from Harvard, the University of Pennsylvania, Sarah Lawrence, Oberlin, Dartmouth, Yale, Georgetown, Columbia, Brown, the University of Michigan, and Université Paris 7-Denis Diderot. In 1993 she was awarded the Nobel Prize for Literature.

Lorie Novak is an artist who has been questioning the relationship between photographs and memory in her work for the past twenty years. Her photographs, installations, and Web projects have been in numerous solo and group exhibitions. In 1996, she launched Collected Visions (*www.cvisions.nyu.edu*), an interactive Web project exploring how photographs shape our memories. Over twenty-five hundred family photographs are in a searchable database, and more than two hundred stories are posted throughout the site. Her awards include a National Endowment for the Arts Fellowship, a New York Foundation for the Arts Fellowship, and residencies at Bellagio, MacDowell, and Yaddo. She is the chair of photography and imaging at Tisch School of the Arts at New York University.

Susannah Radstone teaches cultural theory and film studies in the School of Cultural and Innovations Studies at the University of East London. Her recent publications include *Memory and Methodology* (Berg, 1998) and "Special Debate: Trauma and Film Studies" in *Screen* (summer 2001); she has three books forthcoming from Routledge: *Contested Pasts* and *Regimes of Memory* (both coedited with Katharine Hodgkin) and *On Memory and Confession*.

Michael Rothberg is an associate professor of English and comparative literature at the University of Illinois at Urbana-Champaign and a member of Teachers for

Peace and Justice. He is the author of *Traumatic Realism: The Demands of Holocaust Representation* (University of Minnesota Press, 2000) and coeditor, with Neil Levi, of *The Holocaust: Theoretical Readings in History, Memory, and Criticism* (Edinburgh University Press, forthcoming). His recent publications include essays on W. E. B. Du Bois and Toni Morrison.

Richard Stamelman, professor of Romance and comparative literatures at Williams College, is the author of *Lost Beyond Telling: Representations of Death and Absence in Modern French Poetry* (Cornell University Press, 1990) and the editor of *The Lure and the Truth of Painting: Selected Essays on Art by Yves Bonnefoy* (University of Chicago Press, 1995). He is currently completing a book on the poetics of perfume in nineteenth- and twentieth-century French literature, culture, and fashion.

Patricia Yaeger teaches in the Departments of English and Women's Studies at the University of Michigan. She is the author of *Dirt and Desire: Reconstructing Southern Women's Writing, 1930–1990* (Chicago: University of Chicago Press, 2000), winner of the Society for the Study of Southern Literature and the Narrative Society prizes for 2000; editor of *The Geography of Identity* (University of Michigan Press, 1996); and coeditor of *Nationalisms and Sexualities* (Routledge, 1991). She is currently at work on "American Detritus: Trash and Ethnicity in American Literature."

James Young is a professor in and the chair of the Department of Judaic and Near Eastern Studies at the University of Massachusetts, Amherst. He is the author of *At Memory's Edge* (Yale University Press, 2000) and *The Texture of Memory* (Yale University Press, 1993), among other works, and was appointed by the Berlin Senate to the *Findungskommission* that chose a design for Germany's national Holocaust memorial, now under construction in Berlin.